Between Warrior Brother
and Veiled Sister

Between Warrior Brother and Veiled Sister

Islamic Fundamentalism
and the Politics of Patriarchy in Iran

Minoo Moallem

UNIVERSITY OF CALIFORNIA PRESS

Berkeley / Los Angeles / London

An earlier version of chapter 2 appeared as "Universalization of Particulars: The Civic Body and Gendered Citizenship in Iran." *Citizenship Studies* 3, no. 3 (November 1999), reprinted by kind permission of Taylor and Francis Ltd. An earlier version of chapter 3 appeared as "The Representation of the Mostaz'af/'the Disempowered' in Revolutionary and Postrevolutionary Iran" in *Feminist Futures: Re-Imagining Women, Culture and Development,* edited by Kum-Kum Bhavnani, John Foran, and Priya Kurian (Zed Books, 2003), reprinted with the permission of Zed Books. An earlier version of chapter 5 appeared as "Transnationalism, Feminism, and Fundamentalism" in *Between Woman and Nation: Nationalisms, Transnational Feminisms, and the State,* edited by Caren Kaplan, Norma Alarcón, and Minoo Moallem (Duke University Press, 1999).

University of California Press
Berkeley and Los Angeles, California

University of California Press, Ltd.
London, England

Library of Congress Cataloging-in-Publication Data

Moallem, Minoo.
    Between warrior brother and veiled sister : Islamic fundamentalism and the politics of patriarchy in Iran / Minoo Moallem.
        p.   cm.
    Includes bibliographical references and index.
    ISBN 0-520-24344-7 (cloth) — ISBN 0-520-24345-5 (pbk.)
    1. Feminism—Iran.   2. Colonialism—Iran.   3. Islamic fundamentalism—Iran.   I. Title.
HQ1735.2.M62   2005
305.42'0955—dc22   2004012262

Manufactured in the United States of America
13   12   11   10   09   08   07   06   05
10   9   8   7   6   5   4   3   2   1

Printed on Ecobook 50 containing a minimum 50% post-consumer waste, processed chlorine free. The balance contains virgin pulp, including 25% Forest Stewardship Council Certified for no old growth tree cutting, processed either TCF or ECF. The sheet is acid-free and meets the minimum requirements of ANSI/NISO Z39.48–1992 (R 1997) (Permanence of Paper).∞

Contents

Acknowledgments

Coercive displacement is a desubjectifying process. One loses her sense of continuity in time and space, threatened by the thought of being deleted from history. This process, sometimes romanticized as exile, is unsettling, disorienting, and risky. One might easily get trapped between borders where one could disappear. Displacement makes you a broker of time and space, always failing to remember yet not being able to forget. In this journey, thinking and feeling keep you connected to various communities somewhere between longing and belonging. No matter how violent the loss of place, those who accept the radical singularity of your being and becoming provide you with a sense of history, both affective and intellectual. However, it is in the collapse of belonging that I have found intellectually and emotionally supportive communities.

Writing is a collective endeavor. No one writes in isolation—writing in isolation is a modernist illusion. However, in these instances of amalgamation in the world of words, there are some moments of creativity when one discovers a tiny new line or a new idea that makes the entire process of writing exciting and astonishing. The dancing of the pen or the music of the computer keyboard grasping the compelling excitement of these moments by pouring it onto the page may be the most significant aspect of writing. These extraordinary moments do not emerge without the vitality of one's affective and intellectual communities.

I am indebted to many people along the way. I would like to thank Caren Kaplan and Inderpal Grewal for their friendship, critical feedback, and encouragement. Caren was a precious *parrhesia,* in the Foucauldian sense. She enthusiastically, thoroughly, and patiently read various drafts of the manuscript and gave me the most valuable comments and feedback. Inderpal, both as my friend and as my former department chair, never failed to support me and always encouraged me to take risks in saying what was unpopular. She also gave me useful feedback on the manuscript. Both Caren and Inderpal have been great friends and inspired me for many years with their pioneering work on transnational feminist practices. I also wish to thank Parama Roy for her friendship, inspiration, and great comments on several versions of the manuscript. The brilliant and courageous contributions of Ella Shohat to the field of feminist Middle Eastern studies have stimulated and inspired me significantly, and I am indebted to her support of this project and her encouragement. My gratitude goes to Eric Smoodin for his historical work in film studies and for supporting this project and its publication with University of California Press. My thanks to James Clifford, whose suggestions helped me to improve the manuscript. The intellectual and collegial support of Norma Alarcón, Danielle Juteau, and Arlie Hochschild has meant much to me. Colette Guillaumin's brilliant interventions on race relations have always inspired me.

This book profited greatly from the comments and suggestions of the two anonymous readers of the manuscript at the University of California Press. Also, I am very grateful to Naomi Schneider, my editor at UC Press, who supported this project. Without her encouragement, support, and understanding of the field, I would not have been able to finish this project. My thanks to Sierra Fillucci for suggesting the cover picture and to Chalon Emmons and Elizabeth Berg for their help in getting the book through publication at UC Press. I started to work on this project when I was a postdoctoral fellow in the Beatrice M. Bain Research Group and the Department of Sociology at the University of California at Berkeley, where I exchanged ideas with a number of scholars. Many colleagues supported this project by conversing with me and by reading and commenting on particular chapters. My warmest thanks go to Halleh Afshar, Tani Barrlow, Iain Boal, Kum-Kum Bhavnani, Lisa Bloom, Elizabeth Castelli, John Foran, Suad Joseph, Abdul JanMohamed, Vassant Kaiwar, Brinda Metha, Sucheta Mazumdar, Elizabeth Potter, Raka Ray, and Robyn Wiegman. A number of colleagues invited me to give talks and presentations in the United States, Canada, Sweden, Japan, Germany, and Tunisia, and helped me refine my ideas and writing. My thanks go to Åsa Andersson, Ali Behdad, Tina Campt,

Laura Donaldson, Joseba Gabilondo, Gayatri Gopinah, Frances Hasso, Monia Hejaiej, Lois Hombold, Janet Jakobsen, Behrooz Ghamari Tabrizi, Toru Tani, Nora Räthzel, and Joseba Zuleka. I am deeply grateful to my hosts and my audiences for their support and critical engagement with my work. I also want to thank Paola Baccheta, Shelly Feldman, Anne Marie Fortier, Deniz Gökturk, Kristin Huffine, Alfred Jessel, Surina Khan, Laura Kuo, Rachel Lee, Elspeth Probyn, Renate Sadrozinski, Pam Smith, Parnian Taidi, and Jennifer Terry for their friendship and support. Leyla Etzinili and Julie Lewis supplied valuable editorial help. I am also thankful to colleagues Deborah Cohler, Jim Qusada, Loretta Stec, Julyana Peard, and Jillian Sandell at San Francisco State University. My deepest thanks go to my students at SFSU, who supported me and cheered me on through all these years, when I had to juggle writing, teaching, and chairing the department. Sima Shakhsari and Leah Veldhuizen provided conscientious research assistance.

I have received generous institutional support from SFSU to complete this project. I benefited from a Presidential Award, an Affirmative Action Faculty Award, and a Research and Professional Development Award. Also, I am grateful to the current dean of humanities, Paul Sherwin, and the retired dean of humanities, Nancy McDermid, for their interest in and support of this project.

My family, both in Iran and in diaspora, was a great support to me. I wish to thank Mehraneh, Mahnaz, Abbas, Ali, and Ahmad for their love and support. I am grateful to my husband and *yar*, Shahin Bayatmakou, who has taken a great interest in my work and my well-being. I also thank my son, Arash, for his joyful presence and for keeping track of where I was in my writing. My mother, Mohtaram Sharyatpanahi, and my father, Abdollah Moallem—who did not live to see this book—offered me their unconditional love, even if I was a disobedient daughter.

I dedicate this book to a generation of Iranian women who found meaning in the freedom to revolt, those who did not claim to be sisters but learned to treasure friendship.

Introduction

In 2000, while on a research trip to Paris, I visited an Iranian friend. During our conversation about the Iranian diaspora in Paris, my friend insisted that I visit the new Middle Eastern section of the Louvre Museum. With excitement and enthusiasm, she reminded me that the objects exhibited in the museum included a number of forks and spoons, demonstrating that Persians had civilized manners early in their history. With a sense of relief, she made the point that French people would no longer have any excuse to accuse Iranians of being uncivilized. This conversation reminded me of the stereotypical depiction of Iranian manners in the Hollywood film *Not Without My Daughter,* in which Iranians eat with their hands, sacrifice sheep in the streets, and lack hygiene. I kept thinking about the extent to which modern notions of civilization and barbarism continue to give meaning to the notions of self and other in today's globalized society. I kept thinking about my friend's notion of what it meant to be a Persian[1] in diaspora, and the extent to which colonial modernity—an era, a project, a politico-economic formation distinct in its evolutionary historicity and marked by the experience of European colonialism—has defined the Persian diaspora through a framework of cultural and racial humiliation. Needless to say, colonial modernity bears traces of colonial epistemology and is a precursor to postcoloniality. I thought of the importance of race and culture, not only in relation to the modern Iranian construction of a pre-Islamic Persian identity proximate to Europe, but also in terms of the return to Islamic culture as an authentic and oppositional identity.

At the Intersection of Culture and Identity: Hailed as a Sister in a Semiotic War

My passion for the project that has taken form as *Between Warrior Brother and Veiled Sister* comes from the convergence of many factors in my life: experience and scholarship, emotion and reflection, location and displacement, changing conditions of (be)longing that have created temporal and spatial disjunction, and the ensuing fissures and gaps in identity. I refer to my experience here not to position myself as an empirical site of truth and so invoke a range of assumptions contingent on the physical presence of the author's body, but rather to acknowledge how, by being physically present at a particular space and time and then revisiting that experience, one comes to understand oneself as a subject in time. The moment of writing about an experience is always a representational moment in which both remembering and forgetting are at stake. The opening and closing of one's experiences I consider a reflective moment, a moment of risk taking, of realizing that one's identity and one's acts belong to no one else.

In Iran during the second decade and a half of the twentieth century, called the postconstitutional period (1911–25), the modernizing and Westernizing nation-state was established by Reza Shah Pahlavi, replacing the Qajar dynasty. In 1925, Reza Shah became shah, ruling until 1941, when his son, Mohammad Reza Pahlavi, replaced him. During the ensuing years, Western influence increased in Iran. In 1951, Muhammad Mossadeq, the leader of the national front, was elected prime minister, and with the support of the nationalist movement, he nationalized the Iranian oil industry. In August 1953, pressured by the nationalist movement, Mohammad Reza Shah was forced to flee Iran. Within days, however, with the backing of the U.S. Central Intelligence Agency, there was a military coup d'état by the royalists, and the shah returned to power.

The Pahlavi regime was based on the ideology of modernization and Westernization and offered endless dichotomies revolving around the racial and civilizing tropes of the modern in contrast to the traditional. The women of my generation were born into an uncompromising world of binaries in the middle of a cultural war. We learned to identify with what Connell calls an emphasized model of femininity, defined in subordination to masculinity and organized as women's adoption of men's power rather than an exercise of power over other forms of femininity (1987, 183–87). It was not until my displacement from Iran (and certainly not through tourism) that I became aware, both in theory and through experience, of modernization as a process of racialization, in which the local is rejected and the West declared superior.[2] In the modernist Pahlavi regime, the boundaries of tradition and modernity were rigidly drawn, so that moving from one world to the other required particular strategies of copying, passing, and mimicking. The codes of conduct were either rigidly defined or so deeply embedded that they became naturalized. The proximity or distance between one world and the other was not an issue, since what counted was the staging of identity. The agents of discipline and control were not the same for both. While modernist forms of femininity were disciplined by the state through national performance, modernist education, and print and media representations, it was family and community members who policed the so-called world of tradition, the world confined to the private sphere (the household, community spaces, neighborhoods, particular urban spaces). Modernization and Westernization neither challenged patriarchy in Iran nor changed it. Indeed, they merely divided patriarchy into hegemonic and subordinated semiotic regimes positioned to compete for control of women's bodies and minds.

Growing up in the post–coup d'état era of the Pahlavi regime, I rapidly learned to distrust the official narratives of events and began to seek out what was not said. "Things said" was the space for the performance of legitimate speech.[3] In contrast, the unattainable, outlawed, and underground forms of knowing and feeling became places where one could escape the dictatorship's positioning of the public as imbeciles. Oppositional subjectivities offered an attractive alternative for many women in my generation by promising social change through social movements and revolution (although our optimism was later shattered when women were marginalized by most anticolonial and nationalist movements in the postrevolutionary era). The arena of social movements was also a space where we could distance ourselves from colonial and modernist civilizing models concerning femininity and seek refuge in a world where relations were less rigidly patriarchal and gender identities were more ambiguous. Our need to participate in these social movements allowed for all kinds of imaginary and material transgressions and overruled the cultural pressures to conform to certain gender identities. The collapse of the normative self into the contingent conditions of what was needed for the collective good of the people led to an abandoning of gender performance at the family and community levels. Iranian women's rejection of rules, laws, norms, and values, along with their rejection of the state and the authority of the family, led to a massive revolt, which was channeled into the social revolution of 1979, in which masses of women of all ages, classes, and ethnicities took part. Paradoxically, the revolution both rejected and affirmed the state, for it was a revolution against the existing state that nevertheless laid the groundwork for a new version of the state. Yet the moment of revolt was also a moment of rupture, filled with possibilities emerging from the collision between desires and the infeasibility of dialogue. While many in my generation paid with their lives for daring to articulate their desire, others hesitated and chose to live in uncertainty, their wavering creating a pedagogical momentum of wait and see.

The revolutionary conditions soon circumvented or surpassed the framing of Iranian modernity, and Iran entered a postmodern world characterized by the collapse of boundaries between modern and traditional, secular and religious, West and East, elite and popular, scripture and image, and national and transnational, leading to new forms of subject formation. This collapse of dichotomies created space for all kinds of transgressions and various forms of resistance. Both material conditions and a new, revolutionary orchestration of representational gender practices created previously unimaginable connections among what had seemed unrelated concepts: The participation of a generation of women in the events of the revolution made it possible for modernist gendered representational practices to become denaturalized. Long lines for fuel and gas connected consumers to the striking oil workers in the south, thus bringing the metaphor of "black gold," used historically by Iranian intellectuals to make the nation aware of its territorial wealth, into the everyday lives of citizens as consumers. The collapse of the preacher, the popular Shia entertainer,[4] and the media reporter into a revolutionary actor enabled the re-presentation of the revolution. The print culture of modernity was gradually replaced by popular, mass-mediated communication. This was a semiotic war that gained popularity over the guerrilla war fought for almost a decade to overthrow the shah's regime. As women, we were both object and subject of this war, for even though the conflict included the issue of who had the power to control women's bodies, some women veiled themselves in protest of Westernized models of femininity. (Much later, I realized that the semiotic war was in fact much older than the guerrilla war, and that it was inscribed on women's bodies.)

Caught in the middle of this semiotic war, women were called to be sisters to brothers in an emerging imagined community, that of an

Islamic ummat. The ummat's relationship to its secular counterpart, the nation, is evident in its call for personhood and its hyphenated relationship with the state. The terms of this semiotic war grew out of the transnational and translational moments of colonial modernity and its failure to concurrently represent and repress the people. The Islamic call for the constitution of this new imagined community in Iran—defined as a transnational ethnicity, positioned oppositionally in relation to the global hegemony of the West, and capable of moving within and beyond the territorial boundaries of the nation—appealed to the Iranian masses, men and women alike.

The ummat was represented as uniquely Islamic, yet it was fashioned from identities borrowed from the Western imaginary, a fact that led to numerous contradictions and conflicts. The desire for an original identity is inevitable, since the act of copying always presupposes the existence of an original. Copying in the context of identity formation was already present in relation to one original—that of the Western, imperialist global order. The search for an indigenous original could only lead away from the copy but would necessarily remain linked to the copy, causing the moment of revolution to emerge as the moment when the original came into existence. What came into meaning as the original then had to be distinguished from the copy. It is this recourse to an Islamic identity and a selective reading of Islam that creates a basis for the emergence of an Islamic nationalism and fundamentalism. As a result, a complex set of overlapping discourses, dialogues, and imagery about Islam and colonial modernity in relation to gender constructions and identities were mobilized to give meaning to Iranian modernity and postmodernity.[5]

Iranian women responded in various ways to the call to be sisters to brothers in the community of ummat. Some were interpellated by the call, while some opposed it, and some took the position of the subject in-between. The call divided my generation of women and determined the conditions of our belonging—staying in the homeland to either join or resist, or becoming diasporic. The comforting idea of the nation was there to naturalize this hailing as a sister, and many women spoke before they knew what they meant by being or not being a sister. Part of my challenge in writing this book has been to examine this moment of division and to interrogate the various responses to the call to be sisters, especially those of women who joined.

I was among those who left. Epistemologically, I wish to account for my position as a subject in-between, meaning my position as a subject constituted by the modern notions of home and location and their post-modern debunking in homelessness and dislocation.[6] I wish to explore the links between inside and outside Iran as proximities, rather than view them as internal and external space and thus loci for dichotomies of traditional and modern, oppressive and free, fundamentalist and secular. Far from being a romanticized, exilic space, the in-between location escapes neither the coercive practices of nation-states nor their surveillance apparatuses. Yet it is a potentially desubjectifying space, for, in the terms of Kaplan, Alarcón, and Moallem (1999, 12), it is a zone of deconstruction of the two monoliths of "woman" and "nation."

Western Representations of Islamic Fundamentalism

During the Iranian revolution of 1979, various oppositional groups in Iran revisited Islam in order to mobilize masses of people. While some articulated an Islamic vision significantly influenced by global social movements, including Marxism, socialism, and anarchism, others worked to bring nationalism into dialogue with Islam. What eventually won the hearts and minds of masses of people was Khomeini's representation of the Islamic community, which brought together particular notions of religion with modern forms of nationalism and transnationalism. However, despite the hegemony of Khomeini's vision, in the postrevolutionary era, Iranian civil society continued to be a battleground for the proponents of various ideologies, with most of them claiming their own interpretation of Islam.

The 1979 revolution was also a turning point in terms of the representation of Islamic fundamentalism outside of Iran. Since then, the Western media in general, and the U.S. media in particular, have shaped the Western view of Islam by depicting Iran as a society that exemplifies an antimodern impulse of the Arab and Muslim world that longs to return to the unchanging world of Islam. However, the reductiveness of the Western media's representational practices blatantly disregards both geopolitical differences in the Muslim world and the cultural significance of Iran. As a non-Arab country, Iran has its own complex historical relationship to Islam that cannot be reduced to a generalized transhistorical and transcultural notion of Islamic fundamentalism.

My dislocation from Iran to the West placed me in a world where no distinction was made between differentiated and sometimes opposing views of Islam, and where a unifying notion of Islam as the "other" of

the West held sway. All Muslims were portrayed as fundamentalist, traditional, backward, and fanatically religious.[7] In response to this
difficult situation, very few scholars or members of the Iranian diaspora
in the West have tried to map out the similarities and differences between the racialization of Iranians with Arabs and the history of race
and immigration in the United States. Many, however, have aligned
themselves with the prevailing anti-Islamic racism by claiming the radical separation of Iranian culture from Islam. The romantic notion of
"Persianness" and a selective belonging to the glorious age of the Persian empire, removed from modern Iran, have become the most conve-
nient means of ethnic identification and of protection from the everyday racism experienced by the Iranian diaspora. Modern forms of
Iranian secular nationalism in Iran itself are also rooted in the idea of an
Iranian identity that is uncontaminated by Islam. Finding the path to
assimilation through the disowning of Islam and Islamic culture, many
Iranians in the West even took a missionary role vis-à-vis Iranians in
Iran. A number of Iranian television programs, magazines, and websites
in diaspora have invested in the mission of "saving Iran" from the Muslim fundamentalists, using gender signifiers as a site of distinction between "the oppressed Iran" and the "liberated diaspora."[8] Such notions
have become an obstacle for the interrogation of patriarchal discourses
and practices that are at work not only in Iran but in the diaspora. However, there has been little interest in examining or challenging the various forms of fundamentalism and their political implications for the
production and reproduction of particular notions of race, nation, gender, and sexuality as they relate to immigrant communities in the West.

In the post 9/11 era, it is hard to ignore the everyday forms of racism
and its multiple expressions in the popular media, in social institutions,
and in common ideologies vis-à-vis Muslims. Iranians living in the West
are constantly being put in the imaginary cultural zone where a civilizational battle between the Muslims as "them" and the Westerners as "us"
has been taking place for centuries. A selective reading of particular
events in historical time and space has been used to authenticate the
construction of this civilizational and cultural war.

Glancing beyond this particular arena of civilizational confrontation,
we see that it is not unique. It is one conflicted territory in a complex
world of cultural interactions, linguistic translations, and social transac-
tions where the modernist dichotomous notions of us and them, the
West and the Rest, civilized and barbaric, tradition and modernity, and
good and evil have been taken to their limits. This new, global world is

haunted by the legacies of colonialism and the uneven exchanges of postcolonial and neocolonial formations.

Islamic fundamentalism has become a generic signifier used relentlessly to single out the Muslim other in its irrational, morally inferior, and barbaric masculinity and its passive, victimized, and submissive femininity.[9] Such new forms of Orientalist discourse not only legitimize Western intervention and the protection of Western economic and political interests in the "Middle East," but also justify discrimination against Middle Eastern and Muslim immigrants in diasporic locations.[10] There are serious consequences to this problem. First, it legitimizes imperialist and militarist intervention of the West in general, and the United States in particular, in the Middle East. Second, it is used to maintain racism of discrimination and extermination against Arabs and Muslims in the United States, and legitimizes various forms of exclusionary and racist practices. Third, it makes various forms of fundamentalism and cultural nationalism attractive or appealing to the masses of people in the Middle East; in other words, it creates a situation where claiming an "us" or making certain claims to authenticity becomes a site of resistance and identity formation.

Phrases such as "the Muslim rage," "the threat of Islam," "what is inside the Muslim fundamentalist mind," and numerous others used in mainstream scholarly and journalistic writings in the United States reveal Orientalist and racist depictions of Islam and Muslims. Words such as *jihad, fatwa, faghih, imam, ayatollah, chador, shahid,* and *sharia* are frequently (mis)used to refer to Islam as a world of religious fixities, rigidities, and barbaric traditions that is tyrannical, violent, patriarchal, and antimodern by nature. Such discourses reduce all Muslims to fundamentalists and all fundamentalists to fanatical antimodern traditionalists and terrorists.[11] These totalizing discourses not only deny the presence of diverse social movements in the Muslim world, but also disregard lively discussions around the meaning of Islam taking place in many Muslim countries. Said's discussion of Orientalism (1979) sheds light on the power/knowledge connection of such a framework and on Western symbolic and material hegemony over the Middle East. Furthermore, the depiction of Islam as a static system transcending cultures and peoples has made it possible for scholars to refer to the reinvention of Islam in the context of modernity and postmodernity as "Islamic revival" or "Islamic resurgence," which suggests a return to a fixed way of life (Bernal 1992, 2). At the same time, dualistic and demonizing representations of fundamentalism have generated resistance to the term among other scholars, who avoid the concept completely or replace it with some other term, such as "political Islam," "Islamic militancy," "communalism," or "orthodoxy."[12]

The central intent of this book is to historicize what is becoming fixed in the notion of Islamic fundamentalism and Iranian identity. It looks, in particular, at the modernist constructions of race, gender, and sexuality as major components of such notions. It shows how Islamic fundamentalism is a by-product of colonial modernity and the process of modernization and Westernization, and how it is fed by a hybrid blend of images, signifiers, icons, and myths of both pre-Islamic and Islamic Iran, as well as globally circulated meanings, images, and modern patriarchal ideologies. In the course of this discussion, this book addresses the larger question of how both representational practices of "othering" and the identitarian claims of "we-ness" are inseparable from the modern history of race, gender, religion, and nation.

The Production of Fundamentalism out of Modernity

Fundamentalism is not peculiar to an Islamic context. Recent scholarship on fundamentalism locates it as a global phenomenon that emerges in many social and religious contexts. While some scholars equate right-wing and conservative religious movements with fundamentalism (Kintz 1997; Sarkar and Butalia 1995), others apply the concept to a wider range of religious movements (Hawley 1994; Marty and Appleby 1991). Well-informed comparative accounts of fundamentalism, such as Marty and Appleby's *Fundamentalisms Observed* project, have brought to light the othering effects of the term vis-à-vis Muslims. In these accounts, fundamentalism emerges as modern secularism's other to perpetuate modernist notions of religion as a fixed object that is "a troubled category," in Castelli's terms (2001, 4). Castelli argues that the attempt to separate religion from other aspects of social life, including historical contexts, social frameworks, political struggles, and institutional practices, masks the conditions by which religion is produced for study (5–6). As Asad notes, there can be no universal definition of religion, since not only are the historical constituents of religion specific but the definition of religion is itself produced by discursive processes (1993, 29). Postcolonial critics, feminist scholars, and critical race theorists have argued against the separation of religion from the domain of power, demonstrating the complicated role of religion in shaping identities, political cultures, and social relations. In this book, I situate fundamentalism as a modern discursive formation (no less modern than "progress" or "development") with a genealogy and a history of representation. In agreement with the views of the scholars just mentioned, I examine the historical and representational processes within which a particular notion of religion is produced. This discursive formation, I will argue, cannot be limited to religion and is produced in various discursive sites.

The concept of fundamentalism is problematic since it remains tied to religion, and to the history of Christianity in particular. Not surprisingly, the analytic application of fundamentalism to non-Christian contexts has been the subject of much controversy. Calling such an application a misnomer, Naderveen Pieterse argues that the term *fundamentalism* signals an essentializing, demonizing, and polarizing conceptual approach that ignores multiple currents, internal divisions, and change over time (1994, 5). While I agree with Pieterse that the application of the term *fundamentalism* is problematic in a non-Christian context and runs the risk of essentializing and demonizing Islam, I find fundamentalism as an analytical concept and as a modern discourse useful for an understanding of both religion and secularism. I define fundamentalism as a regime of truth based on discourses identified with or ordained by God (understood metaphorically or literally), which binds its observers to it. I believe, therefore, that any understanding of fundamentalism based on religion must be challenged and replaced by an analytical definition that enables critical intervention in both religious and secularist forms of fundamentalism. An example of secular fundamentalism is the modernist theory of identity formation and race that considers religion a key determinant in the discourse of racial inferiority. This imputation of an intrinsic nature to a cultural or religious system has roots in European race theory, in particular, in the discourse of anti-Semitism. Horkheimer and Adorno assert that the idea of an "opposing race as the embodiment of the negative principle" is key to the construction of racialization (1987, 168). I share Guillaumin's view that modernist racial constructions rely on "the idea of nature that is no longer reduced to a simple finality about the place objects should have, but further claims that each of them, like the whole group of them, is internally organized to do what it does, to be where it is" (1995, 211).

Modernity would leave us with the impression that there is a radical evolutionary and revolutionary rupture between the archaic, irrational world of religious and cultural traditions and the modern world of secularism. Yet contra this naive notion of secularization, religion persists as an important part of meaning-making. The reappearance of religion at the forefront of cultural and political spheres in various geopolitical locations challenges modernity's claim of being a postreligious and post-traditional world.[13] In fact, in the context of these emerging localized forms of religious nationalism, the collective concept of moral community is being reconstructed through religion. What Derrida calls "globalatinization" (the impact of modern Christianity's external forces—and Christianity's perception of the relationship of religion to secularism—on the internal dynamism of particular localities) has brought such local religious and cultural meanings onto the global stage (2001, 70). The result has been a crisis for both modernity and religion, as exemplified in the concurrent existence of modernist secularism and religious fundamentalism in the West.

Far from being free of religion, the discourse of secularism in the West defines itself by using religion as a discursive object. As Asad points out, "What is distinctive about secularism is that it presupposes new concepts of 'religion,' 'ethics,' and 'politics,' and new imperatives associated with them" (2003, 2). Secularism's representation of religion allows secularism to produce what is in fact a Christianized public space where tradition is reinvented through the framework of Christian tradition. This hegemony of a masculine Christianity and its Eurocentric way of looking at other faiths, as Nandy notes, was integrated into the colonial states themselves and subsumed a set of clear polarities, including true faith versus its distortions, civil versus primordial, and great traditions versus local cultures (1998a, 323). My use of the word *religion* relies on this understanding of religion as a discursive formation produced by Western hegemonic discourses.

In secularism's terms, religion is defined as a matter of faith that is located beyond public space.[14] Critiques of Eurocentrism and Westernization have warned against the separation of the concept of the secular from its Christian history and of the concept of religion from the discourse of progress and enlightenment.[15] As Nandy states, both the belief that the public realm can be managed through a science that is essentially rational and universal and the idea that religion is an ideology opposed to the modern state are by definition ethnophobic and ethnocidal (1998a, 324–27).[16] The secular space is in fact an amalgamation of religion, culture, and power. As Asad argues, it is only a particular history of knowledge and power in the modern West that has conceptually separated religion from the domain of power, insisting on the transhistorical and transcultural autonomous essence of religion (1993, 28–29).

Moreover, the very mapping of religion in private space, beyond the politics, commerce, and messiness of everyday life, has produced a desire on the part of believers for the return of religion to the public sphere as a force enabling the unification of private, religious belief and public, secular behavior.

Outside the Christian West, modernity collapses religious belief and religious practice—which, unlike in the modern West, exist as separable entities in cultures such as Islam—into a single, unitary "tradition" and maps it as opposed to modernity. Thus the cleansing of religion was high on the agenda of Reza Shah in Iran and Ataturk in Turkey in their projects of modernization and Westernization. In Iran, the promodernizing elite of the Pahlavi regime believed in Westernization literally from head to toe. Westernization meant the redisciplining of the body through the process of nation-state building. The redisciplining project made it necessary to invoke the category of the traditional as the other of modernity to mark what was distinctive about the modern. In the language of colonialism, modernity's encounter with tradition was structured as a civilizing mission; in the language of postcolonialism, it entailed cultural imperialism. In both views, being modern necessitated the rejection of tradition. That is, in order to be modern, one had to reject one's tradition. Given the logic of this civilizational thinking, the return of Islam—whether as Islamism, Islamic fundamentalism, or militant Islam, not to mention other permutations, even in its most "Christianized form"[17]—is doomed to be seen negatively by the West.

While in the Islamic world in general, and Iran in particular, the concept of tradition was used to depict religion as the other of modernity and modernization, in the context of Western modernity it was used to refer to the translational and transactional relations of religion and secularism. Within the context of Western modernity, tradition is of course present in secularist guise—"reinvented," in the well-known phrase of Ranger and Hobsbawm (1983). By this ruse, a particular kind of tradition is reserved for the West, while the Rest are told to abandon their own traditions as fast as possible. Such representations reinvent new religious identities by attributing barbarism and otherness to Islam and Muslims. This is why an understanding of fundamentalist and foundationalist interpretations of religion requires an investigation of the ways in which collective identities are constructed and diffused.

The articulation of religion as an essence also allows modernists to think of religion in fundamentalist ways. In the case of Islam, references by journalists, scholars, and activists to the "reality" of religion—which implicitly argues for religion as a culturally encoded experience in a space beyond language and culture immune to any form of cultural contamination—has allowed a continual fundamentalist revisiting of religion.[18] The construction of religion in general, and Islam in particular, as explainable only in terms of an internal logic sets the stage for a conception of religion that does not take into consideration external factors, including political, economic, technoscientific, and biotechnological forces.

In the case of postrevolutionary Iran, as well as the late-twentieth-century Islamic world generally, the notion that tradition and modernity are dichotomous created a need for the renewal of the industry around the colonial discourse of a civilizing mission (on the part of the West), while provoking, in return, a desire to claim authenticity on the part of Muslims.

The return of Islam to claim national identity or to articulate oppositional politics is not only a reaction to the demonization of Islam by the West. It also produces particular notions of religion and religious identity, such as "resurgence," "revivalism," and the "return" of religion, in Muslims' own discourse. These in turn produce fundamentalist analytical frameworks, which separate religion from the geopolitics of colonial modernity and its globalization in the Islamic world itself.

However, such a psychic investment is also influenced by postmodern regimes of national and transnational governmentality, which increasingly require the production of a subject position—a self—able to successfully negotiate distinctions between voluntary and involuntary, as for instance with regard to participation in the ummat. This notion of the self has become increasingly dependent upon the rearticulation of the personal and the political; it is constructed in the disjunction between cultural and political citizenship. Postmodernism relies extensively on consumerism, where Islamic culture is increasingly commodified and opened to uncertainty, multiplicity, intertextuality, and the collapse of time-space with no foundation. In this context, any fundamentalist claim to a particular interpretation of religion is also subjected to discontinuity and fragmentation once it is read in relation to specific discourses, contexts, or groups (including women, youth, minority groups, and so on).

Islamic fundamentalism has been portrayed as belonging to an archaic and traditional world of Islam and Muslims. However, as a regime of truth, fundamentalism is not premodern but rather a by-product of the process of modernization. As such, it is in dialogue with modernity.

In one sense, fundamentalism's impulse is to counter modernity, though in doing so it stands in the place of neither the premodern nor the postmodern. As a moment of modernity, it is not coterminous with premodern discourses. Since it claims cultural unity and homogeneity for itself, it thus locates itself as oppositional to postmodernism's insistence on cultural difference.

Interrogating Fundamentalism

Limiting fundamentalism to religious meanings presupposes modernist notions of an easily discernable space outside modernity for religion and also undermines the commonalities among various forms of fundamentalism, both religious and secular. I draw on the work of Jakobsen and Pellegrini to argue that religion and reason participate in the same regime of knowledge and power. In addition, applying the concept of fundamentalism to the context of Islamic countries in general and Iran in particular is problematic, since it imposes a definition of fundamentalism that is historically produced in the West and in the context of Christianity. As an analytical tool, I use *fundamentalism* in the particular context of Iran to refer to three converging phenomena: Sometimes, I refer to Islamic nationalism along with Islamic fundamentalism to discuss the territorial and national framing of fundamentalism in Iran and to examine various negotiations and interpretations emerging in the context of the Islamic nation-state. I also turn to fundamentalism to talk about a transnational phenomenon as the concomitant national and transnational identitarian claims to authenticity in Iran, which are based on ethnic absolutism and what is called the "right" tradition or religious dogma. Finally, I refer to fundamentalism to talk about a system of representation that moves in and out of Iran by way of global networks of communication, trade, and travel. Its vectors are money, ideas, bodies, and consumer goods. Gender meanings and signifiers are critical to the plausibility of all three concepts.

In their attempt to respond to the crisis of modernity, Islamic nationalism and transnationalism have created new sites of subject formation as well as new spaces of resistance to the assimilative forces of global capitalism. Nevertheless, their positions remain imprisoned and self-contained because of their own complicity in the suppression of alterity and their claim to be free from contradictions. In Iran, any understanding of the "nation" demands engagement with the issue of religion, since the invention of the nation in Anderson's (1991) terms does not abide by a universal pattern. As Balibar suggests, nationalism, despite its universalist character, is particularistic because of its claim to different national roots and its call for the separation of nations in order to preserve their identities (1994, 193–95). Islamic nationalism and transnationalism have been successful not only in reinventing an Islamic nation but also in sacralizing citizenship through the participation of both men and women as citizen-subjects in the modern political entity of the nation-state. However, the invention of the nation is based on particular narratives that transgress the boundary between secularism and religion—as well as the borders between domestic and nondomestic, territorial and nonterritorial, rational and irrational, and mythical and historical—to create a state of population, a form of personhood.

By focusing on the disjunctive temporalities present in Islamic nationalism and transnationalism, we can see that social contradictions and cultural differences, which have been overridden for the sake of creating a unified national identity, are indeed related to the disjunctive space of modernity and the continuous problem of what Bhabha calls the ambivalent temporality of modernity (1994, 239). While time is an important component of modernity—one that has been secularized and then placed at the disposal of imperial and national projects—the projection of time onto space as history has taken on the character of a spectacle as multiple antagonistic and conflicting discourses have converged (McClintock 1995, 359).

In this book, I argue that cultural and nationalist Islamic claims have provided space for monolithic, masculinist narratives of an Islamic ummat that ignore the diversity and multiplicity of discourses and practices actually present in the Islamic world. The ummat is neither an archaic phenomenon transcending time and space, definable through an Islamic semiotic system, nor the antithesis of modernity, as suggested in certain analyses of Islamic fundamentalism. On the contrary, it is a modern construction based on the reinvention of an imagined Islamic community that is active both in opposing the state and in sustaining it through the nation. As with other forms of nationalism, fundamentalism and ethnic absolutism are components of the reinvention of the ummat. Furthermore, the narrative of an Islamic ummat, both national and transnational, relies heavily on the bodies of women and their mediation between the "we-ness" of the Islamic ummat and the "other." Indeed, women become ideological subjects (Lazreg 1994, 96), and their bodies are engaged or "ideologized" to rework the disappointments and failures of overarching dichotomous notions of identity in modernity by suppressing cultural hybridity or forms of in-betweenness. Consumer capitalism has incorporated this transnational reworking of the nation in its inexorable march to produce new consumer subjects.

Western representational practices, as well as fundamentalism itself, have complied with the consumerist impulses pervasive in global capitalism in creating and maintaining consumer subject positions, turning people, in Deleuze and Guattari's terms, into desiring machines. Many examples attest to the successful incorporation of Orientalism and Islamism in the promotion of consumerist culture both in Iran and in the West. Using the analytical framework of transnational feminism, I argue that the dichotomous notions of the veiled Muslim woman and the Western woman, and their juxtaposition as signifiers of unfreedom and freedom, respectively, are incorporated into consumerist capitalism.[19] Both in Iran and in the diaspora, through dichotomous notions of veiled/unveiled, Islamic/secular, Western/non-Western, and free/unfree, different and sometimes oppositional models of femininity are asserted and performed through the consumption of goods and ideas.

Fundamentalism is a useful site for comparing unfreedom and freedom, with important implications for women's movements. It is not only used to dismiss the gender crisis of modernity—comprising the dual crises of rationality and masculinity—but is also a site for expressing the paradoxical desire for the freedom to be "unfree." It is an important place for the systematic production of discursive enclosures, since it defines women's othering and legitimizes day-to-day oppressive gender practices. In feminist scholarship, fundamentalism has been used descriptively to characterize the most conservative elements of religious gender ideologies.[20] An essentialized notion of womanhood justifies the collective legal and political control of women's bodies and sexualities in a number of religious fundamentalist discourses.[21] However, recent scholarship has shown that women are not just victims of these movements but are also participants in the formation and upholding of fundamentalist discourses.[22]

Middle Eastern Studies

Whereas the history of Middle Eastern studies in Europe is much more connected to European colonialism and Orientalist scholarship, Middle

Eastern studies in the United States, like other area studies, emerged in the context of the Cold War out of the determination of the United States to assert its hegemonic position in the world order in relation to "problem-generating areas" and as an investment in those "areas" where U.S. economic and political interests are at stake.

However, Middle Eastern studies in particular, and area studies in general, as spaces of research and scholarship have been challenged by the reality of postcolonialism and neocolonialism and their effects on the modernist paradigms of knowledge production: canonicity, rationality, and Eurocentrism. Feminist scholarship in particular has pushed modernity's masculinist and patriarchal paradigms to their conceptual limits.

As Appadurai has argued, areas are not facts but artifacts created by the academic imagination (2001a, 7). With the expansion of globalization in the post–Cold War era, the definition of *area* in area studies has been seriously challenged by new forms of information technology, mass migrations, the expansion of cyberspace, and mass-mediated spaces. I have argued elsewhere that, with regard to the Middle East in particular, in the last two decades the "threatening" presence of "Islamic fundamentalists" and the relocation of "Muslim immigrants" in the West have created new "security" concerns, leading to the emergence of a significant body of literature on new forms of globalization and the Middle East (Moallem 2001, 1266).[23] The military's security concerns in relation to new forms of imperialism and colonialism have created an increasing need for an ideologically legitimized expertise, incorporating the testimony of journalists, academics, administrative officers, and military and security officials, that is able to intervene in producing political, academic, and media discourses. A number of conferences, books, and articles have found an audience in academia and beyond under the rubric of the new global threat of Islamic fundamentalism, while in the world of visual media, depictions of the "Islamic other" have filled the void created by the disappearance of the old, post–Cold War version of friend/enemy.

The arrival of masses of new immigrants and refugees from Muslim cultures has created new anxieties about hosting the Muslim other in Western countries. Far from being utopian sites of hybridity, the cosmopolitan centers of the contemporary global village are marked by the twin traditions of asylum and xenophobia that still compete today, according to Gurnah (2000, 1). He argues that the modern construction of the narrative of the foreigner is accompanied by a discourse of asylum and coexists with a xenophobic narrative that constructs foreigners as eternally alien and tragic.[24] Indeed, these narratives are displaying the violence of borders and the limits of border-crossing. The daily pressure on these immigrants to identify or disidentify with their cultural and religious traditions as sources of threat, contamination, and barbarism is manifesting in new forms of racism. As Etienne Balibar argues in the case of Europe, the combination of colonial and anti-Semitic schemes, with their imageries of racial superiority and cultural and religious rivalry, works against the populations of Arab-Islamic origin who have settled there (1991a, 12).

These immigrants are casualties of the fragmented reality of a post/ neocolonial era. As they struggle to find space to engage critically with cultural and political issues, they find themselves constantly pushed to find meaning in old paradigms. They have difficulty fitting into the modernist framework of a homogenous self, since they claim to be from both here and there. Even as they lay claim to such a complicated identification, they are subjected to policing by the security concerns and the disciplinary measures of nation-states.

Emerging scholarly paradigms such as "Muslim and Arab studies," "Muslims in Europe," "West Asians," and "Muslim immigrants" depict the complexity of postcolonial convergences among the racialized immigrants from Middle Eastern, North African, and South Asian Muslim countries who find themselves in the West. At the same time, when I see them designated as yet another identity group in ethnic studies, I become concerned about what Spivak calls "the privileging of speech on the ground of the subject's self-presence" (1999, 321). While self-recognition of Arabs, Muslims, or other groups from the area as racialized creates all kinds of possibilities for understanding the linkages between the history of race and immigration in the United States, this does not necessarily incite an interrogation of the history of colonial modernity or the production of the United States as an "area" in itself and its relationship as such with the other areas of the world. I see here a kind of unrecognized hesitation about redefining *area* to include the history of both emplacement and displacement, which is parallel to that of the bodies living in the compression of time and space that it entails.

The very meaning of *area* has been called into question by the presence of immigrant communities from the Middle East and North Africa in Europe and North America. In fact, through social movements such as those centered on women, sexuality, and identity, those who were once objects of area studies are now themselves agents of social change and social transformation, challenging Middle Eastern studies as well as many other area studies. New scholarly paradigms are needed to study Muslims in the West, since neither modernist notions of identity nor taken-for-granted notions of area studies are able to grasp the complexity of an unstable and contested world of meanings, identities, and subjectivities.

As a field of knowledge production, Middle Eastern studies is marked by the absence of a certain postmodern scholarship that could potentially equip it to meet these challenges—in particular, colonial and postcolonial studies, transnational feminist theories, and transnational cultural studies. A fixation on what Immanuel Wallerstein calls "the historically frozen Oriental high civilizations" (1997, 198) is still a defining component of Middle Eastern studies. In recent years, new forms of Orientalism, along with racism vis-à-vis Middle Eastern peoples and cultures, have found currency in a reinvestment in the civilizational tropes of Islam and the West. However, the inability of Middle Eastern studies to catch up with the transnational nature of such transformations has kept it in a space/time where it is protected from the risk of its own disciplinary undoing.

The production of knowledge of the Middle East, and on the Middle East, is still governed by the political, cultural, and economic divisions of the particular nation-states. Appadurai argues eloquently that the geographical and geopolitical paradigms of area studies, in this case Middle Eastern studies, have affixed permanent associations between space, territory, and cultural organization (2001a, 8). As Said says, areas are also the material constructions of particular forms of power relationships (1979). Given the complexity of the present world situation, area studies now frequently overlap with international relations or globalization studies. However, the scope of the issues concerning the Middle East now surpasses even the disciplinary frameworks of international and area studies. This is why Middle Eastern studies now sometimes finds a home in such programs as security studies, peace and conflict studies, and immigration and diaspora studies. Again, the racialization of Muslims and Arabs, which cannot be separated from the notion of fundamentalism, has become a prominent topic in the study of U.S. (and European) race relations, but it has been dismissed by scholars in the fields of Middle Eastern studies and U.S. ethnic studies.

The underrepresentation of scholarship on transnational constructions of gender, sexuality, class, race, and religion in Middle Eastern studies has been crucial to the upholding of masculinist and Orientalist traditions of knowledge formation in the field. Middle Eastern feminist studies, however, is still placed in the context of development studies, modernization theories, and, increasingly, in the context of global feminist claims to international solidarity. Yet Eurocentric feminist discourses have been crucial in encouraging Western imperialism's current civilizational thinking, as they claim to save Muslim women from their barbaric societies. As I demonstrate in these pages, the Western trope of the Muslim woman as the ultimate victim of a timeless patriarchy defined by the barbarism of the Islamic religion, which is in need of civilizing, has become a very important component of Western regimes of knowledge. The need to engage with the gender underpinnings of Orientalism is no longer merely a rhetorical gesture of postcolonial criticism but has become its sine qua non, since it is under the sign of a veiled woman that "we" increasingly come to recognize ourselves not only as gendered and heteronormative subjects but also as located in the free West, where women are not imprisoned.

An interrogation of new frames of knowledge and representational practices is crucial for a critical intervention in the ways in which the notion of *Muslim* is circulated along with bodies and capital in a neocolonial, postcolonial context.

A Postmodern, Transnational Feminist Framework

This book investigates the overlapping of gender and fundamentalism in the context of Iran through a postmodern and transnational feminist framework. What I mean by *postmodern* is what Caren Kaplan calls a nonidealized but useful framing that can produce conversations and debates signifying the material conditions of critical practice (1996, 21). I also agree with Grewal and Kaplan's assessment that postmodernity is a useful model for understanding the production of modernity in non-Euro-American locations (1994, 5)—what Rofel (1999) calls the "other modernities," a term that includes the distribution, circulation, reception, and commodification of cultural productions both material and symbolic. Rofel notes that these other modernities are neither produced entirely locally nor reducible to a universal model (xii). Focusing on the case of India, Parama Roy elaborates on the process of subject formation in light of Rofel's observation and argues that indigenous subject constitution and nation formation require the establishment of specific symbolic orders and discursive formations as well as the subject's impersonation of what is imagined or imaginable (1998, 5). The plurality of

such symbolic orders, cultural productions, and social identities challenges modernity's unitary notions and demonstrates social formations
that are marked by plurality and multiplicity. It is in light of such theoretical contributions that this book examines the specific case of Iranian
modernity and postmodernity.

Analytically speaking, the concept of the postmodern has provided
space for the critique of modernity across various cultures and locations.
A postmodern approach is helpful in breaking with modernity's construct of the traditional as its other.[25] However, the concept of the postmodern often falls short of addressing the connections between colonialism and modernity. To account for this omission, some scholars use
the expression "colonial modernity" when speaking of modernity outside the West, especially with regard to modernity's construction of
gender and race (Barlow 1993; Grewal 1996). Although Middle Eastern
feminist scholarship has expanded, by not engaging with colonial
modernity and its racial and sexual formations it has contributed to
both heteronormative and ethnocentric practices of knowledge production and the reproduction of "tradition" and "modernity" as dichotomous notions, creating an apparent legitimacy for—in this case—a *feminist* civilizing mission. As Kaplan and Grewal have argued, the
civilizing mission of modern European imperialism relied on non-Western women's lives and on practices such as *suttee,* seclusion, foot binding, veiling, arranged marriages, and female circumcision to symbolize
the "barbarism" of non-Western cultures (1996, 14).[26] The dichotomous notions of "civilized" and "barbaric" are essential in the historical construction of colonialist racism, and in the production and reproduction of both Eurocentrism and masculinist citizenship in the context
of colonial modernity and postcolonial nationalisms. By not engaging
with colonial modernity, Middle Eastern and Iranian feminist studies
have in fact supported the very modernist structures that contribute to
the othering of non-Western women.

While some recent postcolonial feminist scholarship elaborates on
the "woman question" by locating it in the context of modernity and
colonialism in the Middle East, there is still no discussion of the specificity of modernity—the distinctive ways modernity was imagined, materialized, and experienced—in Middle Eastern societies. Abu-Lughod
goes so far as to argue that the woman question in the Middle East
needs to be explored in relation to the cultural dimensions of the colonial encounter and the relationship between the constructs of "East"
and "West" as they fashioned anticolonial nationalism (1998, 5). I agree

with Abu-Lughod that the reflection and scholarship that have developed around postcolonialism are relevant to the colonized, the semicolonized, and those who looked westward and followed its power. Most scholars in the field of gender and Middle Eastern studies, however, are still either taking modernity for granted or limiting themselves to the discourse of development or modernization (Göle 1996; Moghadam 1994; Paider 1995).

A number of feminist scholars have focused on the notion of citizenship (Joseph 1999; Hale 1999) and the formation of the nation-state (Kandiyoti 1991; Afshar 1987 and 1998) in the Middle East, either to distance themselves from cultural or economic approaches or to analyze the relationship between patriarchy and the state and the ways in which the state is a site of ongoing struggles. However, this literature is limited in scope, since it is invested primarily in political definitions of citizenship. I agree with Pettman (1996) that local, national, state, and wider political identities are increasingly located within global structures of power.

My claim is that transnational notions of citizenship are extremely important for an understanding of Islamic nationalism and fundamentalism, since, as Grewal, Gupta, and Ong argue, located and dislocated forms of belonging are connected through the movements of media, markets, and labor (1999, 664). In this context, I argue that in order to understand Islamic nationalism and fundamentalism, one must examine various forms of governmentality and citizenship as typical of modern nation-state formations and postmodern circuits of goods, technologies, and ideas. The theoretical contributions of transnational cultural studies are useful in delineating how modern Islamic forms of governmentality incorporate information technologies, consumer culture, and transnational media in both national and diasporic spaces.

Rofel points out that gender is not simply a factor added to the discourse of modernity; rather, it contributes to the very power relations constituting modernity (1999, 4). To break with the universalizing impulses of dominant masculinized Western cultures, we need theories and practices that are transnational and feminist in nature. As Grewal and Kaplan note, transnational feminist practices intervene critically in the imperialism of a Westernized global feminism that favors a universalized model of women's liberation (1994, 17). The notion of transnational cannot be reduced to modernist notions of international and internationalism since it is informed by the historical specificity of multiple modernities and patriarchies as well as global circulations of

labor, capital, and systems of representation within, between, and beyond the nation-states. In addition, transnational feminism does not
refer to yet another set of utopian discourses and practices but, as argued by Grewal and Kaplan, "involve[s] forms of alliance, subversion,
and complicities within which asymmetries and inequalities can be cri-
tiqued" (2000, 2).

Transnational feminist theories have been crucial not only in seeking
to understand the links between what Grewal and Kaplan call "scattered
cultural and economic hegemonies" (1994), which include various
forms of nationalisms and fundamentalisms, but also in exploring the
possibilities of feminist resistance to patriarchal regimes of power and
knowledge in a global world. Tani Barlow asserts that investigating the
history of contests over signifiers of gendered subject positionalities in
social and political terms is essential in developing a feminist politics
that is "rooted in difference without identity" (1994, 173–74)—or, in
Chandra Mohanty's terms, an analysis that does not reproduce the
hegemony of the idea of the West's superiority (1991b, 73).

To grasp the complexity of the political crisis before us—the new and
expanding forms of globalization, the massive presence of Middle Eastern diasporic communities in Western countries, and the new forms of
racism directed against Muslims and Arabs—we need a transnational
perspective now more than ever. Seeking to help fill this need, I analyze
racial, sexual, and gender formations in the context of Iranian modernity and postmodernity through a transnational framework. I argue that
the signifier of Muslim women, so prevalent in current Western representational practices, cannot be truly examined without stepping outside of the limitations of civilizational thinking; for, to put it bluntly, the
borders of barbarism and civilization—and thus the terms of entry into
the civilized world—are drawn by women's bodies, signifying their association with, or possession by, either a civilized or a barbaric community of men.

Even recent Middle Eastern feminist scholarship fails to examine
gender in the context of modern nation-state building, where particular notions of national community are invented to include men and
women as gendered, sexualized, and racialized subjects. Most of the
current literature in Middle Eastern studies is limited to the national
contexts of each country in the region, or else it employs comparative
international or inter-regional frameworks to examine gender issues,
which are articulated predominantly as women's issues. It fails to
examine gender in relation to the construction of masculinity and

femininity, sexuality and race, in the formation of modern subjects and their particular notions of belonging in the context of nation-state building or nationalism. Many problems remain unexplored—problems such as the emasculation of Muslim men produced by neocolonial modernity and the remasculinization permitted by nationalist and fundamentalist political movements. Fischer and Abedi's analysis of the implication of the fear of *différance* and the defensive anxiety about manhood that insists on subordinating women in the rhetoric of contemporary, politicized Islam is a productive point of departure (1990, 150–220). Parama Roy's recent book *Indian Traffic* (1999), which elaborates on the project of imagining India and Hinduness simultaneously in relation to the Hindu concept of masculinity and the displacement of religious, sexual, and nationalist imperatives, is one of the very few works in postcolonial feminist scholarship to engage with the dynamism of masculinity and heterosexuality under colonialism and nationalism.

I maintain that religious discourses, including fundamentalism, are both constitutive of and constituted by modern notions of gender and sexuality. I refer to sexuality in order to emphasize negotiations and contestations over the regimes of sexual knowledge and the meaning of eroticism, particular forms of desire, and the definitions of what is permitted or prohibited. Historically, religious discourses have significantly influenced cultural conditions of knowledge by articulating social practices in terms of what is culturally normative and what is considered perverse. In this sense it is very difficult to separate religions from their wider historical and social contexts. The patriarchal control of women's bodies and sexuality as a major subject of religious and cultural discourses converges with hegemonic notions of sexuality that privilege heteronormativity in the context of modernity and postmodernity. Thus, both gendered and sexual citizenship are created (and of course contested) as sites of exclusion and inclusion.

Religion and culture are not only inseparable from each other, they cannot be divorced from the historical conditions in which they emerge; nor can they be separated from the law, interpretations of the law, or an understanding of religion that accounts for sexualized bodies and desiring subjects. In other words, along with a number of other feminist scholars, I contend that gender is related to the ways in which power is distributed, mediated, and produced within modern culture, and as a result, we cannot separate religion from these processes or from what one might call the politics of religion. It is impossible to understand Islam and gender without locating them in the context of old and new forms of globalization, colonialism, postcolonial formations (including modernization and Westernization discourses and practices), nation-state formation, nationalism, and citizenship.

Methodological Considerations

In my examination of gender and fundamentalism in Iran, I draw on scholarship from a number of fields: transnational and postcolonial feminism, cultural studies, queer theory, and Middle Eastern and Iranian women's studies. My approach is transnational, enabling me to analyze historical, discursive, and media productions at both the macro and micro levels and to bring the past and the present, the global and the local, and the national and the transnational into the same frame of reference. This study incorporates a wide range of cultural and historical documents, including books, journals, daily newspapers, films, plays, poems, autobiographies, religious sermons, government propaganda, and popular slogans. By investigating the cultural meanings invested in the tropes, images, signifiers, and narratives that became sources of social knowledge and grist for the mill of political intervention, I seek to elucidate the ways in which a gendered Islamic subject was formed during the time of the Iranian revolution of 1979 by tracing the history of subject formation in Iranian modernity since the late nineteenth century. Since it contests the generalized and reductive terms in which Iran is often represented in the U.S. media, this book also makes a case for the cultural and historical significance of Iran.[27]

I utilize key concepts from several disciplines. I deploy the Foucauldian concept of a "discursive formation" and combine it with the notion of systems of representation familiar from cultural studies to examine what I call "fields of visibility" within Iranian modernity. The discursive formation model illuminates the way meanings and knowledge are produced to construct particular subject positions. Concepts and tools from cultural studies are important in my analysis of visual material and image-based discourses. My argument is that, although Iranian modernity and postmodernity have produced specific images of gendered, sexualized, and racialized bodies, these images are not produced with any degree of finality. What we need is an investigation of the dynamic, historically specific processes through which visual imageries of bodies are framed and coded by gender and race against the background of institutional practices across various domains, such as the family, the state, and political and religious organizations. I invoke Hamilton's notion of the "dominant representational paradigm" (1997, 76) and Gramsci's theory of hegemony (1971) to obtain critical purchase on the ways in which certain discourses and images are produced, circulated, consumed, and resisted. Fields of visibility are at once symbolic and material, that is, they are assumed by as well as inscribed on bodies. By arguing that these fields are discursively constructed and representationally organized, I elaborate on the complex forms of dialogue set up between gendered and race-based constructions of Persianness in colonial modernity, as well as between countercultural paradigms of Islamic nationalism and fundamentalism. If modern Westernized cultural meanings of Persianness claimed hegemony over the meaning of national identity before the revolution of 1979, in the postrevolutionary era the meaning of identity was countered and then replaced by Islamic notions of community.

To accomplish this study, I examine a wide range of discursive and visual cultural productions that circulate both nationally and internationally. I analyze the discursive and visual representations of each genre not for their literary style and value but as "research documents"[28] displaying recurring tropes, concepts, signifiers, and images that produce knowledge about the practices of gender identity in Iranian modernity. These discourses, visual images, film narratives, and civic performances are historically constructed to offer an analysis of subject positions within which individuals are able to recognize themselves in relation to others. Such is the case, for instance, in the first chapter, where I look at numerous texts on Persia published between the mid-nineteenth century and early twentieth century, mostly by French and English travelers, traders, military officers, missionaries, and social scientists. My intention is not to offer a detailed and comparative examination of these accounts but rather to examine those civilizational tropes that appear repeatedly in such texts. In my interpretation of these texts, I draw upon the notion of discourse as a system of representation and a regime of power and knowledge that produces and constitutes the subject in any particular historical period.

This project divides itself naturally into four periods according to four specific historical moments in Iranian modernity. The first period embraces the late nineteenth and early twentieth centuries, when civilizational imperialism, in its quest for cultural and economic hegemony in Iran, became a dominant part of a regime of power and knowledge produced, accumulated, and circulated via print media both by

Westerners and a Westernized local elite. The second period covers the years between 1921 and 1953, from the coup d'état of Reza Shah Pahlavi, when the nation-state was established, to the movement for the nationalization of oil, which was followed by a second coup reestablishing the Pahlavi regime after an attempted insurrection. The third period is after the coup d'état of 1953 up to the Iranian revolution of 1979. The fourth period, which begins with the Iranian revolution of 1979 and the establishment of an Islamic republic, continues to the present.

The book shifts from an analysis of print media in the earlier years to an analysis of film production in more recent decades because, in postrevolutionary Iran, filmic spaces have become an important site of transnational cultural, political, and critical intervention. The nationalist and anti-Western politics of the postrevolutionary Islamic state enabled a reversal of the filmic flow, which used to move from the West into Iran, so it now also moves out from Iran as an exporting of Iranian films to various Western and non-Western markets, including the Iranian diaspora in the West. I bring this reversal to bear on this discussion not to argue that it is in any measure comparable to the global hegemonic role of American cinema, but because Iranian cinema is now playing a significant role in bringing local Iranian issues to a transnational and global audience. As a space of mass media, cinematic space has allowed Iranians, both in Iran and in the diaspora, to engage with gender issues as directors, producers, and consumers. From a transnational feminist perspective, I find the opening of the new mass-mediated spaces extremely important for feminist political intervention in the context of a transnational civil society. While the scope of this project does not directly include the effect of the new electronic media and cyberspace, and their significance in the creation of new forms of governmentality and citizenship, my analyses of film production will raise issues that overlap with ones raised by these media.[29]

In the Fraternal Community of Ummat

Between Warrior Brother and Veiled Sister looks at fundamentalism as a crisis of modernity, rationality, and gender rather than simply one of tradition. My project is to examine feminist political activism within and outside of fundamentalist regimes of meaning-making; the representation of fundamentalism in the context of the transnational movement of capital, labor, and commodities; and the production of new religious subject positions. Throughout this book I am deeply interested in the politics of the image and the ways in which it dominates and seduces by investing power in particular signifiers, tropes, and descriptions. Seeking to understand this investment of power by problematizing its historical and textual context, I wish to open up space for a critique of patriarchal notions of community and solidarity, as well as global notions of sisterhood. The title of the volume, *Between Warrior Brother and Veiled Sister,* refers to the gendered notions of sister and brother as keys to understanding the invention of the ummat as a preexisting fraternal and patriarchal Muslim community. The word *between* interrogates the relationship between the warrior brother and the veiled sister as they evoke gender solidarity between the sexes and stage gender performance by maintaining the continuity and cohesion of a unified Islamic community.

Chapter 1 explores the "woman question" in light of what was called the "Persian question" by examining discursive formations of race, gender, and sexuality in the late nineteenth and early twentieth centuries. These discursive formations frame specific forms of representation, which institute and demand the subject's compliance with identifiable subject positions. I argue that the formation of modern disciplinary subjects in Iran must be understood in relation to colonial modernity and the configuration of the categories of both Persianness[30] and femininity as simultaneously unified within themselves and differentiated from others. I argue that representational practices of modernist tropes of gender and race in relation to Persianness have been crucial in the process of nation-state building and citizenship formation in Iran. The signifier of *hijab,* or the veil, has been crucial in staging difference and in giving meaning to a series of dichotomies that underlie gender, power, and authority in Iranian modernity. I argue that "civilizational thinking"—with its discursive regimes, images, tropes, icons, and metaphors—has been crucial in staging gender and religion in Iran. I also show how a number of discourses, including secular nationalism, religious nationalism, fundamentalism, and transnationalism, are related intertextually with civilizational thinking.

Chapter 2 elaborates the ways the discourses of gender and national difference in Iranian modernity after the coup d'état of Reza Shah in 1924 were invested in what I call the civic body—an abstract body that is made public and politicized in a way that displays the connections between individual and collective identities, and that is marked as a place of inclusion or exclusion. In the process of nation-state building, such

corporeal inscriptions put in place a system of signs that marked transgressive and dangerous bodies to delegitimize and criminalize them.
Gender has been crucial in allowing Islam to become a unified religious
and political system. In order to mimic European civilizational thinking,
Persian national chauvinists filtered Islam out of their system of invented tradition by investing in the veil as a signifier of barbarism, unveiling women, and inventing a golden pre-Islamic age of racial and cultural superiority. Although this endeavor was a failure, it paved the way
for Islamic nationalism to turn itself into an oppositional entity, syn-
cretizing the pre-Islamic mythos of Seyavash and the tragedy of Imam
Hussein.[31] It is through the construction of a unified community of
brothers and sisters, or the ummat, that Islamic nationalists and fundamentalists gained membership in the fraternal communities of nation
and state.

Chapter 3 examines the emergence of the gendered revolutionary
subject in the period before and during the Iranian revolution of 1979
through the circulation and legitimization of knowledge not controlled
by the West or the Westernized local elite. As discourse, fashion, spectacle, and historical event, the Iranian revolution presents an interesting
case, since gendered and Muslim bodies provided the surface for the inscription of an Islamic nation, a surface on which cultural and religious
nationalists were able to write their own meanings for the events of the
revolution. While multiple contestations were the order of the day, the
work of hegemony made it possible for the discourse of the revolution
to invest power in particular values and concepts by winning the consent of those who participated in the revolution for varied and sometimes antagonistic reasons. Along with the convergence of religion and
secularism, popular and elite culture, and the identities of Persian and
Muslim, the extensive application of information technologies by the
Islamic movement enabled the emergence of a specific Islamic subject.
I argue that through popular and religious cultural tropes, narratives,
and signifiers, this revolutionary subject drew attention away from the
self as different, ancient, or oppositional to make the Islamic ummat a
mythical yet historical community of brothers and sisters. By recourse
to an antimodern staging of death as a public matter in the day-to-day
theater of the revolution, and through the staging of local rituals such
as Muharam[32] and Karbala-ye Husseini,[33] a revolutionary self was fashioned that was situated anterior to the events of the revolution.

Chapter 4 focuses on the limits of an Islamic nationalism that relies on
a centralized, modern nation-state ruling in the name of a transnational

Islamic ummat. Transnational Islam uses the media and representational tropes familiar in the West to talk about subjectivity, identity, and power. It is political and deploys tropes that are substantially gendered. Membership in transnational Islam is based not on religiosity but on adoption of a particular view of Islam (both from the outside and the inside) and the willingness to (dis)identify with it, fight for it, or fight against it. Thus, what I call Islamic transnational fundamentalism is a coproduction of the conditions of consumer capitalism and new regimes of governmentality. I argue that in both political and cultural citizenship, the collective will of the Islamic ummat is challenged by the expression of fragmented willing subjects. The fragmentation of this collective will is expressed through various practices, from the discussion of the "woman question"—both in the discursive space opened up by colonial modernity and in the mundane spaces where women find themselves negotiating day-to-day legal, economic, and political obstacles—to filmic commentaries on gender, class, and religious hierarchies. In addition, this chapter elaborates on the ways the rigid narratives of nation and religion are thrown into crisis by the display of a fragmented subject who disrupts Islamic nationalism and fundamentalism by "passing"—taking an ambiguous position vis-à-vis not only Islamic narratives of gender, nation, and religion but also modernity's foundational myths of subjectivity and identity.

Chapter 5 looks at both feminism and fundamentalism as major forces responsive to the crisis of rationality, as well as the crisis of masculinity, in prerevolutionary Iran. I argue that both feminism and fundamentalism arise within the problematic of modernity, since it deals with relations between men and women with respect to the universal and the particular, the public and the private, the family and the state, and the individual and the community. I contend that the convergence of feminism and fundamentalism has brought into being fundamentalist feminism and feminist fundamentalism. By calling for the reconciliation of feminism and Islam, as well as the articulation of an indigenous Islamic feminism, Iranian women have been able to negotiate various cultural, legal, and economic expressions of patriarchy. Thus an Islamic feminism has emerged out of Islamic fundamentalism by distancing itself from the antifeminist agenda of fundamentalism and by referring to both Islam and feminism as contested sites of political intervention.

CHAPTER I

Fields of Visibility

The ultimate aim of colonial mimicry is not simply to constitute natives as objects to be studied; it must also produce natives as self-reflexive subjects, who know themselves as others (the colonizers) know them.

Parama Roy (1998, 39)

How are the sounds of the past to be met as they emerge from the well of bygone centuries? What love must still be sought, what future be planned despite the call of the dead? And my body reverberates with sounds from the endless landslide of generations of my lineage.

Assia Djebar (1993, 46)

To understand Islamic nationalism and fundamentalism in Iran, we need to investigate the ways in which Iranian modernity is articulated and the ways in which it has inserted Iran into circuits of global capitalism and modern regimes of governmentality. Iranian modernity cannot be studied without an understanding of its connection to European and Third World modernities, as well as to the process of cultural borrowing, which influenced both modern nation-state building in Iran and various oppositional reform and revolutionary movements. I argue that historical narratives of Iranian modernity diminish the importance of what Ashis Nandy calls "civilizational imperialism." Nandy's expression foregrounds the ways in which imperialism is based on the opposition of civilization to savagery. As such, it resonates more closely with my analysis than the more common "cultural imperialism." Narratives of Iranian modernity incorporate the rhetoric of Orientalism and nationalism, yet refuse to engage directly with colonial and postcolonial reflections on issues of identity. As a result, these narratives have failed to produce an understanding of the humiliating effects of the discourse of race and of the role of gender and sexuality in the invention and reinvention of the nation, in this particular case the Islamic nation. Consequently, tropes such as the veil have become both a global and local sign of identity and of resistance in the postcolonial era. In order to deepen our understanding of the complicated global and national dynamics surrounding the discourse of Islamic nationalism, I have chosen to analyze the impact of civilizational imperialism in the construction of what Foucault calls "a state of population," and what Etienne Balibar refers to as the institution of *homo nationalis*.

In this chapter, I will examine those discursive sites where the Islamic ummat has been able to successfully reinvent its will to assert a collective identity, demanding recognition of its people, and where power can be disguised by creating an "outside" to itself.[1] I am particularly interested in looking at sites of repetition and national performances where the will to nationhood is claimed, reclaimed, or contested. In this context, the Islamic ummat is defined intertextually through modern concepts such as nation, people, ethnic group, and tribe.[2]

To understand this process, we need to investigate the main discursive sites of both Westernization and nation-state building to engage with race and gender as important signifiers in the textualization of Iranian modernity and its reinvention and reconstruction in the space of the Islamic ummat. I use textualization to refer to specific forms of representation that institute and demand the subject's compliance with identifiable subject positions. In Foucault's formulation (1980), subject positions are produced through/as discursive formations. That is, textualization permits meaning to be repeated through the creation of what I call "fields of visibility," or specific representational frames. The subject must comply with identifiable subject positions. Visibility functions as a site of regulation and disciplining. As Foucault asserts, "Discipline produces subjected and practiced bodies, docile bodies" (1979a, 138). In light of Gramsci's idea of hegemony as the ideological power struggle between particular social groups to win the consent of other groups, fields of visibility include both the coercive and seductive forces engaged in the struggle over representation, ideas, cultural leadership, and authority.[3]

Afsaneh Najmabadi, a prominent Iranian feminist, argues that post-coloniality has been an "unavailable space" for Iranian scholars because colonial and postcolonial studies' dichotomous notions of colonizer and colonized make a speaking position impossible for the "neither-nor" zones, such as Iran, Thailand, and other so-called imperial oddities set at the zero time of colonization.[4] In response to Najmabadi's contention, I would argue that Iranian modernity is defined in significant ways by the constructions of race and gender found in the traveling notions that accompany the civilizational imperialism of Western modernity.[5] Since colonialism and postcolonialism are an integral part of modernity, it is impossible for any discussion of modernity—even in "neither-nor" zones like Iran—to avoid confronting modern constructions of race and gender. Indeed, both the translational discourse of the modernist and reformist Iranian elite from the late nineteenth and early twentieth centuries to the present and the coercive modernizing discourse of the Pahlavi regime are intertextually related to Western concepts of civilization and discourses about Persia. The zoning of Persia in the discourse of colonial modernity led to a linguistic shift in the discourses of oppositional movements.

Close reading of European writings on Persia reveals the importance of race and gender to the production of this discourse. Alarcón argues that racialization operates through the dichotomous notions of "civilized" and "barbaric," reinforcing "whiteness" as the "absolute idea of goodness and value" (1998, 377). At the same time however, hegemonic notions of masculinity and femininity have defined the creation of a normative Persian culture for both civilized and barbaric conceptions of the culture. Balibar describes the function of difference in colonialism in the following terms:

We must, however, observe that the *exteriority* of the "native" population in colonization, or rather the representation of that state as *racial* exteriority, though it recuperates and assimilates into its discourse very old images of "difference," is by no means a given state of affairs. It was in fact produced and reproduced within the very space constituted by conquest and colonization with its concrete structures of administration, forced labor and sexual oppression, and therefore on the basis of a certain *interiority*. Otherwise one could not explain the ambivalence of the dual movement of assimilation and exclusion of the "natives" nor the way in which the subhuman nature attributed to the colonized comes to determine the self-image developed within the colonized nations in the period when the world was being divided up. (1991c, 42–43)

This dichotomy of interiority and exteriority is established and functions through the idea of the collective barbarism and immorality of Persians, an idea based on the absence of a Persian rule of law and on the Persian adoption of Islam. This dichotomy also depends on a gendered construction of Persian character in which men are depicted as violent and cruel, women as subordinate, passive, lazy, and obsessed with food and sex. These discourses include academic texts as well as fiction, children's books, and, increasingly, visual media. In addition, they are not limited to the colonial era but are very much present in contemporary society. The producers and agents of such discourses are from both the West and the Middle East; their consumers are both Iranians and non-Iranians of different classes, ethnicities, and religions. Clearly, the cultural representation of otherness cannot be separated from what Said refers to as "a created body of theory and practice in which, for many generations, there has been a considerable material investment" (1979, 6).

My project focuses on two historical periods: first, the late nineteenth and early twentieth centuries, the period of heightened European colonialism and imperialism, and, second, the period from Reza Shah's coup d'état in 1921 to the Iranian revolution of 1979 and the establishment of the Islamic Republic (the period in which the modern nation-state was established in Iran).[6] This chapter examines the gendered construction of the Orientalist notions of Persia and Persians, the invention and reinvention of these notions by a modernizing Iranian intelligentsia, and their adoption, rejection, and contestation by Islamic nationalists and fundamentalists. I would argue, echoing Said (1979), that one of the reasons why religion becomes a site of mimicry and contestation in the Islamic version of European modernity is because religion mobilizes the discourse of anti-Semitism. The discourse of Christianity constitutes both Jews and Muslims as believers in so-called primitive religions (to use Renan's terms), who lack any concept of spirituality or transcendence. Throughout the twentieth century, many Iranian secular modernists incorporated religion into their writings as a component of modernity. By including religion in the "ethos" of modernity, secular modernists were able to counter emerging religious nationalism by locating religion as a coherent ideological system and a normative discourse. Either religion was regarded instrumentally—as part of a discourse to be used for secular purposes—or it was consigned to tradition and thus to the past. In this view, religion exists in the temporality of the premodern, doomed to be forgotten or, at most, subordinate to evolution and progress.

Civilizational Thinking and Persian Otherness

It is essential to note that while Orientalism has been extremely important as a regime of "othering," fundamental to colonial modernity and postcoloniality, the representation of otherness has not been identical everywhere. Although representational practices have been constructed and contested differently in different geopolitical locations, nevertheless, all forms of otherness and "we-ness" have relied on gender and sexuality as markers of Westernization or anti-West oppositional identities. In the case of Iran, these constructions have been framed by three major discursive formations: (1) the disciplinary-academic matrix within which knowledge of particular regions of the world is produced—from the now obsolete Oriental studies to contemporary area studies; (2) global racial formations based on culture and religion rather than biological categories of race; and (3) cultural or religious nationalist and fundamentalist claims to particularity and authenticity.

It is primarily through claiming or disavowing colonial modernity that the discourse of race remains intact through its mutual constitution by Westerners and local elites. A systematic reliance on the discourse of civilization and barbarism can be seen in the use of a number of interchangeable paired tropes, such as modern versus traditional, developed versus underdeveloped, and progressive versus backward. The essentialization of Persian culture through the idea of "Persian character" provided space for the production of a national character. Cultural essentialism, in complicity with the modern discourses of eugenics and biological determinism, deployed gender and sexuality in order to ascribe a particularity to Persianness. These constructions are still active today. Against the backdrop of global geopolitical inequalities and the rapid circulation of cultural products through global media, the racialization of culture has become an important mode for the production of otherness and the fabrication of the foundational myth of authenticity and difference in the discourses of nationalism, religious and secular alike.

What is interesting about this colonial period is the production of a privileged subject position that allows for the emergence of a locally gendered subjectivity. Either in its mimicry of or its opposition to the West, this subject position, far from being that of a passive consumer of meaning, is rather that of a historical subject able to "make meaning" by stepping out of predefined frames. As Foucault notes, "One has to dispense with the constituent subject, to get rid of the subject itself, that is to say, to arrive at an analysis which can account for the constitution of the subject within a historical framework" (1980, 115). Foucault's theoretical insight is useful in tracing the historical formation of the Islamic subject that is "outed" from an ahistorical, quasi-mythological closet.

My work draws on recent feminist postcolonial criticism on the gendering of Orientalism. The contributions of Alloula (1986), Graham-Brown (1988), and Shohat and Stam (1994) have been crucial in illustrating the symbolic and material colonial appropriation of gendered bodies. It is crucial to investigate particular civilizational tropes, signifiers, and representations that constitute the discourse of Persia as the other of Europe. In the field of Iranian studies, the circulation, exchange, and consumption of such meanings are either naturalized or described by an evolutionary framework that refers to the West in civilizational or countercivilizational terms. In her study of the history of translingual practices in China, Lydia Liu (1995) argues that a careful examination of the complex processes of translation, adoption, appropriation, domination, and resistance that constitute the Chinese image/conception of modernity is crucial to an understanding of discursive practices that determine relations between the West and the East. Such an analysis is also crucial for understanding Iranian modernity. The political economy of the symbolic and material circulation of meanings, goods, and bodies between Iran and various Western countries is still wide open for further research and investigation.

As a discourse, civilizational imperialism was essential in the production of Iranian modern subjectivities. There are two sets of texts representing civilizational imperialism, those produced by Western (mostly French and English) travelers, traders, colonial officials, missionaries, and social scientists and those produced by the Iranian local elite who positioned themselves with respect to Western discourses. I have chosen to focus on particular frames of meaning and the tropes operating within what Foucault calls the limits of the episteme, the discursive formation, and the regime of truth (1980). For Foucault, man was born in the nineteenth century, when "one made of man an object of knowledge so that man could become subject of his own liberty and of his own existence" (1989, 36–37).

Many of the authors from the mid-nineteenth and early twentieth centuries whose texts I study make reference to Persian women and their particular situation. The texts authored by women, however, tend to include more extensive accounts of Persian women's circumstances. I do not offer a detailed examination of these accounts, but rather aim to uncover the civilizational tropes that appear repeatedly in such texts.

I also examine a series of late-nineteenth-century adventure books set in—among other places—Persia and written in English for young people, as well as other fiction focused on Persia.[7] These discourses contain two common features: the transnationality of the tropes that link the local to the global (and vice versa) and their systematic production through the construction of gendered bodies.

Recent scholarship on gender, sexuality, and travel narratives provides many insights into the complexities of imperialist discourse.[8] As Caren Kaplan argues, the taken-for-granted categories of home and away, placement and displacement, dwelling and travel, and location and dislocation are inseparable from the historical phenomenon of modern imperialism (1996, 1). In a careful examination of the cultural formations of imperialism and nationalism in India, Inderpal Grewal shows how the female body was written into the nation through the discourse of travel (1996, 230). Any project that analyzes the phenomenon of modern imperialism must address the relationship between colonialism and the postcolonial, masculinist, cultural, and religious nationalisms that are invested in the institutionalization of gender power, since colonialism is the residual content of postcolonial nationalism.[9] In my mapping of national identity, I am committed to exposing the gendered, racialized, and sexualized tropes operative in the invention of Persian character.

Nation and the Invention of the "Persian Character"

> Dr. Euselius sat by Alice's side and gave way to gloomy thoughts.
>
> "I hope we shall not be wrecked," said Alice. "Persia is an almost barbarous country, and I cannot speak a word of the language."
>
> "I have heard that in the case of ladies being wrecked, the young and pretty are sold to great chiefs."
>
> "And the old and ugly?"
>
> "They are made into slaves or killed outright."
>
> *Alice: The Adventures of an English Girl in Persia* (1890, 10)

In the novel *Alice,* published in England in 1890, the protagonist, a poor orphaned English girl, goes on a voyage with her aunt. The ship on which they sail to India to visit her uncle is called *The City of Tehran.*

On the way to India, the ship calls in to "the mysterious kingdom of Persia," where "women are beaten and tortured in Zenana and there is no rule of law but barbaric hierarchy" (10). So begins Alice's adventure in the land of Persian barbarians, who are "believers of Mohametan's religion." Alice is protected by the heroic English sailor Ralph, with whom she falls in love. The story proceeds by way of a series of conversations interspersed with illustrations that portray all Persians—men and women—as dark and barbaric figures of disorder and violence. Through the crude gaze of a Persian prince who longs to possess Alice (Alice's body), Alice becomes "a dream of beauty" with her skin as "white as snow; eyes like the blue sky" (55). Through the tropes of whiteness, Englishness, and heterosexual romantic love, Alice, formerly poor and orphaned in England, not only escapes her destiny as a poor young woman but also comes to appreciate the English treatment of women. A dialogue between Alice and Fanny (a French woman enslaved by the same prince who lusts after Alice) brings Alice's new appreciation of England to light. Fanny tells Alice, "It seems to me in this country, from what I have seen, that they don't treat women as we do in Europe." Alice replies, "Certainly not, . . . they are kept here as ornamental dolls. The mind is neglected, and only the personal or bodily charms cultivated" (115). This story illustrates contrasting symbolic and geographical imaginary lines between dark places, such as barbaric Persia, and civilized White England.

The development of a world market for trade in the eighteenth and nineteenth centuries is closely correlated with the idea of a dominant ethnicity.[10] The exotic other emerges in this context as the object of both hatred and desire. The politics of power infiltrate spheres of knowledge and allow a certain kind of historiography, largely Orientalist, to display "the world as an exhibition."[11] The representation of Persia in the story of Alice is intertextually related to the cultural production of Orientalism in Europe (in literature, painting, drama, the decorative arts, and other media).

The construction of an Iranian nation cannot be separated from the construction of the Persian character by travelers, social scientists, geographers, missionaries, and colonial officers. References to "Persian character" or "Iranian essence" *(Jenss-e Irani)* in the discourse of the modernizing and modernized local Iranian elites intertextually evoked this European discourse (Malkum Khan 1976). Furthermore, analysis of the discourse on Persia reveals the pivotal role Persia played in the development of Western notions of civilization and modernity. These discourses produce a normative code of conduct that reaffirms Europe as a source of inspiration. Travel writings in particular make a space for such codes of conduct and normative conceptions of European identity by creating an "us," which is opposed to "them," and by constructing the superiority of this "us."

Persian otherness is established in and through various genres of writing, all of which have two functions: to produce a culturally dynamic, progressive Europe free from traditional bonds and to cast Persia as a historical prison house, an ancient high civilization of the non-West, "frozen historically and incapable of proceeding autonomously to modernity" (Wallerstein 1997, 198–99). In the European imagination, then, Persia comes to be a place of absolutism and positively barbaric manners and yet, at the same time, a place that is radically lacking—it is without law and order, without motivation or desire to evolve, without any rupture with regard to its past. This representation legitimizes, even demands, European intervention. Margaret L. Gertrude Bell, in her book on her travels to Iran, writes:

It has been said before, and repeated until it should be familiar, that the swift current of Western life is an exception to the general rule, and not the rule itself—said and repeated, and yet when you are brought face to face with tiny towns and remote fishing villages, for whose birth there seems to be no reason but caprice, for whose continuance even caprice can scarcely be alleged, and which may yet boast two thousand years of life, you will stand aghast at such hoar conservative antiquity. Where is progress? Where is the march of civilization? Where the evolution of race? (1894, 261–62)

In this quote, Bell strongly identifies with racial and cultural narratives of progress as the main components of European modernity and with modern Europe as distinct from both premodern Europe and from non-European societies. When she discusses women, her claim that a culturally distinguished, European lifestyle is by definition superior to all other lifestyles is influenced by her racial and class positions as well as by the dominant discourses of race and culture in Europe. Bell's depiction of Iranian women is determined by her identification with the bias of the bourgeoisie, which denigrates peasant life as "capricious" because peasants do not have a decisive social purpose in the bourgeois view of life. While Iran has its own long history of urbanism and class structure, Bell's depiction of the Iranian peasant woman's lifestyle as radically distinguished from her own or from that of the urban, bourgeois European woman demonstrates her ideological complicity with Eurocentric portrayals of an urban Europe that stands in opposition to a rural Iran.

Many nineteenth-century European writers argue that the adoption of the Mohammedan religion and the absence of a culture of "home" (including Persian women's lack of proper notions of motherhood) are essential to the explanation of Persian barbarism and backwardness. While the absence of home represents a utopian harem for certain female travelers, such as Lady Montagne, because of the association of home with domesticity, home and harem have always been defined as binary notions.[12] Such dichotomous thinking produces a pedagogical framework for men and women to share the dream of the civilizing mission, or "la mission civilisatrice." As we will see, these two components of Persian backwardness become important discursive frames in the construction of a unified Iranian character and remain discursively central to the modernization imposed by the Pahlavi regime, to revolutionary oppositional movements, and to the postrevolutionary discourses in both Iran and the Iranian diaspora.

The Orientalist concept of a "Persian character" remained an important site of othering by Western powers and was used to justify Western intervention in the Iranian political sphere. In her detailed historical account of the Iranian oil crisis of the early 1950s, Mary Ann Heiss asserts that Anglo-American officials, reacting to the movement for the nationalization of oil between 1950 and 1953, quite frequently used phrases such as "Iranian mentality" and the "Oriental mind" to rationalize the failure to reach an acceptable oil agreement (1997, 231).[13] According to Heiss, the Iranian prime minister, Mossadeq, was characterized by Anglo-American officials as a "wily Oriental" whose approach to oil was "almost mystical," and the Iranian people were considered incapable of choosing and following the right leader (230). Gender-based language was used to feminize prime minister Mossadeq as "an irrational and fickle adversary who was prone to emotional outbursts, likely to change his mind, and could not be trusted." Such justifications were used to legitimize the CIA-assisted coup d'état of 1953 that replaced the nationalist state of Prime Minister Mossadeq with Pahlavi's dictatorship. Similar characterizations of Iranians also emerge in the context of postrevolutionary Iran, especially in the context of the hostage crisis, and are still used in contemporary Europe and North America to single out Iranians, both in Iran and in the Iranian diaspora.

Race, Religion, and Islamic Otherness

> Generally speaking, Persians are not improved by their
> religious ideas, for the stronger their religious ideas are, the
> worse their lives are, and what one most admires in Persian
> character is least in accordance with their religious belief.
>
> Mrs. Napier Malcolm (1911, 58)

> But Islamism has produced nothing like that on this
> fundamental point. Everywhere there is vagueness,
> uncertainty, an infinite fear of God's judgments, which there is
> no way to anticipate and the absolute originality with which
> they claim to submit themselves to them [God's judgments]—
> that is all that it is able to talk about.
>
> Conte de Gobineau (1865, 53)

For Europeans, the major putative factor in the notion of Persian immorality and cultural inferiority is the Persian adoption of the Mohammedan religion. This logic, however, assumes that all Persians practice one religion and thus excludes non-Muslim Persians. In addition, it presupposes that religion can be identified as a unified, foundational belief system and that Mohammedanism is representative of all forms of Islamic practices, including all branches of Sufism, Shiism, and Sunnism. In the Western view, Mohammedanism in Persia has an anticivilizational effect leading to the cultural degeneration of Persians and the barbaric treatment of women. For Europeans, Islam represents a homogenous doctrine that is essentialized as a force that limits the mental capacities of its adherents. Modern forms of racialization consider religion—Islam, in this case—to be intrinsic to the determination of group inferiority.[14] The idea that a cultural or religious system can be intrinsic has its roots in European race relations and, in particular, in the discourse of anti-Semitism. Horkheimer and Adorno argue that the idea of an "opposing race as the embodiment of the negative principle" is key to the process of racialization (1987, 168).

Sir John Malcolm's *Sketches of Persia* provides a salient example of the way in which Persians are cast as the embodiment of the negative principle:

The intellectual acquirements of the Persians are very limited indeed; consequently their minds are not imbued with anything noble or elevated. They receive no philosophical training, and they know nothing of metaphysics. To be well read in the Koran is the height of their literary acquirements. The modern arts and sciences they know nothing of; but, in my opinion, the cause of this ignorance, and their deficiencies generally, is not the want of mental capacity, but the want of training. No Mohammedan country can ever be great, or far advanced in art, science, and literature, for their religion is the great barrier that keeps them back and binds the mind in a shroud of mental darkness. (1827, 189)

Malcolm's depiction of Persians as intellectually backward is grounded in European race theory and its legal and scientific foundations. Along with many other Western travelers, Malcolm locates Persian backwardness in its religion. The assumption here is that, as a Mohammedan country contaminated by Islam, Persia can never advance in art, science, and literature. The degeneration of Persia is taken to be a by-product of its adoption of Islam.

In the context of modern colonial racial formations, religion becomes not only a means of racialization but also a theoretical tool for justifying the assessment of Islamic inferiority and thus the need for European intervention. A report titled *How to Win Over Moslem Races*, presented at the First Missionary Conference on Behalf of the Mohammedan World, which was held at Cairo in the spring of 1906, contains the statement: "We should win Moslems by showing them a new way of life" (1906, 117). This report includes a section written by Miss G. Y. Holliday on Muslim women in Persia. She states:

The religion of Islam is the cause of special suffering to women. To alleviate and deaden her misery, she resorts to narcotics and stimulants. The Moslem woman suffers physically from her religion; she suffers mentally from a sense of degradation and inferiority ground into her by the veil and to the curtain which never allow her for a moment to forget herself; she suffers from fear of her husband, her family and society, the fear of marriage, of divorce, the fear of unseen malevolent powers, and the fear of death; she suffers from ignorance and from her own follies. (111–12)

This statement is a typical example of how religion is implicated in the process of racialization. In this case, Enlightenment philosophy, with its emphasis on reason over religion, creates a hierarchy of cultures, ranked from barbaric to civilized, which situates Muslims as religiously different but inferior. In addition, women's suffering and inferior position were blamed on the Islamic religion and its barbaric laws. Reference to the "Moslem race" depicts a non-Christian world defined by racial and religious difference. The signifier of race equates religion and race to create what Stuart Hall calls "the spectacle of the 'Other'" (1997, 225),

which enables the connection between fields of visibility and the production of racialized knowledge.[15]

According to Gobineau, the major nineteenth-century scholar of
Oriental religions who, along with Renan, was extremely influential in
the formation of racialism and the propagation of French cultural
racism, Islam is not compatible with the civilized world because it is a
religion that lacks coherence. In Gobineau's words: "As there is not any
sizable group united by the bonds of a strictly accepted doctrine, there
is not collective enthusiasm or well-defined, common hatred either"
(1865, 21).

For Gobineau, Islam is a religion characterized by "a sectarian spirit
with these inconsistent formulas, which seemed to invite everyone to
acknowledge [Islam] without asking anyone to abandon any part of
what he thought" (53). Gobineau then makes an astonishing statement—scarcely credible in these days, when fundamentalism is applied
primarily to Islam and the Muslim world. He writes: "Fanaticism, as a
persuasion tolerates no religion whatsoever, was antithetical to the spirit
of Orientals and does not exist among them" (21). The depiction of
Islam by Gobineau shows to what extent the perception of Islam in the
West has changed since the nineteenth century and proves that the representation of Islam is always formulated within a historical and geopolitical framework.

In March 1883, in his famous paper titled "Islam and Science," Ernest
Renan declared, "Anyone even somewhat acquainted with our times
clearly sees the present inferiority of the Islamic countries, the decadence of the states governed by Islam, the intellectual insignificance of
the races that derive their culture and education from this religion
alone" (1883, 2–3). For Renan, Arabs are neither receptive to nor capable of metaphysics and philosophy, which for him, in a kind of spatial-
ized division of intellectual labor, remain specialties of the Aryan race
(cited by Wessels 1984, 193).

Racialization of Muslims works together with the representation of
gender relations in Western discourse. Women and gender issues become the main signifiers of Muslim backwardness and difference. The
condition of women in Muslim countries, in this case Iran, also serves
to define the boundaries between the civilized world of Europe and the
barbaric world of Islam. The alliance of what Donaldson calls "God,
gold, and gender" plays a crucial role in the representation of Muslim
women in general and Persian women in particular (Donaldson and
Kwok 2002, 5). Consider this quotation from Sir John Malcolm: "I have

had frequent discussions with my Persian friends upon the general condition of the female sex in this country and cannot better illustrate the subject than by relating what passed on an occasion when I made a violent attack on their usages in this particular, and brought them into strong contrast with those of the civilized nations of Europe" (1827, 34).

Here, religion represents a source of moral decadence and a signifier of women's oppression. Through the racialization of Persians and the sexual objectification of Persian women, Europeans construct themselves as racially superior subjects. The depiction of Persian women both as victims of cultural and religious traditions and as accomplices enjoying their own slavery opens up a space for the emergence of a "discourse of protection." I use this term to capture what Pathak and Rajan describe as the creation of "an alliance between protector and protected against a common opponent from whom danger is perceived and protection offered or sought, and this alliance tends to efface the will to power exercised by the protector" (1989, 566).

This discourse of protection is evident in the following passage from *Children of Persia,* a travelogue by Mrs. Napier Malcolm:

Yes, Persia has indeed fallen into a pit, and we must pull her out, but the pit is not simply one of political difficulty, and we must annex Persia for the King of Kings. As long as Persians are Muhammadans, lying and dishonesty will be the rule, cruelty and injustice will go hand in hand, the poor will be oppressed, the girls and women will be treated as inferior creatures, the children will be liable to overwork and cruelty and religious persecution will continue. And the Persians are finding out that they are in a pit and they are struggling to get out, they are crying to us for help. Are we going to help them? (1911, 93)

The feminization of Persia, positioned as a woman who has fallen into a pit, and the depiction of Persian women as being in need of protection from injustice and cruelty serve to legitimize two subject positions—one for Western men and the other for Western women. A masculine Christianity is legitimized through the naturalization of colonialism to rescue a feminized Muslim Persia. European women, meanwhile, are called to collaborate with European men to save Persian women and children from poverty and injustice. The depiction of Persian women as passive victims who are in need of protection continues to be the principal constituent of current forms of neocolonialism in the Middle East. The discourse of protection, I would argue, creates an alliance between European men and women. Although many European women who travel to Iran express sympathy and solidarity with, if not pity for, Persian women, to a greater extent they feel empowered by belonging to a civilized European order of things. As Grewal suggests, "For the English women the harem became an example of the consequence of the denial of freedom to women as well as the problem of the inferior races" (1996, 82).

The civilizing mission targeted Islamic religion as a source of Persian backwardness and women as its main victims. These discourses stimulated complicity with the temporality of colonial modernity and its particular discourses vis-à-vis Persians. At the same time, they triggered a local contest over who could or should take charge of bringing Persia into the modern, civilized world. As a sign, veiling brought together these two components of Persian character in a move that continues to invent masculinity and femininity in the void created by colonial forms of subjection, as well as in nationalist and fundamentalist oppositional movements. Although Iran was not directly colonized, its encounter with the Western world necessitated its engagement with civilizational imperialist discourses.

In the course of the twentieth century, local Persian elites articulated significant responses to civilizational imperialism. These responses serve as defining factors of Iranian modernity and have motivated both secular and religious nationalism. Westerners' ascription of barbarism and lack of knowledge to Muslims generated a debate among Muslim reformers, who disapproved of such accusations while inviting Muslims to reform Islam. For example, in his response to Renan in the *Journal des Débats*, Sayyid Jamal ud-Din Asadabadi (Al-Afghani) makes two important contributions to the debate.[16] First, he refutes Renan's depiction of Muslims as "living in barbarism and ignorance," and second, he calls upon Muslims to overcome the divisions that hold them apart, in essence calling on them to reform Islam (Keddie 1983, 84–95). The Quranic slogan "Truly God does not change the situation of people if they do not change it themselves" is a call to Muslims to participate in the project of religious revival.[17] Asadabadi was, in the colonial period, the founder of an Islamic revival movement, but his revivalism had a rather expansive nature, since he was always open to discussion and reform. He invited the Islamic countries to pan-Islamism as a solution by asking them to go beyond ethnic, class, or territorial differences and to unite under the banner of monotheism and prophecy. He believed that religious belonging was more important than territorial belonging, and that nationalism could not be limited to geographical location (Moddaressi Chardehi 1955, 16). Ayatollah Khomeini, the leader of the Iranian revolution of 1979, never addressed Asadabadi as a possible point of reference in the wave of what occurred in Islamic revivalism.[18]

Thus the colonial period marks the invention of an "Islamic otherness," whose essential characteristic is gender stereotyping. The alluring image of the veiled Muslim woman, in particular, is central to Orientalist discourse.[19] In response to the sexism and racism of Orientalism, Iranians produced a counterdiscourse of gendered nationalism, provincialism, and so-called Occidentalism. Islamic revivalism in this period encouraged the mobilization of the sociopolitical resources of the Islamic religion for social reform. The shift from Al-Afghani's brand of revivalism to contemporary Islamic revivalist and fundamentalist movements is conditioned by different historical and social factors functioning at the national, regional, and transnational levels.

Oil, Carpets, and the "Persian Problem"

> European women could certainly do the work more conscientiously and efficiently, and the employment of a few simple devices, such, for instance, as Mr. Lombaers's scissors, would ensure a better result. But then consider the cost of labour. A woman working at a piece two feet wide can finish one line of stitches in half an hour. If the carpet is to be of moderate quality there must be ten lines of stitches to the inch, that is to say, she finishes a piece of carpet two feet wide by one inch in length in five hours: in other words a square foot in thirty hours. . . . That, then, is why carpets are made in Persia under European supervision and transported, at a cost of 30 per cent of their original value, to Europe instead of being made in Birmingham. That there exists any special faculty for the industry or the art in Persia cannot be believed by anyone who examines the method or its results. Fortunately for the British and American householders, the Persian woman is still a slave. If ever she is emancipated or raised out of the Mohammedan abyss to a higher level in the scale of existence Persian carpets will become a thing of the past.
>
> H. J. Whigham (1903, 300–301)

Whigham's depiction of Persian women's labor in the carpet industry in *The Persian Problem* is instructive. On the one hand, he argues that European women would not merely be capable of carpet weaving, but would perform the work in a superior manner. On the other hand, he states that the exploitative conditions of Persian women's labor make it more beneficial for Europeans to supervise carpet weaving in Iran and export it to Europe. While Whigham acknowledges that the moment Persian women become conscious of their condition will mark the end of carpet weaving, he finds carpet weaving and the exploitative conditions of women within it highly beneficial to Europeans. It is thought provoking to observe to what extent a consideration of exploitation, and even consciousness of it, enables multiple forms of continuities and discontinuities between Europeans and the local male elite in their collaboration to maintain gender domination.

It is through the civilizing notion of race that the "Persian problem" was articulated as a situation in need of external and internal intervention. The Persian problem had two integral parts—nation and gender—each marked by a cultural and territorial (land/body) aspect.[20] In each case, the intervention of either colonial subjects or the male local elite was required. The Persian problem was not a pure abstraction, but had a material foundation that underlay the philosophical lack of modern subjects. Persia suffered from a lack of modern institutions and technologies, which ranged from the absence of the apparatus of the nation-state to the absence of railways to facilitate the circulation of labor capital and commodities. The remedy envisaged by European powers was the creation of a disciplinary order to guarantee political continuity and cohesion through a stable relationship with the Britain, France, and Germany and to limit the influence of Russia in northern Iran. A solution to the dilemma required a landscape—imagined and physical—with identifiable borders. The geographical mapping of Iran as a territorial space and the establishment of Iranian women as the embodiment of such territoriality was a defining moment in Iranian modernity. It created what Balibar refers to as "the historical situations in which nationalist movements and policies arise" (1991c, 45).

Persia was a problem for Europeans. Persians themselves accepted the European perception of the Persian problem but attempted their own solution. Part of the trouble was the unstable strategy of the Iranian ruling class in signing contracts with no coherent logical goal with nations such as Russia, Germany, France, and Britain. For Persia to be able to solve this predicament itself, it needed the intervention either of the colonial order or of a local elite able to identify the problem as its own and establish modern institutions, thus making the nation join the "caravan of civilization" (*ghafeleh-e Tamadon*). The strategic location of

Iran in terms of trade in the early twentieth century made it an important battleground for European colonial powers (Britain, France, Germany, Belgium, Holland) as they competed with each other and Russia
in starting banks, obtaining tobacco, oil, and railway concessions, and
controlling trade markets and transportation. It is in the context of
conflicting interest within colonial modernity and local politics that the
"Persian problem" and the "Woman problem" came to be inextricably
linked.

Before securing oil reserves in this area became a priority, trade
routes were the principal attraction for the British in the region and, in
particular, in southern Iran. The critical element in expanding and securing British trade in the Persian Gulf region[21] to the north of Iran was
the construction of railways that would connect the northern, central,
and southern parts of Iran. However, after cornering the market for Iranian oil reserves in the early twentieth century, the British focused their
energy on maintaining control of Iranian petroleum. Such economic
political concerns required Persia to be symbolically unveiled, opening
it up to the penetration of colonial powers—either forcibly or by a process of self-unveiling that accommodated the geographical localization
of modernity and its civilizing mission.

From the Persian Problem to the Woman Problem

> Just as the movement toward domesticating working-class
> English women was an attempt to beautify them into
> disciplined bodies within a patriarchal culture, the move to
> "civilize" "Eastern" women functioned to make them less
> opaque, to strip them of their veils, and to remove them from
> harems where they lived lives hidden from the European male.
>
> Inderpal Grewal (1996, 49)

In order to accommodate British trade, Persia needed to leave the dark,
chaotic, and mysterious space of a feminized East to join the temporal
space of Western modernity. The move from the feminized zone of the
East required centralization and the interconnection of previously separated geographical locations. The space of the feminine had to be re-
located to what was called the "home." This new zone was to be exposed to modern technologies of power and control. The notion of
home as an imagined modern space emerged to put an end to the dark

continent of chaos and mystery, what had previously been described either as a harem or simply a lack of home. The concept of home is extremely important in the context of civilizational imperialism and nation-state building, since it is the locus of new gendered subjects that facilitates emerging forms of consumer capitalism and the modernization of patriarchy.[22]

While there are accounts by male authors about so-called home life and Persian women's problems, most of the detailed accounts are written by European women. Margaret L. Gertrude Bell writes in her travelogue *Safarnameh:* "The East is full of secrets—no one understands their value better than the Oriental; and because she is full of secrets she is full of entrancing surprises" (1894, 29). Chaos and disorder are represented both spatially in the closed architecture of the houses, harems, and *andarouni,* and also in the veiled bodies of women. In another passage, Bell writes:

As it listeth, it comes and goes; it flashes upon you through the open doorway of some blank, windowless house you pass in the street, from under the lifted veil of the beggar woman who lays her hand on your bridle, from the dark, contemptuous eyes of a child; then the east sweeps aside her curtains, flashes a facet of her jewels into your dazzled eyes, and disappears again with a mocking little laugh at your bewilderment; then for a moment it seems to you that you are looking her in the face, but while you are wondering whether she be angel or devil, she is gone. She will not stay—she prefers the unexpected; she will keep her secrets and her tantalizing charm with them, and when you think you have caught at last some of her illusive grace, she will send you back to shrouded figures and blank house-fronts. You must be content to wait, and perhaps someday, when you find her walking in her gardens in the cold of evening she will take a whim to stop and speak to you, and you will go away fascinated by her courteous hospitality. For it is in her gardens that she is most herself, they share her charm, they are as unexpected as she. (29–30)

The architecture of physical space and the veiling of female bodies create obstacles for the European gaze and become a space for the hidden, the transgressive, the mysterious, and the unpredictable. While the Eastern woman becomes an extension of her gardens in exhibiting unpredictability, Bell's description of the charming Eastern woman's ability to mask both her virtue and her diabolism displays (her) ambivalent desire for the Eastern woman. Through a series of internal contradictions, this passage ultimately reveals an ambivalence that suggests a desire to be free of the structure of home. Both the space and its inhabitants become signifiers for the absence of home—home, that is, in modern European terms, "the domestic space that is also a political entity invested with history and tradition represented through female bodies located within it" (Grewal 1996, 230).

Laurie Thomas, a missionary in nineteenth-century Iran, refers to the absence of home both linguistically and physically: "In their language, as in Arabic, the missionaries found no word for *home;* and there was no need of it, for the thing itself was wanting. The house consisted of one large room, and was generally occupied by several generations. In that one room all the work of family was performed" (1863, 14). In order for the modern nation-state to establish itself, the notion of home had to be invented linguistically in order to establish a division of labor between the two central institutions of family and state. Both European and American missionary women considered Iranian women slaves because of the possibility of early marriage, divorce, and polygamy in Islam. They considered it their duty to save Persian women and to spread Western and Christian ways of life.[23]

M. E. Hume-Griffith, the wife of a missionary who spent eight years in Iran, wrote about the absence of home life, depicting the Persian upper-class woman's home as a space of leisure in *Behind the Veil in Persia and Turkish Arabia: An Account of an Englishwoman's Eight Years' Residence amongst the Women of the East:* "Of 'home life' in Persia there is none; there is no word in their language for 'home' and so it plays no part in their lives. Life in the home varies very much according to the rank of the husband, the poorer wives and village women are blessed by being obliged to work, but the better class have absolutely nothing to do, from morning till night, but smoke, drink tea, and talk scandal" (1909, 86–87).

In this passage, Hume-Griffith's reference to middle- and upper-middle-class Persian women as nonworkers reflects the widespread capitalist notion that work is defined by exchange value and not use value, a concept that excludes various forms of domestic work. In another passage describing Persian homes, she writes: "There is no 'home life,' such as we understand the term, in Mosul. The word 'beit' (house) is the only one in Arabic language used for describing home. It would indeed be a mockery to call such by the sacred name so dear to the hearts of English people" (231). This reference to the sacred English home as the opposite of the profane Persian home has several discursive functions. It enables the conceptualization of home as temporal rather than as spatial. It makes home into a signifier that distinguishes between Britain and Persia not as territorial entities, but as imagined and emotional communities. In addition, it attributes a transcendental and sacred nature to the British homeland and legitimizes its moral superiority over other notions of home. As Doreen Massey argues, in the broader, Western mode of dualistic thinking, "it is time which is aligned with history, progress, civilization, politics and transcendence and coded masculine. And it is the opposites of these things which have, in the traditions of Western thought, been coded feminine. The exercise of rescuing space from its position, in this formulation, of stasis, passivity and depoliticization, therefore, connects directly with a wider philosophical debate in which gendering and the construction of gender relations are central" (1994, 6–7).

The absence of home and a culture of home was characterized by the absence of mothering. Persian mothers were portrayed as lazy and careless and Persian children as needing protection from their mothers. Mrs. Napier Malcolm writes in the introduction to *Children of Persia:*

My dear boys and girls, this is a book about Persia, intended to be read by children; and, on this account, much has had to be left out. Do not think, when you have read this book, that you know how bad Muhammadanism is, for a great deal of its sin and cruelty is too terrible to tell to young folks. But I hope enough has been said to show you that Persian children do need to be rescued from Muhammadanism and brought to the Lord Jesus Christ to be His children. He needs them and they need him. So for His sake and theirs we must do all we can to win the Persians for Christ. (1911, 18)

This text mobilizes a feminine pedagogical and socializing space, where the necessity of colonialism is explained to children in a way that is meant both to educate and to scare them. Colonialism is represented as a desirable phenomenon because of its religious duty to rescue children from Mohammedanism and bring them under the protective wing of a universalist and humanist Christianity. In describing the lack of emotional care provided by Persian mothers and their cruelty to their babies, Mrs. Malcolm writes, "Even the grownup mothers are often very careless. One woman I knew laid her baby, not quite a year old, on a chair, and left it there. Of course it fell off—it was sure to; and yet she did this over and over again, and a few days later dropped it into a stream of water" (19). Persian women's barbaric ways of childrearing legitimize Western women's need to protect children from their bad Muslim mothers and push the education of Persian women to the forefront of the modernization project, an education that will focus on turning them into good housewives.

The linguistic and geographical invention of a bourgeois home in Persia would demand an end to the architecture of ambiguity and transgression. In exchange, Persians would be promised the possibility of normativity and cultural coherence. Thus, the invention of the home is integrated into the civilizing project of imperialism as a process requiring intervention by both Europeans (especially women) and civilized Persian men.

In articulating a need for such intervention, Hume-Griffith (1909, 103) asks, "Ought not the cries of distress and agony from the poor women of Persia so to rouse us, their sisters in England, that we shall determine to do all that lies in our power to lighten their burdens and to bring some rays of light into the dark lives of our Eastern sisters?" Sisterhood as a quasi-familial, affective site of connection and action creates a subject position for Western women who see themselves as agents for the enlightenment of Persian women.

The construction of an imagined bourgeois home to contain Persian women has been essential in the construction of the Persian nation as an imagined community and as a source of authority for local men and the masculinist project of citizenship. As Masiello argues for the case of Argentina, the famous quote "One can judge the degree of civilization of a nation by the social position of its women" has been used to create authority for local men (1992, 27). Similar justifications were used to authorize the forced acculturation of women by the Iranian modernist elite. As Grewal argues, this authority required a "movement out and back to home providing a textual structure that creates the subjects and objects of the nation" (1996, 231).

The Spatial Framing of Belonging: From Home to Homeland

> Listen, just king [*shah-e ba edalat*] Aghayoon went on
>   pilgrimage.
> People went to the embassy.
> Women were captured.
> How long the injustice?
> Ayn al Dawlah [appointed to be premier]?!
> The country is robbed.
>
>   Song popular during the constitutional revolution
>   of 1905–1906, cited in Najmabadi (1995, 47)

Iran is poor, Iran is incapacitated, Iran is impoverished.
Iranian reformist Mirza Malkum Khan,
Collected Works (1948, 212)

The imagined notion of home became an important signifier in per
mitting local elites to emerge as subjects invested with the authority to
civilize others while simultaneously protecting two interior territorial
landscapes, both represented as objectified, feminized, and victimized:
the imagined national space of "mother Iran" and the collective body
of Iran's women, who signify the incarnation of cultural inferiority.
Numerous texts published in this era quote European travel writings as
their sources of knowledge about various topics. These constructions
are effective and affective, provoking deep feelings of protection, love,
natural belonging, and biological connection. The affect evoked by the
constructions makes them politically effective tools for social change.
In this process, argues Tavakoli-Taraghi, historians of the modern period, which dates from 1905 to the revolution of 1979, crafted a narrative of the period prior to the constitutional revolution of 1905 as an
age of ignorance *(bikhabari)*, stagnation, and despotism (1998, 9). This
narrative was essential to the creation of a teleology, or a modern temporality, and simultaneously to the facilitation of the redefinition of
historical time. Under the Pahlavi regime, the construction of a civilized and uncontaminated pre-Islamic Persia was essential in extending
this age of ignorance to include the time of the conquest of Iran by the
so-called barbaric Muslims, a gesture intended to reinforce anti-Arab
and anti-Semitic ideologies. Through the construction of the Arab in-
vaders of Iran as barbaric, the imaging of a civilized pre-Islamic Persia
became possible, providing space for modern notions of Iranian secular nationalism.

Sadeq Hedayat, a prominent modernist writer famous for his writings against the hypocrisy and duplicity of the religious clergymen, systematically relies on anti-Semitic and anti-Islamic discourses of colonial
modernity in his work. In his famous novella *Toup-e Morvari* (Pearl's
Ball, published in Germany in 1930), the protagonist responds to the
issue of all the European philosophers and scientists who have praised
Islam in their writings, asserting:

These books are written to promote colonial policies. These books are written
for us the Orientals, to enable them to run us (ride us). Which poison or which
opium is functioning better than the philosophy of destiny *[ghaza va Ghadar]*
of Jews and Muslims for making people insensitive, uncreative and bad

humored? Look at the geographical maps: all Muslim nations are inferior [*tu sari khor*], poor, deceitful, dominated and hacks. To seduce them and divide them, the colonial powers pay these greedy writers to write this nonsense. Which civilization? Arab civilization? Just read the book of Sheik Alligator that is only about the camel milk, and orbicular, *Aba,* and alligator's kebab. The rest is written by inferior and dominated nations and attributed to Arabs. (2001, 60)

Modernist nationalist writers concerned with the development and progress of Iran use anti-Islamic, civilizational, imperialist tropes to dismiss colonial writing. However, the covert operation of colonial forces remains a powerful popular belief in the Iranian popular imagination. The popular political paranoia about the British manipulating the Islamic clergy for their own political ends is still an influential public myth.

An examination of the discourse of the modernist male elite in the early twentieth century—from journalists to poets and writers—is necessary in this context. However, there are also a number of popular stories that provide a frame for representing gender roles by binding gender to national problems and ethnic conflicts through the themes of sexual honor, victimhood, revenge, and protection. In her original investigation, collection, and reconstruction of "The Story of the Daughters of Quchan" (1995), Najmabadi argues that this text was a founding story in the articulation of the victimization of the Iranian people by the state. According to Najmabadi, this story was circulated from mouth to mouth, recited in the mosques, and published in the "Shabnameh" (Night Letter) and "Entebah Nameh" (Letters of Warning) during the constitutional revolution of 1905–1909. It created solidarity and a sense of national belonging among the people. In the recitation of the tale, the daughters of *Quchan* are transformed into Iranian girls and so become figures for the expression of national unity, for signifying Iranianness. The story refers to a group of poor peasants living in the northeastern part of Iran in the spring of 1905 (1323 *hejri/ghamari*) under the government of Asif al-Dawlah, who in desperation sold their daughters to the Turks and Armenians of "Esqabad." This story played a significant role in attracting people to the constitutional revolution and in inventing a national purpose (Najmabadi 1995, 4–5).

As Najmabadi argues, only in light of gender relations in the context of the constitutional revolution can one understand the importance of this story, since both women and children had become powerless in the cultural climate of that time (1995, 39–57). Fear of "losing sexual honor"

(Namouse-jensi) and the Islamic ethic mobilized people to fight for national unity. I agree with Najmabadi that this story is not only about injustice to women, but also about injustice to the men who had ownership of women vis-à-vis other men. It also signifies the emasculation of Iranian Muslim men and their lack of *mardanegi*, or virility. This story has other functions as well, including merging the discourse of territorial nationalism with the discourse of protection and creating a site of agency and subjectivity for Iranian men in their opposition to despotism *(estebdad)* and in their reappropriation of Iran from oppressors, external and internal alike.[24] Nationalist paternalism is a gendered conflict. The story calls upon Iranian men to overcome "emasculation," to mobilize their masculinity, and to save their national homeland. What is fascinating about this story is not only its gender dynamics but also its significance for the emergence of a majority/minority discourse in Iran through which two groups of men are constructed: the unvirile Muslim *(na-mard)* men on the side of *estebdad,* or despotism, who act as collaborators, and the non-Muslim men, such as Armenians, who were able to buy the "Quchan girls " The transgression of national and religious borders through the choice of Esqabad as the city where the girls are purchased—a city that was part of Iran until 1881 and afterward became part of Russia—symbolizes the powerlessness and inability of Iranian people to prevent such injustices (Najmabadi 1995, 53). By bringing together the two notions of selling the daughters of Quchan and selling out Iran, the language of the constitutional revolution produces a field of action for the Iranian Muslim man to rise up to protect his honor by protecting what he owns, that is to say, Iran as a national territory and Iran as a feminized body.

In the story of the Quchan girls, masculinist historiography not only manages to create national hegemony, but also enables it to emerge as an imagined community, in Anderson's terms (1991). This imagined community is based on a unification of the rich and the poor that comes about via the creation of the category of the victimized who are in need of protection. An alliance is created between the protected and the protector to transcend their class differences. Gender and sexual signifiers are crucial to the intelligibility of this alliance, since they provide space for the emergence of a dominated ethnicity, for the category of "disempowered Muslims." Emasculation makes the disempowered Muslims clearly gendered subjects. In this context emasculation becomes the ultimate form of injustice and cultural poverty. Women are present as objects of national, sexual, and ethnic transgression, objects in need of protection, to give meaning to men's agency and remasculation. The formulation of a heteronormative narrative in which women are owned and protected by men against other men works to naturalize the nation.

One of the important sites for these constructions is the discourse of the modernized, Westernized Iranian intelligentsia, including poets, writers, and reformists, who articulated a national will. As Tavakoli-Taraghi argues with regard to the global hegemony of the West, an Iranian national historiography revering progress, development, and growth sought real, albeit normative, solutions to perceived abnormalities in Iran's development by promoting modernization, meaning Westernization (1998, 4). One of the very first advocates of Westernization in Iran was Mirza Malkum Khan, who elaborated a number of key modern concepts, such as progress *(taragi)*, civilization, law, and religion, in a number of publications, including the *Qanun* newspaper (forty-three issues, 1890–1898).[25]

Malkum Khan invokes the notion of "bearing or accepting progress" *(taraghip Paziri),* a term that alludes to the gap in consciousness between humans and animals, in his description of Iranians' capacity to adapt to progress (1948, 102). Progress for him is what can be imported from the West, notably *Farhang,* or governmentality; to leave the age of savagery behind requires government intervention. Central to progress is *Ussul-e nazm,* or the absolute sovereignty of the law and the principles of order, which must be adopted from Europe (*Qanun,* no. 8, p. 3). He describes the Iranian government as permissive *(ekhtiari),* rather than based on law and order, as in the West (1948, 105). In addition, he calls for the codification of Islamic law (sharia) in an effort to reconcile European and Islamic law, which Malkum Khan considers "a revised version of Christianity"(Algar 1973, 228).[26] The discourse of the Iranian elite intertextually evokes the European construction of the Persian character.

By isolating Iranian nature as receptive to progress and Iran's backwardness as an external accident, Malkum Khan calls on Iranians to adopt Western notions of law and order. For Malkum Khan, the move toward civilization also requires dealing with women's problems, since any national project necessarily involves women's cooperation. Moreover, for Malkum Khan, this cooperation requires civilized women to educate men about masculinity: "Now that many men in Iran have turned into women, women should teach their husbands lessons on manhood" (*Qanun,* no. 7, p. 3). The language of honor, masculinity, manhood, and "self-help" is an integral part of the intelligentsia's pro-West discourse. To become a national subject, the Iranian man had to overcome his lack of virility *(bi gayrati)* and claim his masculine honor through the collective project of self-help or self-civilizing.

While men are invited to return to their sexual virility to take charge of their Westernization, Iranian women are continually depicted as backward by the local male elite who read women through the repertoire of textual and visual representations of the Western discourse on Persian women. For example, Ahmad-e Kasravi (1890–1945), a well-known Iranian secularist modernist who was an advocate and admirer of the constitutional revolution and the author of numerous essays on women, reprinted a number of sketches depicting Iranian women from the works of various European travel writers in his book *Khaharan va Dokhtaran-e Ma* (Our Sisters and Daughters [1946]), which was published after his assassination. A secularist with anticlerical opinions and a supporter of women's unveiling, Kasravi promoted monogamy, modesty, and education for women. He called upon women to be a visible presence in Iranian society, but in their natural roles as mothers, sisters, and wives (45). While he was very critical of what he called Islamic traditional culture, he was, nevertheless, a sexual Puritan who encouraged only domestic education for women and who argued that it was appropriate for women to get an education only in housekeeping, childcare, health issues, and cooking.

The late nineteenth and early twentieth centuries were a period when civilizational imperialism, in its quest for cultural and economic hegemony in Iran, became the dominant part of a regime of power and knowledge produced, accumulated, and circulated via print media both by Westerners and by a Westernized local elite. An examination of the intertexuality of racial and civilizational tropes in various genres of writing in Iranian modernity reveals the discursive constructions of a Persian character in need of civilization. To become part of the civilizational process, this subject needed to resolve two problems simultaneously: the Persian Problem and the Woman Problem. Both problems called upon male citizens to leave the age of barbarism and to join civilization through identification with a Westernized masculinity represented as capable of resolving these problems. It is within the context of such discourses that the Iranian nation was invented as an imagined community.

CHAPTER 2

The Civic Body and
the Order of the Visible

And sometimes it seems to me that it is only in the teeth of
violence that we can speak the unstable truths of our bodies.

Meena Alexander (1996, 78)

I only know how to work with a philosophy of detail. Then,
on the surface of being, in that region where being *wants* to
be both visible and hidden, the movements of opening and
closing are so numerous, so frequently inverted, and so
charged with hesitation, that we could conclude on the
following formula: man is a half-open being.

Gaston Bachelard (1969, 222)

In prerevolutionary Iran, the civic body becomes the unifying object of
the nation-state in its process of modernization and Westernization.
This is expressed in the Pahlavi regime's national anthem, which affirms
the connection between the individual and the state: "Cho iran
nabashad tan-e man mabad [Without Iran, my body would not exist]."
In the postrevolutionary period (after 1979), the civic body is represented as a site of both the nationalization and transnationalization of
gendered universalism on behalf of the Islamic ummat (blood and message / *khoon va payam*).[1] Both pre- and postrevolutionary discourses
commemorate specific bodies—through gendered and heterosexist
practices, gestures, and postures—serving not only to facilitate modern
disciplinary control of the body but also to create gendered citizenship,
both national and transnational.

Theoretically speaking, the body has always been a site where culture acts on individuals to turn them into subjects (Foucault 1979a). The objectification of the subject happens through what Foucault calls "dividing practices," meaning the differentiation between good and bad, or normal and abnormal, which awakens consciousness of the body as an "instrument of power." This theoretical point is significant for my argument not only because it relates to the colonial construction of bodies and underlies the nationalist and fundamentalist remapping of these bodies, but also because the very idea of citizenship depends upon the notion of a civic body. Especially important to me is the way in which citizenship becomes a site of exclusion and marginalization, as Adorno and Horkheimer put it, in the profound relation between freedom and practices of cruelty (1987, 232). The issues surrounding the relationship between the individual and the body—his or her own or that of others, the separation between the body and work in modern capitalist economies, the love-hate relationship with the body, and state intervention in the punishment of stigmatized bodies through the rights of citizenship—are all of crucial importance to my project.[2]

Eurocentric and Orientalist theoretical frameworks have systematically ignored the body and power in marginalized locations, while at the very same time they have deployed them to perpetuate what Foucault calls dividing practices. It is essential to examine the ways in which Orientalist discourse eliminates traces of the apparatuses of modernity, state-building, and citizenship in Middle Eastern societies through its obsessional focus on an essentialized Islam.[3] As Joseph argues, "We need to identify and explain the ways in which citizenship and gender interact within the constructs of the state, religion, the individual and communities, without relying upon stereotypes of the region, its states or its peoples" (1996, 4). The racist, colonialist image of Muslim women as eternal victims, characterized by ignorance and passivity, has become Westerners' most comforting cliché. The decoding of such spaces of representation and their historicization by Third World and Middle Eastern feminists is still resisted by both Western and Middle Eastern Orientalists. However, the recent contributions of postcolonial and antiracist feminists, such as Inderpal Grewal, Ella Shohat, Marnia Lazreg, and Mary Layoun, have elucidated historical relations, transnationality, and the interconnections between race, gender, sexuality, national imaginings, and power relations in the Muslim world.[4]

I am not interested in the body as a sociological field of inquiry but rather in the political images, symbols, metaphors, and representations that help to create the body as a site of political performance in the particular context of modern nationalist and fundamentalist movements. In other words, while I am interested in the production of the civic body, I want to show its instability over time in Iran. Although there is a growing body of theoretical scholarship on the body within feminist and queer studies, very little has been written on the national and transnational imagining of the body and how this imagining is invested in notions of motherhood, sisterhood, and wifehood as sites of empowerment, political mobilization, and participation.[5]

While man as a "half-open being" can achieve status as a subject only in a philosophy of becoming, the logic of nation-state building and modern citizenship is founded on two lines of thought that define each other in contradictory ways. The first line is based on the equality of citizens, while the second posits the subjugation of the citizen to religious morality. In other words, the first line of thought is based on the notion of disciplined citizen-subjects who actively participate in their own governance as citizens of the nation-states, while the second founds politics on the basis of a series of binary pairings—public and private, rights and needs, reason and passion—that tie politics to a secularized, theological notion of responsibility.[6] The theological-political notion of responsibility described by John Stuart Mill is defined by discourses of civilization, secularism, and progress, which grow out of a Christian culture (Connolly 1999, 77).

Such binary concepts are intrinsically linked to temporal and spatial metaphors, which naturalize the spheres of family and civil society and distinguish them from the sphere of politics; these concepts are essential in the construction of modern rational subjectivities and liberal citizenship.[7] For example, oppositional spatial metaphors of home versus market, family versus state, and private versus public distinguish two spheres, one regulated by nature and the other by culture. As a number of feminist scholars have shown, beyond the realm of what is usually called political there is sexual division of labor with disciplinary practices that determine the feminine body and normative femininity. While the embodied citizens of modern nation-states are subjected to various forms of governmentality and their concomitant disciplinary practices, it is only through the rationalized denunciation of the markings of social status and through their disembodiment that citizens become legitimate inhabitants of the state. The liberal state erases differences in order to claim that all citizens are equal. In order to enter the political sphere, the citizen-subject of the modern nation-state must transcend the political economy of the body and the work that sustains that body.

The civic body produces and regulates racialized, gendered citizenship. The civic body is both universal and particular, since it is marked as white and masculine. It establishes a superior, sovereign moral economy in which circular exchange is subordinated to a "noble" surplus value obtained inequitably through faith and sacrifice. Embodied particulars compose a unity, creating a transcendental subjectivity that seeks to comprehend all entities within itself, thereby perpetuating a "logic of identity"—an identity that seeks to eliminate all uncertainty by eliminating otherness. This logic lies behind the idea of an impartial reason at work in the machinery of citizenship and militates against the recognition of differentiated moral subjects. The civic body creates a site of visibility and exhibition, which expresses the will to unity even as it suppresses corporeality, ambiguity, and fragmentation. To become a citizen of such a visible order is also to become a consumer of meanings and of commodities.[8] The imagining of an abstract citizenry that sustains the authority and power of the nation-state is inseparable from gendered and racial constructions. I would like to argue that it is through the notion of the civic body that the parallel processes of embodiment and disembodiment take place. I use the term *civic body* to describe what in Western modern political thought is referred to as an effort of will to create political rights in opposition to natural rights and in relation to natural law, as Hobbes, Spinoza, and Locke have described. The civic body, I argue, functions as a site of both subordination and resistance to normative prescriptions and laws of citizenship where dependence on state power is the very condition leading to the formation of citizen-subjects.[9] While such a politicized body is crucial to the creation of an imagined community where citizens are sovereign, this body nonetheless bears the marks of racialization, genderization, and sexualization.[10] In the case of prerevolutionary (before 1978), revolutionary (1978–1979), and postrevolutionary (after 1979) Iran, the civic body not only becomes a site of gender performances and national particularism—an undivided adherence to one particular system—but also a site of revolutionary hermeneutic practice and transnational particularism.

The civic body makes it possible for national and transnational forms of governmentality to contain the disruptive influences of history, class, race, gender, and sexuality by creating sites of repetition. It also allows for the strategic manipulation of identity by creating a space for the universalization of individuals and for its opposite concept—cultural specificity. While normative patterns and normalized subjects remain central to the perpetuation of the civic body and to the regulation of citizenship, transnational constructions contain the contradictions of the multiple contingent identities of globalized markets within and beyond the territorial spaces of the nation-state. These contradictory processes cause difficulty for the expression of a transnational Islamic femininity, an identity that is negotiated differently by Muslim women who are citizens of Islamic nation-states and by Muslim women in diasporic locations.[11]

Orderly Patriarchy: The Rule of the Father in the Motherland

> Each of us lives at home. At home we love and respect our father. We also have a bigger house. This big house of ours is our country Iran. In this big house we are like one family. The Shah is like the father of this large family and we are like his children. The Shah loves all of us. We love our kind Shah like our own father. We respect our Shah.
>
> From the first grade textbook used in prerevolutionary Iran, cited in Chelkowski and Dabashi (1999, 128–29)

The coming to power of Reza Khan in 1921 soon after the establishment of the Pahlavi dynasty (1925–1979) and the establishment of a centralized state was based on multiple foundational axes. The first axis entailed the construction of a patriotic, pseudo-nationalist ideology predicated on the revival of the pre-Islamic past and acceptance of a sacred notion of monarchy, the aim of which was to weaken the strength of religious ideology and to legitimize the hegemony of the state over other institutions, especially religious institutions.[12] Such patriotic nationalism drew extensively on the Orientalist views of Gobineau on the Aryan[13] race and produced a new terminology. Such discursive civilizing notions have worked through both seduction and coercion in Iran. Before the coup d'état of Reza Shah, the Westernized elite used civilizing rhetorical tropes to legitimize modernization. Under Reza Shah, the state took the initiative to impose the ideology of European civilization through the construction of a unified Iranian national will to progress and modernization.

The motherland—*Mam-e Vatan*—was eternally married to and ruled by a father/king who came to be the procreator of the "Irani," or the descendants of the Aryans, and the nurturer of "Iraniyat," a particular kind of cultural being.[14] The territorial name Iran, which refers to Aryan, replaced the name Persia. Farsi was proclaimed the national language.[15] Declaring Farsi the national language created a dominant ethnicity for the Fars—Iranians who supposedly originated from the region of Fars or Pars—and subordinated various ethnic languages, including Azari Turkish, which was the language of the Qajars (a Turkish-speaking people originally from central Asia), who created the Qajar dynasty and ruled from 1785 to 1925.

These measures used race to mark gender and gender to mark race. The adoption of European dresses, suits, jackets, and trousers, along with the design of a new hat called the Pahlavi hat (copied from the French military cap) for men in 1929, was used to distinguish modern, civilized Iranian men from their seemingly backward counterparts. A European dress code displaced the religious coding of masculinity (wearing traditional garb, having a beard, and carrying religious honorable titles such as *Haji*)[16] and discouraged culturally valued Islamic manners for men.[17]

In a similar manner, the veiled female body became the incarnation of cultural barbarism with the invention of a unified category of women victimized by local patriarchies and in need of emancipation.[18] The call for revelation of the secrets of women's bodies dates back to the eighteenth century in Persia, yet only enters the discourse of the Iranian cultural elite at the beginning of twentieth century. Women's secrets refer to women's sexual experiences, which were shielded from masculine and community surveillance. Veiling facilitated women's anonymity and movement. Elite women met with their lovers wearing servants' veils. Women of various classes veiled their faces to engage in sexual acts while hiding their identities. Also, veiling protected women from the community's accusations because it made a woman indistinguishable from others, so a woman could deny her presence in a particular place. In the popular literature, sayings, and jokes, there are many references to women's ruses *(Makr-e Zanan)* and secrets. Because men needed to claim agency as the subjects of these acts of disclosure, voluntary acts of unveiling on women's part were suppressed. The act of unveiling had to be initiated by men—subjects recognized as moral agents with the power to unveil women and to reveal their secrets.

The second foundational axis centered on the construction of an orderly, coercive patriarchy. Given the ethnic and religious plurality of Iran, the centralization of the political system enabled the king to become the sole focus of national loyalty, a position never before enjoyed by such a personage. Loyalty to the king imitated filial piety in its ability to motivate people to obey or to conform to the will of a superior authority. Such a cultural move facilitated the process of modernization. The state became the sacred father/king, but coercion and violence were necessary to guarantee obedience. An important component of this coercive patriarchy was a redefinition of gender roles, which the state effected by imposing a heteronormative order characterized by a hegemonic masculinity and an emphasized femininity as the appropriate gender identities for the social subjects of a modernized country.

The newly created hegemonic masculinity liberated itself from its aristocratic bonds. Reza Shah always identified himself first as a soldier and then as a king, creating a model for the emergence of new military classes. The new system of gender identification provided a frame of reference for the newly emerged state-related classes (military, bureaucratic, bourgeois) in two ways. First of all, a hierarchical system of social categorization was established by distinguishing the urban from the rural, the tribal and ethnic from the national, the secular from the religious, and the traditional from the modern. Secondly, new models of femininity facilitated the entry of women into the public sphere and into previously gender-segregated segments of the market, especially educational institutions.

The forced unveiling of Iranian women, along with the encouragement of men to dress in a Western way during the time of Reza Shah, contributed to these gendered and racialized notions of state-initiated modernization. Fashion became an important site of both gender and national identification. These new kinds of identification were distinguished from the prior forms of social differentiation based on family name, wealth, religious filiation, land ownership, and so on. The signs of modernization were written on the body, as dress became the focal point of such identification.

An authoritarian state was imposed through the construction of a coercive public patriarchy, which was regulated by the state rather than the family and based on obedience and loyalty to the father/king. However, the lack of a civil society, combined with the imposition of a modern state from above and its violent insertion into daily life, intensified the gap between public and private patriarchy. The state had a dualistic and contradictory approach to civil society. It prohibited certain discussions to avoid social crises. For example, it closed down independent women's journals and magazines while bringing women to the center of its nation-building project. However, despite this shift of power and the invasion of the private sphere by the public sphere, the state stopped short of affecting the private sphere. Public and private spheres became sharply separated and came to represent different interests within patriarchy. As a result, there emerged a distinction between patriarchs vis-à-vis the nation and patriarchs vis-à-vis private families. The new state-based patriarchs publicized their discourse, while the private patriarchs continued to protect their power in the private sphere and in those spaces where the state's access was either limited or contested, including religious spaces, such as mosques. From this situation was born a potential for revolt that waited for a day when the regime could be overthrown and the nation-state could be replaced by a collective "will to state." Indeed, the contours of the normative public sphere were drawn by the will of a particular segment of the local elite. As a result, internal tension, contradiction, and antagonism between the public and the private spheres continued to haunt the modernizing state during the revolution of 1979.

With the marginalization of *ulama* (religious scholars) from centers of power and with the expansion of the role of the state into education and the regulation of sexuality, the state became the direct adversary of religion.[19] Reza Shah's nation-state building project focused on the expansion of the railroad; the modernization of army; the spread of public education, including student exchange programs that sent students abroad; the consolidation of a national heritage by building memorial monuments for poets and writers; and finally the regularization of imports and exports, along with participation in international trade exhibitions. For example the 1934 (1313 in the Iranian calendar) *Amta'eh vatan* (goods of the country) exhibition publicized Iranian products from agricultural goods to carpets for an international audience and was one of the first moves toward the formal commercialization of national products.[20]

Under Reza Shah and Mohammad Reza Shah, the gap grew between state-related classes, such as the government functionaries, which started to be heavily defined by the world capitalist market under the hegemonic power of the West, and the bourgeoisie, whose participation in the nation-state was conditional upon their obedience to the identitarian rule of the state. Rapid urbanization, stemming from the migration of hundreds of thousands of poor peasants to urban areas, occurred after the 1963 land reform and increased the size of the urban lower middle classes and the underclasses. In addition, because of gender stratification in the class system, disparities emerged between the new upper- and middle-class educated women present in the public sphere and lower-middle-class and underclass men. The 1970 fall of oil prices in the world market reinforced the tension between unemployed men and employed women.

These divisions were followed by a widening of the gap between the pro-West culture of local elites and the anti-West sentiments of popular culture enjoyed by the masses. This gap was, however, a site of ambiguity and contradiction, since popular culture became a source of inspiration for other classes, including the local elite. The local elite tried to encourage the production of a high-culture version of popular culture for consumption in national ceremonies and opera and theater houses. However, the same cultural practices increasingly became sources of political empowerment for the masses. For example, under Reza Shah, *ta'zieh* (the popular Shia performance of Karbala) and the ceremonies of the month of Muharam were outlawed as a sign of traditionality and fanaticism, yet in the 1970s the politicization of the masses allowed for a return to indigenous theater and art, such as *ta'zieh,* by modernist artists and performers. The extension of capitalism and the gradual inclusion of women in the labor market did not, in the long run, bring more equality for women, but rather created a double burden shared by women in different parts of the world.[21] A gender-based division of labor opened up feminized segments of the labor market, such as nursing, teaching, and service, including sex work. In addition, the modernization of domestic work created new expectations for skills in the performance of housework while simultaneously defining it as unpaid work and as a natural extension of women's bodies, especially among the modern, urban middle class.

This new definition of women's work went against the common cultural practices associated with Islamic customs, including the definition of marriage as a contract and practices such as the dowry (*mahr,* or the economic obligation of the husband to pay the wife a certain amount agreed upon by both parties), *nafaqa* (the economic support provided by the husband to the wife during the waiting period for a divorce), and *shirbaha* (literally translated as the value of a woman's breastfeeding). It also disrupted the concept of the husband's financial support of the wife in exchange for her housework, including, in the case of middle-class women, the husband's provision of a level of comfort to the wife based on her class position (e.g., hiring domestic help for her). These traditional practices radically unsettled the expansion of modern views of domestic work and created great dissonance between women's desire to be modern and the common practices providing them with a limited level of protection in the marriage contract.[22] It was not until the establishment of the Family Protection Act of 1967 and its amendment in 1975 that the modern civil code provided some leverage to protect women's position within marriage. What the Family Protection Act accomplished was the removal of the man's unconditional right to divorce and the regulation of polygamous marriages, the custody of children, and the man's right to prevent his wife from taking a job. It created equal rights for both men and women to apply for official divorces to be approved by the family protection court. As far as polygamy was concerned, it required both the wife's written permission and the court's authorization for a second marriage. It authorized the courts to make decisions about the custody of children. An amendment to the Family Protection Act further limited men's power by curtailing polygamous marriages.[23] However, the Family Protection Act was ineffective in regulating customary and religious practices because it was accused of being illegitimate and un-Islamic by the Islamic oppositional movements. Islamic fundamentalist women's return to Islamic law, or sharia, must be understood in relation to the failure of personal status laws vis-à-vis women's issues.

As a result of structural and cultural changes due to rapid urbanization and industrialization, as well as to the failure of the nationalist and the socialist movements, a new generation of educated young men and women from the middle and lower middle classes emerged with a religious zeal for making sense of the culture and society in which they had been raised, a zeal that was grounded in popular culture. This generation of university students, composed of alienated men and women discontented with social repression and injustice, was concerned with finding a sense of identity and empowerment. This group played a peculiar and powerful role in the contemporary Islamic movement.[24] What distinguished this generation of revolutionary Iranians was its adherence to militant political ideologies, which were constructed in a profoundly intertextual, transnational, translational, and transactional relationship with other oppositional and revolutionary movements in other parts of the world and particularly in other parts of the Middle East. However, such a modernist oppositional movement failed to determine the course of the revolution.

Unveiling and Reveiling: Corporeal Inscriptions of Citizenship

In 1934 and 1935 a forced unveiling took place in Iran, a historic episode that marked a turning point in the construction of the civic body marked by gendered notions of citizenship. My grandmother was from an upper-middle-class background. My grandfather was well known for his social and political status. Here is my grandmother's story:

> It was early in the evening, we were coming back from the public bath, I was with my mother, my kids, and their nannies. When we got to Manoucherhri Square, a number of policemen approached us and asked us to unveil. I started to talk to them, reminding them who I was. At that time my husband was a well-known political figure, and he was in favor of Reza Shah's regime. The policemen disregarded my explanation, repeating that it was a government order, and started to be more coercive. I removed my veil while keeping my bath scarf. Our nannies did not want to unveil. They started to cry, curse, and beg the police to let them go. Their gestures made the policemen angry; they started to chase them and pull their veils off. We were all shocked and scared.

My grandmother's body—like my own later—was marked by corporeal inscriptions of citizenship. Both of us share an incorporated traumatic memory of citizenship in the modern nation-state. She was forced to unveil; I was forced to reveil. Living in different times, we were obliged by our fellow countrymen respectively to reject and adopt veiling. Our bodies were othered by civic necessity. We were coerced by the order of the visible and were concealed in the realm of the invisible. Her body's lived experience was forgotten in the state commemoration of the day of unveiling, which was celebrated as Women's Liberation Day (the "day of uncovering of the veil," *kasf-e-hijab*); my body was displaced and became diasporic. The diasporic subject is incessantly subjected to the disciplinary practices of veiling, unveiling, and reveiling, with their nationalist and racist connotations. Veiling haunts Iranian women both in Iran and in the diaspora. While women in Iran must veil to be legitimate members of the nation-state, the veil as a signifier of Muslim women's passivity and victimization influences women's identification and citizenship in various diasporic locations.

This positioning of the body in the order of the visible has been instrumental in the emergence of the pedagogical discourses and practices of freedom and enthrallment in their positioning relative to dominant models of femininity.

Both unveiling and reveiling created sites where the history of state intervention in the performance and perpetuation of particular forms of femininity was imprinted on female bodies. These practices created social authority for local men. Through the direct coercion of female bodies, first unveiling and later reveiling created spaces of social agency for male citizen-soldiers. Under Reza Shah, the state commemoration of such intervention authorized male citizen-soldiers to civilize women, thereby suppressing women's resistance to colonial and local patriarchal order. Women were discouraged from publicly unveiling themselves— the public self-unveiling of women like Tahirih Qurrat al-ayn, who in 1849 removed her veil to signal the equality of women and men as a basic principle of the new Babi religion, was suppressed. Instead men became the moral subjects of this ritual while women were objectified through domestication and denial of their free will.[25]

With submission to the triangular power of *Khoda, Shah,* and *Mihan* (God, king, and homeland) at the center of a secular, sacrificial national ideology, the sacred army of Allah submitted to the collective will of an Islamic ummat under the leadership of Khomeini.[26] Under Reza Shah's regime, two discourses functioned in conjunction with each other to authorize male citizen-soldiers to civilize women: the discourse of a modernizing state elite and the discourse of a modernist intelligentsia (of poets, writers, and scholars). While the discourse of the state elite emphasized the value of modernization and Westernization for women, the discourse of the modernist intelligentsia focused either on the victimization of women by the local patriarchy or the possible hypocrisy and duplicity of veiled women.[27]

After the state-imposed ritual of unveiling, women became complicit in the principle of state authority: they started to dress in European fashions and were invited to accompany their husbands to formal and official gatherings. State-regulated fashion not only created new feminized subjects but also required them to assume heterosexuality in official social gatherings. Negotiations over veiling and unveiling were at the core of Iranian modernity. Although a number of urban and educated women stopped wearing the veil long before the state imposed unveiling, the state's intervention in this process predisposed women to obedience and submission to the will of the state.[28] The imposition of modernized fashion not only marginalized customary clothing for men and women, but also established a hierarchical dichotomy, both spatial and social, between modern and traditional, progressive and fanatic, urban and rural, secular and religious, upper class and lower class, and male and female. In this manner, clothing created a hegemonic masculinity, distinguished the religious from the secular, and valorized state secularism as a moral code.[29] This process had a significant impact on social tolerance for gender ambiguity and for transgendered persons in the political sphere. For example, because they were permitted to enter feminine spaces, transgendered men previously had an important role in negotiating the relationship between the private and the public in the Qajar dynasty.[30] These transgendered men were no longer permitted to function in the same way after unveiling, which widened the social consequences of the gendered coding of who was permitted or prohibited from political participation.

The masculinity of the secular nationalist elite was elevated above religious, rural, tribal, and other locally defined versions of masculinity. This new model of hegemonic masculinity was constructed by a nexus of writers, poets, and political leaders positioned in different relationships to the state. In its discourse and performance, the key feature of this masculinity was a self-definition that excluded any association with the Muslim elite. The model of modern masculinity thus defined itself through the othering of religiously defined masculinity. In the popular novel *Haji Agha,* by the prominent Iranian writer Sadeq-e Hedayat, first published in 1945, the eponymous main character, Haji Agha, is portrayed as a filthy, polygamous, misogynist glutton, that is to say, as the other of modern masculinity, which projected all that it wished to disavow onto a character designated primarily through the religious title *Haji.* An ostensibly pious and religious man who has made the pilgrimage to Mecca, Haji Agha is later revealed as a hypocrite who conceals his cunning and greed behind a pious persona. In the space between the mask of piety and Haji Agha's perversity lies the possibility— by way of a critique of religion—of the construction of a modern, secular masculinity.

The character of Haji Agha has passed into popular culture as the personification of a religious masculinity that continues to have currency in Iran and even more widely in the Iranian diaspora. These contrasting masculinities have been used to conceal patriarchal relations and norms critical to both secular and religious systems of meaning. *Haji Agha* functions precisely to obstruct a critique of patriarchy in its multiple cultural forms and locations. The protagonist—manipulative, duplicitous, violent, frustrated, obsessively self-interested, and focused on his "lower trunk"—signifies a contrast to modern masculinity's family man—honest, secular, selfless, and willing to sacrifice himself for the protection of the mother country. In contrast, Haji Agha, a member of the Bazar commercial elite whose wealth comes from trade and the exploitation of the workers, is depicted as a polygamous, sexually perverse opium smoker.

This production of hegemonic masculinity was inseparable from the national ideology of security and militarism. For men who underwent cultural emasculation in their voluntary assimilation to Westernization, and who rejected their local, ostensibly backward traditions, the position of citizen-soldier promised access to the will to power. This process was instrumental in distinguishing between the normative bodies of respectable citizen-soldiers and unveiled women and the particularized bodies of peasants, workers, and tribal ethno-religious groups. The abstraction of bodies—their genderization and nationalization—provided space for the representation of gender as a civic necessity and as a site of both coercion and conviction.[31]

Once the category of women in need of unveiling had been invented, unveiling and self-sacrifice reenacted a homogenized image of the past. In other words, it is through the unified notion of Iranian women as all veiled and in need of civilizing (unveiling) that a unified notion of masculinity is created to define subjects whose will to power breaks. Masculinity was created as a site of subject formation, as a site of willing subjects in charge of both civilizing women and protecting the motherland. This moment was followed by the suppression of many forms of women's clothing (that of peasants, tribal women, and women of other ethno-religious groups), by the predominance of military dress for men, and by the categorization of all men as soldiers, ready to sacrifice their lives for the mother country, regardless of class, ethnicity, and local political ties.

For my generation of women, raised with Western technologies (such as photography, films, television shows) of femininity and a modernized body-image, women's poses in the photographs of my grandmother's era represent the uncertainty of this moment of gender adjustment. A socio-cultural malaise in the face of the subordination of female bodies to the modern orders of visibility and normativity results in women sitting with their legs wide apart, their posture overly rigid or relaxed, their heads raised high or completely lowered, their eyes averted or staring ahead. Modern techniques of recording and imaging played a role in the rituals of state commemoration of the nation.

With the expansion of visual media in the late 1960s and 1970s, followed by extreme state control of the media, new spaces of domination and resistance were created. As Behruz Turani has argued, this process started earlier, in the aftermath of the 1953 coup d'état, when movies offered an escape from people's deep sense of political despair (1999 [1378], 92–93). In addition to state-regulated media, a number of radio stations located outside Iran became a platform for the expression of oppositional political voices in the early 1970s.

The civic body made it possible for gendered citizenship to legitimate itself through law as incorporation and inscription. Through femininity, the law was connected to the essence of women's selves, consciences, and desires; it created continuity between a European civil code and an Islamic family code. In the postrevolutionary state, the law, which was exercised externally, became internalized as the essence of the female body.

The Civilized City: Unveiling, Heteronormativity, and the Abjection of Urban Space

> Entering a market requires a movement in space, a "location moment."
>
> Schivelbusch (1986, xiv)

Corporeal inscription of citizenship puts in place a system of signs that delegitimizes and even criminalizes certain bodies; it functions as a spatial marker of the transgressive, the dangerous, and the endangered.[32] As Elizabeth Grosz has noted, "The inscriptions on the subject's body coagulate corporeal signifiers into signs, producing all the effects of meaning, representation, depth, within or subtending our social order" (1994, 141). By disguising heterogeneity, such a political body contains the distinctions and boundaries that maintain the organization of a society based on class, race, ethnicity, religion, and gender/sex. This arrangement relies on what Spivak calls the discourse of "protection" (1988b). The discourse of protection serves to distinguish an "inside" and an "outside"—to assign positions to the protected and the protectors. The gendered metaphors of private and domesticated are defined in opposition to public and political. This discursive construction relies on the spatial and physical metaphor of home as a domesticated, bordered space and a territorial homeland. These spaces are characterized by the performance of socially useful work, yet one is defined by the natural division of labor and the other by the social division of labor. Women are considered the natural agents of the work of mothering; the socialization of children is given new value and meaning in the building of a well-informed, educated nation. Indeed the naturalness of mothering justifies the naturalness of the nation; Iran was referred to as "Mam-e Vatan," or the mother country. The spatial metaphor, a reference to both home and homeland, creates an inside and an outside, which must be treated with passion and protected at any price.[33] The institutionalization of state surveillance (through borders, prisons, psychiatric institutions) and of the ideology of the patriarchal family is related to such temporal and spatial metaphors and the discourse of protection in Iran.[34] Gender locations and meanings define agency within the discourse of protection. In the modern Iranian nation-state, while submission to normative respectability was fundamental for all members of society, gender notions assigned different positions to men as protectors and to women as the protected.

The discourse of protection relies on the process of abjection of the urban space and the systematic criminalization, separation, and isolation of perverse and transgressive bodies. For example, while unveiling was forced on respectable women, the state discouraged and even took initiatives to prevent the unveiling of prostitutes. A secret document from the Ministry of the Interior to the Cabinet Direction, dated 1942 (15-2-1321), states: "In reference to letter number 90, with regard to 'Maroofeh women' [prostitutes], the office of the provincial and presidial garrison was ordered to limit them and not let them be seen in the public spaces. However, if any of them get married, they should give them permission to unveil."[35] The modern state tried to contain transgressive sexuality by abjectifying the urban space associated with these acts. There are very few historical documents pertaining to the development of Iranian cities. This is especially true in the case of Tehran in the early twentieth century. There are a few revealing studies, including the socio-historical study of Jafar Shahri on "the old Tehran." When Tehran became a modern urban space in the early twentieth century, various forms of transgression surfaced. In his account of the development of Tehran, Shahri refers to the public display of transgressive gender behaviors. For example, in his description of the steam car station, he refers to "a woman called Bilghais who used to entertain people in the station. She was someone who dropped the veil for the pleasure of travelers" (1978, 171). He also characterizes "Laleh zar," a famous commercial street in Tehran, as a lovers' street where "boys who epilated their face, who put on makeup, with their sideways looks, flirtatiously and girlishly appeared in the street" (147).

New urban developments led to the construction of railroad and bus stations and the expansion of new urban commercial districts outside the limits of the traditional bazaar, which offered consumer goods to new, modernized classes. These commercial spaces were characteristic of the "leisure," "entertainment," and "pleasure" of urban life around which hotels, cabarets, and bars were constructed. While the traditional space of the bazaar resisted indulging patrons in new forms of consumerism, these new commercial spaces displayed gender mixing and class and ethnic intermingling. Both female entertainers and the non-Muslim entrepreneurs who sold food and alcohol found fresh possibilities for survival and success in these spaces. The blurring of the boundaries of *haram* (prohibited according to Islamic law), *halal* (permitted by Islamic law), and modern regimes of respectability based on bourgeois morality occurred within this commercial zone.

Further development transformed Tehran into a bordered city in the 1960s and 1970s. The city's coming of age was marked by the spatial division between the north, which was enclosed by the Alborz mountains and had a high concentration of the rich classes, and the south, which was open to the arrival of rural migrants seeking work in the industrialized capital and saw the emergence of the new urban poor. While the different moral frameworks of modern bourgeois and Islamic values competed for hegemony, consumer capitalism sought new subjects by exploiting sexual and gender ideologies that both encouraged and criminalized gender and sexual transgressions. The expansion of the film industry, media production, and entertainment relied heavily on such transgressive spaces, for in these spaces the recruitment of a labor force—especially females—was possible. Cinema, cabaret, and other entertainment venues were off limits to modest women, and women workers in these spaces were often characterized as potential prostitutes.

The expansion of the railroad brought modernization and new ideologies of respectability to remote places, yet also encouraged transgressive modes of life; by facilitating movement from one location to another, the railroad made it possible for people to lead an anonymous life. Railroad stations gradually became new sites of urban promenades, gender mixing, and encounters between locals and strangers. In addition, the distances opened up by modern transportation facilitated the uprooting of bodies, especially those of deviant women.

Prior to the revolution of 1979, the "New City" (*Shahr-e now*), where the prostitutes lived, was one of the most important of the abject and bordered places in Tehran. The life of its inhabitants was supervised by numerous state agencies, including the police department. The old city was protected from the New City, which was seen as contaminated by immorality, disease, and sexual transgressions. Located in the middle of one of the busiest parts of Tehran, the New City had a primary entrance point, a *darvazeh,* that maintained the border between the abject city and the normative city. During the revolutionary period (1978–1979), the New City was demolished to clear it of prostitution. The collapse of the boundaries between the abject city and the normative city created a lot of anxiety. The massive participation of women in demonstrations against imposed veiling in Tehran after the revolution in 1980 was condemned by secular and religious branches of the revolutionary movement as an act of collaboration between women and both the Westernized elite of the ancien régime and its ignorant victims, such as entertainers and prostitutes. Women were blamed for betraying revolutionary ideals through their intentional and unintentional collaboration with counterrevolutionary forces that were distracting the revolution from its primary concerns. By blurring the boundaries of respectability that separated pure women from impure ones and by transgressing the boundaries between revolutionary and counterrevolutionary, women became the first social group to need disciplining and containment within revolutionary discourse.

The Civic Body as a Site of Revolutionary Hermeneutic Practices

In the revolutionary and postrevolutionary era (1979 and after), the body became a site of enunciation and agency through the association of its subjection and subordination with a quasi-colonial order. The civic body demarcated a field of action that defined women's political agency in terms of what was tolerable or intolerable within particular political frames of meaning. As sites of agency, these frames of meaning challenged Western liberal feminist notions of the free will of an autonomous individual on behalf of nationalist, anti-imperialist, socialist, or simply antidictatorship agendas. At a time of social upheaval and revolution, the civic body became a site of hermeneutic activity, of revolutionary contestation and mimicry. Both dress code and warfare became frames for political activism, contestation, and the reimagination of femininity and masculinity.

The discourses of modernization and Westernization were subject to interpretation and to what Vattimo calls "a form of participant knowledge that transforms the interpreter" (1999, 9). In 1979, a revolutionary challenge to the social order dislodged hegemonic gender identities, including Westernized and modernized models of femininity and masculinity based on the racialized notion of a pre-Islamic Persian superiority, proximity to the West, and the heterosexist class culture of a modernized local elite. Islam as a religion was included, yet "othered," through its designation as an Arab import, not indigenous to Persia. Hegemonic masculinity and emphasized femininity were countered by oppositional movements, which practiced everyday revolutionary transgressions of gender roles. Revolutionary men and women fought against the dominant models of masculinity and femininity. Subordinated models of masculinity, in which men identified with the Islamic religion or secular oppositional cultures such as socialism, Marxism, and communism, came to the foreground. Women sought new models of femininity by distancing themselves from the emphasized model of femininity predominant under the shah. However, what connected various forms of oppositional gender and class identifications—from Islamic to Marxist and socialist—was a Westernized or "Westoxicated" (euphoric intoxication and poisoning by the West) notion of femininity incarnated in the *gharbzadeh* woman as the locus of sexual objectification, consumerism, and imperialism.[36] The semiotic shift from Westernization to Westoxication mobilized political action for the detoxification of the civic body of *zan-e gharbzadeh,* the ultimate symbol of state legitimacy and its imperialist supporters. The model of emphasized femininity, with its sexual objectification of women, was rejected and replaced by a combative model of femininity in the discourses of the various oppositional groups.

Counterhegemonic feminine performativity became an important source of identification and resistance and so attracted many women, who chose to risk their lives to challenge the oppressive order. Each oppositional group defined a particular dress code for women. Women identifying with leftist urban guerrilla groups wore trousers, long shirts, and sport shoes, while Islamic guerrillas wore head scarves to distinguish themselves from fundamentalist women, who wore the long black *chador* (long covering veil). Fashion was one of the most important tools of revolutionary imagery. However, an analysis of the ramifications of such imagery still needs to be articulated.[37]

At present, as a signifier, veiling has come to function as a form of boundary making, both in Iran and worldwide, a way of negotiating the dress code that reveals the instability of meaning invested in fashion. The visual capacity of clothing to stand for binary opposites was essential in the representation of revolution. As Bourdieu states in his empirical study of taste in French society (1984), one of the functions of fashion is to activate these forces of differentiation. In the context of the Iranian revolution, veiling coupled individuality with conformity. While this form of differentiation enables the successful representation of an Islamic revolutionary subject, in the postrevolutionary era, the focus on Islamic fashion coincides with the consumerism of late capitalism, which defines identity through the activity of buying.

In the prerevolutionary era and under the surveillance of the shah's dictatorship, women who participated in urban guerrilla movements transgressed gender codes and contributed to the construction of a combative model of femininity, becoming secret heroines for many Iranian women. Identification with women guerrillas could not be openly expressed, since they were hunted by the shah's secret police. However, women guerrillas were associated with risk taking, courage, fearlessness, and caring more about the revolutionary cause than family or community expectations. The capacity of combative women to transcend traditional feminine responsibilities—marriage, motherhood, nurturance, protection of the family—gave rise to a new ethic of political responsibility. Women guerillas endured terrible gender-specific forms of torture put in place by the dictatorship to destroy women's resistance—including rape in front of relatives and the introduction of snakes in their prison cells.[38]

Literature about Third World anticolonial revolutions was pivotal in the formation of these revolutionary subjectivities. Stories of revolutionary women, such as Layla Khalid and Jamila Buhrayd in the Middle East, were essential in encouraging women to join the guerrilla movement. In her autobiography, read repeatedly on oppositional radio stations under the shah, Ashraf-e Dehqani,[39] a member of a leftist guerrilla group, describes her torture:

Finally, one of them who had opened the box and who called himself a snake charmer, picked up a snake and brought it close to my head. The snake coiled round my neck. Had I not analyzed their motive and mentality, I would have been surprised at their idiocy. The point was quite simple. The snakes were poisonous, in which case they would kill me, an end I longed for and had tried to achieve, or they were harmless, in which case there was nothing to fear. Yet they expected me to be frightened, for they could imagine "women" as weak and cowardly. Their mentality is a product of their base and ignorant lives. They had indeed found "women" weak, but had never been able to analyze the reason for this. The "woman" in their mind is indeed weak. She has throughout the centuries, in class societies and in the reproduction process, suffered twice: once together *with* a man, she has been "enjoyed" . . . and once again she has suffered the same *from* a man. (1978, 20)

The strategic and instrumental manipulation of femininity and respectability for the sake of the revolution provided a justified opportunity for all forms of transgression. Women's participation in the guerrilla movements required the systematic rejection of emphasized femininity, including fearfulness, emotionality, and sentimentality. A guerrilla had to be ready to live as a comrade with others in group housing, to abandon her children in the revolutionary "cell-houses" in the event of entrapment by counterguerrilla forces or preemptive suicide, to endure torture, and to be capable of disloyalty toward her family and community in order to lead an underground life. Marriage and family as covers for underground activism put many women in the position of adhering to gender in its heteronormative mode while being ready to abandon it when necessary. Ashraf-e Dehqani escaped from one of the most heavily guarded of the shah's prisons and went on to lead a militaristic segment of the same organization by making it her own guerrilla group. Her omnipresence in dangerous urban spaces and her ability to disguise herself and to pass as an ordinary woman greatly influenced revolutionary urban legend making.

The National Spectacle and Gendered Subjects

Discourses of Westernization and modernization, along with their oppositional counterparts, have been invested in determining the meaning of the civic body in Iran. The civic body creates an inside and an outside within the order of the nation-state, which forms boundaries that rationalize and normalize a logic of identity and belonging. This demarcation of inside and outside is instrumental in the institutionalization of Orientalism by the local elite in the process of nation-state building.[40]

Also essential to this process is the will to unity expressed through what Young calls a "deontological self which is not committed to any particular ends, has no particular history, is a member of no communities, and has no body" (1987, 60). This framework provides the modern nation-state with the means to keep citizens under state surveillance, while keeping women under the surveillance of the male elite.[41]

In their assimilatory attempt to be part of the universal, Western rational order and through their acceptance of the necessity to protect Iranian women's bodies, civilized Iranian men were able to gain agency by means of citizenship in a modern world. Through a conscious recognition of the superiority of the European Enlightenment and through rejection of local models of masculinity, the modern Iranian male elite positioned itself as a superior, civilizing moral agent. The political encoding of the body and its representation as an abstract civic body have been essential to the project of modern state-building and to the representation of citizenship as universal.[42] The will to unity of citizens is consolidated in the idea of the civic body as a site of textual, legal, and political practices that transcend particular material bodies.

This process has four steps. First, an imagining of the body occurs through its legal, civic, and political representation. In the colonial and postcolonial order, this abstraction is inseparable from the process of racialization of civilized bodies in the fabrication of a globally hegemonic masculinity and hyperbolic femininity, along with the universalization of cultural institutions of heteronormativity. Second, oppositional nationalist discourses, secular and religious alike, are positioned in relation to these gendered bodies in order to nativize or indigenize this abstract body. This paradoxical process of particularization and universalization relies on the tropes of masculinity and femininity as the embodiment of proximity or distance. In this context, social agents are offered a place for the performance of a political action that sustains normativity through self-governmentality. Third, the imagining of bodies is made possible through a regime of othering where temporal and spatial proximity to and distance from certain bodies become measurements of power and control. This process of imagining and reimagining the body preserves a notion of body: a concept of the body as essence or origin remains behind and beyond the one exhibited as a refuge. Fourth, heteronormativity and its familial metaphors are essential in creating an outside and an inside of the nation and its boundaries. The spatial metaphors of home and homeland rely on the emotional resonance of inside and outside to support the rational spaces of political citizenship, by which I mean that the affective language of love and romance constantly colors modern notions of citizenship.[43] The borders of the nation are drawn and contained not only physically but also emotionally through the heteronormative imagining of the family.

The idea of an undifferentiated and universalized civic body crystallized during the formation of the modern nation-state in Iran. In the nation-state, bodies are subjected to the will of the political community. The civic body, as a politicized body, has the power to forge a connection between individual and collective identities, thereby delineating inclusion and exclusion. By such corporeal inscription, a system of signs is put in place that delegitimizes and criminalizes certain bodies and functions as a spatial marker of the transgressive, the dangerous, and the endangered. Such a political body contains the distinctions and boundaries that maintain the class-, race-, and gender/sex-based organization of society by disguising heterogeneity and calling for social agency within the discourses of protection. The discourse of protection serves to distinguish an inside and an outside, assigning positions to the protected and the protectors. This positioning is defined by the gendered metaphors of the private and the domesticated, which are opposed to the public and the political. Indeed, the very notions of "peoplehood" and "we-ness" create sites of agency for the protection of an "us" in its relation to an "other." The institutionalization of both state surveillance and patriarchal family ideologies is related to such discourses of protection. Agency within these discourses is defined by gender locations and meanings. While submission to normative respectability is fundamental for all members, gender concepts assign positions to men as protectors and women as protected, which require particular definitions of moral agency. In this case, the female body as both civic body and national landscape becomes the site of immanence and domestication with respect to which the male citizen-soldier achieves social agency as a self-sacrificing moral agent.[44] Forced unveiling of women by men made women vulnerable and effaced female agency, along with the subjectivity of women with names and historical trajectories.

The civic body became an important location of both Westernization under the Pahlavi regime and what was dubbed "Westoxication" during the revolutionary and postrevolutionary era. Global and local notions of femininity merged, creating homogeneity through the corporeal practices of Westernization and Westoxication. Both Westernization and Westoxication were inscribed on female bodies, one through the mission to civilize and the other through the return to indigeneity.

Both racialization and genderization, in their attempts to convert the barbaric body of women into a civilized one through male agency, provided material ground for Westernization or Westoxication. In both cases, the female body functioned as a site of possible pollution or contamination, a borderline state marking both marginality and vulnerability.[45] For the Islamic nationalists, a return to indigeneity was conditional upon the detoxification of women's bodies. In this sense, the female body was used to define the boundaries of two separated entities, the inside and the outside of the nation; the West and Islam thus contained the possibility of hybridity.

Identification through dress style is not of course unique to the Iranian revolution; many Third World revolutionaries used clothing as a powerful statement of their revolutionary goals to give the nation and revolutionaries an identifiable look and to present a politically informed style to the West. In Iran, while unveiling was used as a symbol of the civilizing of the nation, reveiling became a politically informed means of indigenizing it.

It is essential to examine how the civic body functions as means of legitimizing images and memories of the past and as a site of gender performance and national specificity. The social function of the civic body is directly related to the regulation of the present social order, that is, to the ways in which femininity and masculinity are conveyed and sustained by ritual performances, such as national commemoration of the past. Furthermore, intertextual racial and gender performance, as defined by its proximity to (or distance from) the white, European, bourgeois body, its habitus, and normativity, constitutes an important component of Westernization and anti-West cultural nationalism alike.

CHAPTER 3

The Tragic Paradox of Revolution

And hence only in so far as it mourns, becoming itself in the labor of infinite mourning, in the indemnification of a spectrality without limit. It is sacred, holy, infinitely respectable only in the name of what is worth more than it and what is not restricted to the naturalness of bio-zoological (sacrificeable)—although true sacrifice ought to sacrifice not only "natural" life, called "animal" or "biological," but also that which is worth more than so-called natural life.

Jacques Derrida (1998, 50–51)

At the center of these experiences that delimit the West is, of course, that of the tragic itself—Nietzsche having shown that the tragic structure from which the history of the Western world is made is not only the refusal, the forgetting and the silent effects of tragedy. Many other experiences revolve around this one, which is central since it ties the tragic to the dialectic of history in the very refusal of tragedy by history. At the boundaries of culture, each draws a limit that signifies, at the same time, an ordinary division.

Michel Foucault (1994a, 161)

But if there are old Shi'ite inflections available for contemporary political use, there are also conditions, scales, and meanings of modernity that are new.

M. J. Fischer and Mehdi Abedi (1990, 168)

In the 1970s, movements of resistance started to grow in Iran and recruited more members to take action against the regime. Guerrilla organizations, both Islamic and Marxist, became popular in rural and urban areas. The student movements gradually became a place where a new generation of young people could learn about the state's repressive policies and could get involved in various social movements. The shah's dictatorship started to respond in two ways: one was to increase students' resources (increasing the student loans and scholarships, improving student food and dormitories, facilitating student travel, and so on) to discourage them from joining the oppositional revolutionary movements; and the second was to intensify repressive measures by arresting masses of students for simple reasons, such as reading an outlawed text, participating in a student protest, or criticizing the regime in the classrooms. The experience of imprisonment was crucial in connecting the student movement to other revolutionary movements, since prisons became an important place for the recruitment of students by these organizations. Moreover, the Iranian student movement in other countries, especially in Europe and the United States, and Iranian religious leaders exiled in Iraq contributed their energy to overthrowing the shah.

In the mid 1970s, there emerged a widespread culture of resistance in the form of oppositional radio stations, as well as through the distribution of tracts, cassettes, publications, and underground anthologies called *Jong* (a collection of different genres of political writing). This revolutionary culture was accompanied by the emergence of a revolutionary style in fashion. This revolutionary culture was a transnational production rooted in Third World revolutionary and anticolonial movements. This transnational revolutionary culture became an umbrella under which various political ideologies and groups led their struggle against the regime. While the older generation of political activists and organizers was focused mostly on political solutions and reform, the younger generation was attracted to more militant, revolutionary modes of resistance. Various ideologies, including socialism, Marxism, and anarchism, as well as revolutionary versions of Islam, were crucial in channeling these movements. In 1977–78, the labor movement, religious officials associated with the mosques, and masses of ordinary people, both in the capital and elsewhere in the country, began to join the revolutionary movement.

Soon the various segments of the avant-garde movements melded into a movement under the leadership of Khomeini that aimed to overthrow the shah and his regime. Khomeini accused the shah of having sold the country to imperialist powers. Recounting the stories of Shia imams' revolts and martyrdom against cruel rulers, audiences remembered and reacted to the injustice and cruelty of the shah's regime. Allegory, symbols, and double meanings were an important part of the pedagogy of resistance in Iran, educating people to always look for hidden political meanings. This pedagogy provided space for various groups to articulate their dissatisfaction with the regime in different levels of language.[1] The anti-Shah movement developed into a massive revolutionary movement.

In 1978, during the military curfew in Iran, which prohibited trespassing on government or military grounds between 6 P.M. and 6 A.M., there emerged a culture of resistance influenced by mass communication and information technologies. This technology of resistance used popular means of diffusing information, mimicking the strategies of mass media. After the announcement of the curfew, word circulated that every night at midnight everyone should turn off the lights, go to the roof of buildings, and shout "God is Great" *(Allah-o Akbar)* as a protest against military rule. The utilization of microphones and cassettes, along with live voices, created confusion between embodied voices and those created through mechanical ventriloquism. Shouting and screaming at a given time of the night—a protest in which everyone participated—broke the silence imposed by military rule. Under the curfew, the Tehran night soon became a site of protest and revolt. The roof (*bam,* or *pohst-ebam*) found a new function as a liminal urban space, neither public nor private. When upper-level windows also became a site for protests, the military was forced to recognize that occupation of these buildings would be a difficult task. The massive participation of voices, some of which were broadcast live and others carried through electronic relay, created a community of protest. The use of the slogan "God is Great"—an ambiguous religious statement that people, religious and nonreligious alike, commonly used in diverse circumstances, including sadness, death, happiness, and anger—was difficult for the military rulers to use as a cause of arrest.

The mass-mediated spaces of the midnight protest became privileged sites for spreading news. News that would have otherwise been limited to a neighborhood circulated around the city. The shouting and screaming of "God is Great" became background music for the revelation of outlawed and censured news, including information about the number of deaths and arrests, as well as the announcement of the date, time, and location of plans for future political demonstrations. The military governor, General Azhari, claimed that only a small group of people were responsible for the breakdown in curfew and that these events were perpetrated by means of tape recorders and cassettes. However, in one of the first mass demonstrations, in which millions of people showed up in the streets of Tehran, one of the popular chants was "Poor Azhari, can you dare to say that this is a tape? Tapes don't walk! You are a four-star donkey."

Visual representation and the mythical construction of reality were quintessential components of the Iranian revolution and continue to be important in Iranian cultural production. The revolution of 1979 produced an extensive body of pictorial and mythological tropes, which helped to create the historical reality of the Islamic revolution.[2] The reinvention of tradition, in Hobsbawm's terms, required recourse to Shia mythology. However, it would be reductionist to read this reinvention as fully defined by Islamic religion and to accept that religion was mobilized in any clear way for the sake of revolution. Shiite mythology includes many cultural productions, including theater, painting, poetry, stories, songs, mourning rituals, festivals, miracles, mythical figures, and sanctuaries. People's relationships to these popular cultural productions and practices are aesthetic, affective, figurative, theatrical, and ethical. During the revolution, the iconographic and dramatic components of Shia mythology mobilized the masses. In Iran, these iconographic and dramatic aspects of Shiism are related to pre-Islamic, Persian myths. For example, Imam Ali (the first imam of Shia Muslims) has a place in Iranian popular culture as a mythical hero rather than a religious figure. The textual and legal aspects of Shiism did not become central until after the establishment of the Islamic state. The iconography of Shiism is still important in Iranian popular culture and has become a significant part of consumer culture. Today in Iran, posters of imams are mass-produced and sold in gift shops next to holy shrines, including the tomb of Imam Khomeini, a newly constructed holy site, a place of pilgrimage and tourism for masses of Iranians.

Shia revolutionaries most frequently drew upon myths that embodied the hybrid nature of Iranian nationalism, integrating pre-Islamic and Islamic mythologies. The Pahlavi regime emphasized the superiority of the pre-Islamic mythologies of a monarchist Persia. Secular Iranian nationalists still insist on the superiority of the Persian pre-Islamic culture and traditions, and consider Islam to have been imposed by Arabs after their invasion of Iran in the seventh century A.D. The revolutionary reliance on such hybrid Shia mythologies transcended the dichotomy between a good, civilized pre-Islamic Persia and a post-Islamic Persia contaminated by Islam and Arab culture. The Pahlavi regime's construction of a nationalism that imagined a glorious age prior to the Arab conquest was challenged in the revolutionary era. The nationalistic Pahlavi regime commemorated Iranian literary traditions of cultural resistance to Arab dominance, glorifying an Iranian culture independent of Arab and Islamic elements. Islamic cultural nationalism, however, bridged pre- and post-Islamic Iran, transcending both Persian chauvinism, with its anti-Arab components, and the communist/socialist focus on the egalitarian vision of the pre-Islamic and prophetic movements of protest led by Mazdak, the Zoroastrian priest who revolted against the Sasanians' rule in 494 A.D. and was put to death along with many of his followers.[3]

Shiite religious dramas are also related to pre-Islamic Persian mythology. For example, the Shiite tragedy of Imam Hussein draws on the pre-Islamic myth of Seyavash.[4] Both Imam Hussein and Seyavash are beloved leaders martyred as a result of a conflict between different sources of power. Both figures are remembered as being killed unjustly. Both tragedies vividly relate the ethical and conscientious conduct of these leaders and their decision to surmount worldliness (family ties, sexual seduction) because of their commitment to social justice. Both figures prophesize their own murder and accept it.

Bringing together the pre-Islamic myth of Seyavash and the Shiite tragedy of Imam Hussein enables a tragic and skeptical view of life. A systematic investigation of the operative historical conditions is necessary to understand the emergence of a hegemonic, tragic view of religion. By "tragic view of religion," I mean a version of Shiism that is, to a great extent, invested in the myth of Karbala and the tragedy of Imam Hussein, the origin of a conflict between the minority forces of Ali's followers and the majority forces of the Umayyad dynasty. The tragedy of Imam Hussein became a central myth in the politicization of Shiism in Iran. Imam Hussein, the third imam of Shia Muslims and the second son of Imam Ali, was martyred in Karbala (Iraq) in 680 A.D. by the army of the Umayyad dynasty. His martyrdom is honored by Shiite Muslims. As Cole and Keddie have argued, Shiite identification with these martyred leaders took an activist, nationalist turn, and was used during the Iranian revolution for political purposes (1986, 28).

Long before the revolution of 1979, the shah's regime used visual media for governmental campaigns and propaganda, commemorating, for example, the "White revolution" and the day of "national resurrection" (*Rastakhiz-e meli Mordad of bist o hasht-e mordad*), as well as the triumphant return of the shah to Iran after five days of forced exile. The Iranian revolution relied on similar media representations to promote oppositional revolutionary ideals, exemplifying the importance of visual media for postmodern social revolutions.[5] Fifteen years before the extensive application of information technologies by the Zapatistas in Chiapas, Iran's "cassette revolution" (to use Foucault's phrase) played a key role in bringing the revolution into focus as a unified event by creating an oppositional collective will and calling upon various groups to take part in the revolutionary process. This oppositional collective will relied on what Khomeini referred to as *Vahdat-e kalemeh,* or the unity of words, and led to a revolutionary discourse that moved beyond agents and actors to encompass phases marking the periods before, during, and after the revolution. In other words, revolutionary discourse became a place where particular subjects were included as revolutionary to the exclusion of those whose perception of the revolution was different. In the prerevolutionary era, avant-garde political organizations were considered revolutionary. During the revolution, masses of people, along with political, cultural, and religious groups, joined the revolution, bringing different ideas of what the revolution was supposed to achieve. In the postrevolutionary era, after a period of struggle among various groups, from Islamic nationalists to social democrats, socialists, and Marxists, the Islamist discourse of revolution became hegemonic. Parvin Paider refers to this discourse as the discourse of Islamization, which sought to attain national independence through the creation of a modern Muslim nation (1995, 265). As a result, the revolution became the domain of all its participants and the burden of "true revolutionaries" in the postrevolutionary era.

An obsession with image—both in the construction of myths, symbols, and revolutionary icons and in the fashioning of a revolutionary "self"—is at the center of the Iranian revolution. Such imagery is interwoven with Orientalist images, in the sense that the Orientalist Other took hold of its own otherness, fabricating a self—or in Foucauldian terms, a "morality style"—subject to attraction and consumption. The morality style of the Iranian revolution is defined by the formation of gendered bodies.

A revolutionary subject was thus formed by two concurrent processes: transgression of the boundaries set up by regulatory forces, which required an understanding of what infringed upon the body, and the exercise of power through the construction and legitimization of knowledge that was not controlled by the West or the Westernized local elite. Two important scenarios exemplify these revolutionary processes. One scenario represents the possibility of death as a radical manifestation of subjectivity, while the other scenario channels revolt into the revolution by opposing self-interest to love of the Islamic ummat, the revolution, and the motherland. In the first instance, death represents revolt, the right to intervene in life at a point at which, in Foucauldian terms, "Death is now going to be, on the contrary, the moment where the individual escapes all power, sinks back into himself, and withdraws" (1997, 221). While modern structures of power tend to hide death by making it a private matter (221), in the revolutionary context, death becomes a public matter in the day-to-day theater of revolution. The staging of local rituals, such as Muharam and Karbala ye Husseini, provided a forum where death could be exposed. Considering the theatricality of the everyday events of revolution, Foucault reminds us of "the terminology, the ceremonial, the historical drama of a people who weigh their existence against the existence of their ruler" (1979b, 230).

In this context, the subject of the revolt assumes the sovereign power previously held by the state. However, this moment is discursively assimilated within and transferred to a second moment where—through a dialectical logic reducing all conflict to a fundamental antagonism—war, conflict, and death become the object of the state and civil order. The creation of a postrevolutionary state established continuity between pre-Islamic and Islamic Iran, as well as a hybrid sense of identity composed of both national and religious discourses. This process, however, has been contradictory. The challenge of the West has led to the search for a style of existence rooted in local knowledge and a familiar, Islamic style of morality, but, at the same time, the very establishment of an Islamic state where the Islamic style became common to everyone, both by force and by choice, has itself provided fertile ground for new forms of global consumerism.[6] The Islamic style has given way to a more secure, religious nationalist identity, represented in fashion, art, theater, film, and music. By performing an indigenous identity based on Islamic nationalism, Iranians have created new opportunities for consumption in the local and global markets. The growth of local and national forms of Islamic consumerism, including Islamic dress, ornaments, art, and literature, as well as Islamic tourism both in Iran and globally (especially in the Muslim populated countries), provides examples of the expansion of transnational consumer citizenship and the increased cultural influence of the working classes and middle classes, who identify with Islamic morality. In Iran, in the postrevolutionary era, new forms of entrepreneurship include regional tourism. The postrevolutionary forms of Islamization are also sites of consumerism and the production of consumer subjects. Indeed, the postmodern subject of revolutionary Iran is not the sole author of its own text or the related modes of representation, since these modes of representations are formed by an endless chain of messages that are always subject to interpretation.

Both the revolutionary movement and the Islamic republic that seized power in its aftermath used visual representation as an important tool of subjectivity and persuasion. Modern technologies of communication, such as posters, slogans, banners, murals, television, and cinema, were utilized to counter the West and create a "we-ness" that represented all the forces involved in the revolution. Before and during the revolution, when the media was still controlled by the shah's regime, the oppositional radio station and widely distributed cassette tapes of Khomeini's speeches were crucial in diffusing news of oppositional movements and in forging connections between localities. During the revolution and under the military curfew, myriad expressions of mass solidarity emerged that sought to break down the isolation imposed by military rule. These included creative, popular ways of circulating information (such as shouting the news of demonstrations from residential rooftops and windows, reciting religious sayings such as *Allah-o Akbar* [God is Great] at a set time of night, and reflecting on the course of events in graffiti in public spaces). Religious expressions were extremely effective in this context because of their ambiguity, which stemmed from having both religious and political connotations.

In this chapter, I will elaborate on five major sites for the formation of an Islamic revolutionary subject. The first site is the construction of an oppositional model of Islamic femininity that allows for active participation in political life and is based on female figures in early Islamic history. Borrowed from early Islam, this model of femininity became a symbol of indigenousness and originality. I argue that it is through the symbolism of this indigenous model of femininity that the Islamic movement was able to represent itself as different, original, and uncontaminated by the Western world. The second site is the mobilization of *ta'zieh* as a genre of popular Islam emphasizing religious practices based in oral, visual, and theatrical performance rather than on the memorization of scriptural components. The third site is the imagining of a unified but gender-divided Islamic community (the ummat) as dynamic, historical, and dialectical. The fourth site is the construction of an Islamic subaltern, or *mostaz'af,* in opposition to the powerful, or *mostakbar.* The last site coincides with the use of tragedy, specifically the Karbala parable, as a site of gendered performance of Islamic subjectivity.

Gender identities and performativities are crucial for the construction of an Islamic revolutionary subject position in all these sites, for a number of reasons: they provide a liberatory discourse that is legitimately used to articulate the suppressed cultural histories of the oppressed groups; they represent the indigenous possibilities ingrained in those histories to empower political action; and they establish a framework for the creation of new forms of identities and subjectivities that are conceived as historically constructed.

From "Zan-e hich va pouch" to Fatima and Zeinab

> *Zeinab:* Brother, you were never like this,
> Never so alarmed and concerned as this . . .
> The *ta'zieh* of the martyrdom of Ali Akbar

Gianni Vattimo describes the formation of an oppositional revolutionary subjectivity as a "time-language" process that incorporates a multiplicity of myths, narrations, and language games that are never definitive but always new.[7] Some of these myths are grounded in modern discourses and the imagery of Orientalism. As I argued in chapter 2, the need to reveil the nation from the voyeuristic eye of the West and the West's modernizing regimes has been essential in the reactivation of certain myths and images. For example, the veiled woman represents the border between outside and inside, the known and the unknown. The taboo pleasure of veiling, the secret hiding behind the veil, and even the strategic use of the veil as a way of passing are all related to symbols and myths that have been at work since the inception of Iranian modernity.

Fatimah Fatimah Ast (Fatima Is Fatima), written by Ali Shari'ati and published in 1971, is one of the most important texts for the formation of an oppositional Islamic femininity, since it identified a new discursive space and influenced women to take action in the indigenous revolution. By questioning both the "old traditional models of femininity" and the "imported models of femininity" in *Fatimah Fatimah Ast,* Shari'ati seeks a role model for women in Shiite history. Fatima—the prophet's favorite daughter, the wife of Ali, and the mother of Imam Hussein—provides inspiration for those women who, according to Shari'ati, need "to create themselves and to be reborn." This rebirth, according to Shari'ati, is about a woman's willingness to be her own midwife rather than being created through either inheritance or mimicry (1971, 2–3).

Fatima, a dutiful daughter, wife, and mother, was subjected to the cruel rule of Umayyad caliphs, who usurped power after Muhammad's death. According to Shari'ati, "Fatima would go with her children to the ruins of the city of Medina called *Bayt al Ahzan* (the house of sadness) and cry for those who attacked Imam Ali and deprived him of his rightful leadership of the Islamic community" (7). Shari'ati uses Fatima's life to examine the parallel world of Iran under the Pahlavi regime and calls for a return to a "belief that requires reason and books as well as blood and sacrifice." He urges a return to the *khaneh* (house) and loyalty to the house of Fatima, which includes a reconnection with the affective—crying, feeling, loving, and suffering (13–14).[8]

Shari'ati's invitation to mourn the suffering of Ali's family—especially Fatima—created a momentum in the reinvention of a gender-based notion of nation. Collective identification with the suffering and tears of Fatima redefines the nation as a family whose members enact gendered roles. The family of the nation is born of two sources: *andisheh* (thinking) and *ehsas* (emotion). Shari'ati's conception of the nation is also interwoven, however, with the discourse of Orientalists on Persians and Muslims. He writes, "They say we are concomitantly both fanatic and stubborn yet persistent and apathetic" (17). Shari'ati's comment describes how the representation of difference or Persian otherness is repeated or altered in another historical moment.

Through the intertextual accumulation of meaning across different texts, where one image refers to another or is read in the context of other images, in Hall's terms (1997, 232), Shari'ati refers to Western women as those who struggle for their rights, as opposed to middle-class Iranian women, who are lazy and only good for childcare and housework. By praising the women in the United States and Europe who fought for freedom, Shari'ati seeks to catch up with modernity and yet indigenize it through Islam. He attacks middle-class women, who have become *Zan-e hich va pouch* (a woman in her nothingness): "A housewife who is only good for housework and childcare, but since she can afford it pays others to do these jobs for her. She is not a peasant, she does not work in the field, she does not work at the office, she does not go to school, or to the hospital, she is not an artist nor interested in science or books or pen, she does not take care of children, she does not cook" (1991, 83). For Shari'ati, *Zan-e hich va pouch* is obsessed with sex, since she is a "woman of Friday nights," that night of the week when Muslim couples are supposed to have sex (1971, 84–85).

By criticizing housewives who hire someone else to do their housework, Shari'ati reveals his modernist and masculinist bias, viewing middle-class women as only good for housework but not even up to doing the housework and so paying others to do this work for them. He also considers women's work to be expressions of individuality rather than forms of labor. Fatima, however, represents an alternative model of femininity for Shari'ati—a woman who is "a model of a daughter before her father, a wife before her husband, a mother before her children, and a responsible and militant woman before her historical time and the destiny of her society" (1971, 186). Shari'ati's reference to Fatima as a model of femininity is an invitation for women to participate in an oppositional community of Muslims.

While Fatima served as an Islamic model of femininity in the discourse of Iranian Islamic oppositional intellectuals and made it possible for a *Zan-e hich va pouch* to reinvent herself through an oppositional, indigenous model of femininity, it was not Fatima, but rather Zeinab, the daughter of Imam Ali and the sister of Imam Hussein, who took leadership after the massacre of Karbala. She emerged as the more revolutionary figure during the Iranian revolution. As a cultural and historical icon, famous for her participation in the tragedy of Karbala and for her rousing speech at a time when the combatants were at their lowest, Zeinab became a political symbol to encourage women's participation in the events of the revolution. Zeinab's story legitimized the participation of masses of young women in the events of the revolution and prevented their families from forbidding them from taking revolutionary action. Zeinab, who was slaughtered along with seventy-two other relatives of Hussein, including babies, children, and their caretakers, was portrayed as a powerful public speaker, a brave combatant, and the confidante of her brother Imam Hussein. However, soon after the revolution, Zeinab was domesticated and marginalized. She was later remembered on Nurses' Day, as a result of her work taking care of the wounded. Instead, it is Fatima whose birth is celebrated on National Women's Day in Iran and who is identified as the ideal Muslim wife and mother.

Women participated in all aspects of the revolution, from demonstrations to acts of political belligerence. However, the visual representations that accompanied the revolution systematically portrayed men as warriors and combatants and women as mourners of the martyrs.

Revolutionary events were narrated through Shiite mythology, and the role of the hero warrior was attributed to men, while women were included only as wives, mothers, and daughters.

Ta'zieh, Tragedy, and the Performance of the Revolution

> The blood of Seyavash a tree rose up
> To touch the clouds; each leaf displayed his likeness,
> And from his love there came the scent of musk.
> It was an evergreen that flourished in
> December's cold as freshly as in springtime,
> A place where those who mourned for Seyavash
> Would gather and bewail his death and worship.
>
> Abulghasem Ferdowsi, *The Legend of Seyavash* (1992, 131)

> Every day is Ashura and the whole earth is *karbala*.
>
> A mural in Hamedan, cited in
> Chelkowski and Dabashi (1999, 120)

> Muharam, the month of victory of the blood over the sword.
>
> A revolutionary banner

One of the most important stories in Shia martyrology is that of Imam Hussein. The widespread popularity of Hussein's drama reflects its capacity to integrate pre-Islamic Iranian mythology into popular Islam. By popular Islam, I refer to those religious practices that address all levels of society via visual and oral culture rather than through scripture. Local heroes and heroines and popular sanctuaries represent these practices more than clerical Islam. Performed in popular sanctuaries, popular Islam represents religion through local heroes and heroines rather than through Islam clerics.

As a form of popular Shia theater, *ta'zieh* was performed in both rural and urban areas by local performers during Muharam, which is the month when Imam Hussein and his family were slaughtered by the army of the Sunni caliph Yazid in Karbala in Iraq. During the Qajar rule, Naser al-Din Shah (1848–96) built a famous royal *tekiyeh* (an arena theater) in which *ta'zieh* was performed. *Ta'zieh* attracted the attention of Orientalists and Western writers as early as the sixteenth century, after the Safavid kings began their patronage of Shia as the state religion. In the nineteenth and twentieth centuries, it became the focus of a number Orientalist writings. In villages and cities where there was no performing troupe, *ta'zieh* was accomplished through the visual representation of the *Pardeh-dari*.[9] While storytelling was used by both men and women for entertainment and instruction, *ta'zieh* performance in public spaces was male-dominated, with men playing the roles of women.

Chelkowski describes *ta'zieh* as a compromise between "the moving procession and the stationary recitation" (1979, 6). He argues that, as a popular form of performance, *ta'zieh* was historically staged at street intersections and squares; in the nineteenth century, it was performed mainly in the *tekiyeh*, or arena theaters. In small towns and rural areas, *ta'zieh* is performed in any space large enough for spectators to gather. In the urban spaces, *ta'zieh* is performed in the *tekiyeh*, which is architecturally different from the mosque, since it includes an open space with two or more openings to the *mahalleh* (residential areas) and platforms where people may sit to watch the performances. In some rural and urban public spaces, temporary structures are built for the Muharam observances. In urban areas, *tekiyeh* are built mostly by the well-to-do and the upper classes as a location for religious and public services. Some *tekiyeh* seat thousands of spectators, but most seat a few hundred. Chelkowski states that in the late nineteenth century even the British and Russian legations were drawn into the competition for the most splendid *tekiyeh* for the annual Muharam celebrations in Tehran (1979, 6). He asserts that *ta'zieh* served as the unconsciously avant-garde theater of the twentieth-century rural poor because of its dynamic flexibility, stemming from the absence of time and space barriers and its textual fluidity (9).

While the primary theme of the *ta'zieh* has always been Imam Hussein and his family, in the Tekiyeh Dawlat during the Qajar dynasty, performers began to use its imagery to portray current events. In the late nineteenth century, Comte de Gobineau described a *ta'zieh* called "The Christian Daughter," which was played in the Royal Tekiyeh and dealt with the advent of modernity. In this particular *ta'zieh*, a young European woman and her servant arrive—with a caravan of horses, carpets, and baggage—in the field of Karbala, which is strewn with the headless bodies of martyrs. Dismounting, the young woman asks her servant to make camp in the field of martyrs. Suddenly, "a great stream of blood sprang from the earth, true, red blood, staining the grass covering the ground" (Gobineau 1865, 444–45). Refusing to remain in that terrible place, the exhausted European woman leaves with her servant to sleep on the *Taghnama* (the false arch). The *ta'zieh* concludes when a Bedouin arrives and discovers the bodies of the martyrs.

This *ta'zieh* is revealing in its depiction of an encounter between Iran and modern Europe characterized by gender and violence. In this scene, the dormant Christian West is represented as a feminine presence horrified by the boiling blood of the Karbala martyrs. I could not find any other accounts of *ta'zieh* dealing with current issues or reconstruction of the Karbala tragedy in the early twentieth century, but Gobineau's description indicates the convergence of religious and modern traditions in art performances. Such a convergence became taboo in modern Iran of the mid-twentieth century. During the Iranian revolution, not only did *ta'zieh* started to incorporate current events, but current events started to incorporate *ta'zieh* elements, including the recitation of *ta'zieh* songs and the wearing of green headbands during demonstrations.

Ta'zieh, along with other Muharam observances, were restricted by Reza Shah's secularist regime. However, they continued to be performed on a local level, and *ta'zieh* and the tragedy of Karbala reemerged in modern visual arts. The coffeehouse school of painting, which began in the late 1950s and continued into the 1960s, portrayed Ashura, *ta'zieh,* and other motifs in the story of Karbala. These motifs also appeared in another tradition of modern painting, the Saqqakhaneh school.[10] In the mid 1970s, *ta'zieh* was revitalized, and in 1976 the first conference on *ta'zieh* was organized at the Shiraz Festival of Arts under the direction of Farrokh Gaffary. This event played a crucial role in the public recognition of the need for preservation of indigenous performing arts and in the formation of the Institute for Traditional Performance and Ritual (Chelkowski 1979, xvi).

The Karbala drama was completely displaced from the stage to the streets during the revolution and the Iran-Iraq conflict. Through the performance of such passion plays, the nation was able to identify itself as a family surrounded by forces of evil. The textual fluidity of *ta'zieh* and the flexibility of its staging in both rural and urban areas created a platform available to every group and locality seeking meaning. This period blurred the boundaries between performer, spectator, image, and reflection. *Ta'zieh* became a staging ground for revolution, making no distinction between the poor and the rich. It provided only two colors to identify with (the red and the green) and two forces to align oneself with: the forces of evil (Shemr and his followers) or the forces of good (Imam Hussein and his family).

As a genre of cultural production, *ta'zieh* has the structure of modern tragedy. Williams argues, "Tragedy, as such, teaches nothing about evil, because it teaches many things about many kinds of action. Yet it can at least be said, against the modern emphasis on transcendent evil, that most of the great tragedies of the world end not with evil absolute, but with evil both experienced and lived through" (1979, 60). As a type of tragedy defined by circular, mythological time (returning every year in the month of Muharam), *ta'zieh* converged with the historical time of modernity and revolution to stage the evil lived through under the dictatorship, promising an end to injustice and evil.[11]

Chelkowski and Dabashi, in their analysis of the Iranian revolution, examine the religious and epic Persian imagery of the revolutionary period and claim that the "Islamic revolution of 1978–79 was such a grand historical moment of self-reunderstanding" (1999, 65). However, they do not take into account the ways in which the modern self represented in painting and miniature was expressed by particular artists, who portrayed these mythologies through modern male biases, for example, the seductive appeal of a tragic version of Shiism, which, along with the death of the Seyavash epic, serves to reactivate masculine cultural forms and traditional practices of identity formation as a process of subjection of the self. The questions that need to be asked here are the following: What makes it possible for the tradition to be reinvented through the genre of tragedy? Which epic stories would have been chosen, and which pre-Islamic or Islamic myths would have been reactivated, had the reinvention of this tradition not happened in the context of political and social oppression?

From the Community of Man
to the Community of God

> But I disagree with whoever would say: "It's useless to rise up; things will always be the same." One doesn't lay down the law to whoever risks his/her life before a power. Is it right or not to revolt? Let's leave the question open. People don't rise up, this is a fact; and it is through this that subjectivity (not that of great men but that of anyone) enters history and gives it breath.
>
> Michel Foucault, "Inutile de soulever?"

I see that the nation has become godly *[Mibinam keh milat ellahi shodeh ast]*.

Imam Khomeini (cited by Chelkowski
and Dabashi 1999, 116)

In the revolutionary period, multiple political ideologies were represented in the various demonstrations against the dominant regime. Thousands of urban inhabitants from the working, lower-middle, and middle classes spontaneously or in a planned way participated in daily political action against the dictatorship. An anti-Western movement was associated with Khomeini and his version of an Islamic republic, which radically distinguished itself from nationalist, radical democratic, Marxist, and socialist visions. This shift in the postrevolutionary era was characterized by the slogan "Neither West nor East, the Islamic Republic." *East* was used as a signifier of the Marxist, socialist, and communist modernities of those oppositional groups that were defending notions such as a people's democratic republic *(Jomhouri democratic Khalq)*.

Ayatollah Khomeini's successful articulation of the concepts of individual and ummat in his reading of Islamic religion in general and Shiism in particular not only reconciled Islam with the concept of the nation-state, but also expanded Islam to include a transnational community. These two very modern constructs are related to a concept of sovereignty based on the idea that God is the ultimate and absolute sovereign of all creation. God, in this sense, is owner and master vis-à-vis the ummat (community of believers) in which each individual is a participant. In his writings, Ayatollah Khomeini makes constant reference to this idea, emphasizing that the entire religion must be in the service of the individual and the individual in the service of religion (1980, 76–78).

There are a number of interconnected ideas at work in the creation of an Islamic community contained within modernity's order of time and space. Entry into the normative time of modernity is predicated on a particular historicity and a bounded spatiality, which, in the context of postmodernity and the recent erosion of the nation-state (owing in part to the expansion of mass media, to migration flows, and to the intensified displacement of capital and labor), can no longer be exclusively defined by recourse to national territoriality.[12]

As a modern entity, the Islamic ummat is mapped out through several crucial ideological elements. One element critical to the creation of an Islamic community is the reference to a common, historicized past. While historicizing the Islamic community, Islamic nationalists and fundamentalists modified its temporality, as the cyclic time of myth replaced the linear time of social and historical struggles (Shayegan 1989, 139). Shiism provided the symbolic capital for such revisiting of history. Two episodes in the history of Shia Islam become especially important—the usurpation of power by illegitimate caliphs and the Karbala uprising.[13] Both episodes provided ideological grounding for a call to Islamic revolution by showing the illegitimacy of the state and the need to mobilize a mass movement.

The second critical element is a transnational idea of territory. This idea is based on the emergence of an Islamic subject, located in a space where the national and the transnational converge, a location that is in the geographical mapping of neither the West nor the East. Khomeini refers to an Islamic space between the "imperialism of the left and imperialism of the right" (1981a, 210). This transnational spatial metaphor is characterized by the emerging subjectivity of Muslims in alliance with the disempowered (the *mostaz'afan* of the Quran) in their opposition to the oppressive powers of the imperialists. The imagined nation of Muslims was invented in opposition to the powerful *(mostakbaran)*.

The third element is the cultural cohesion of Islam as *tassavor* (vision), realizable through an Islamic revolution and a commitment to collectivity. This vision recalls Jahiliyya, an age of ignorance located in the past, and idolatry *(taghut)*, its contemporary manifestation, where man rules over man, an order opposed to a society in which believers achieve equality and justice through realization of an Islamic praxis. The real significance of Islam, according to this schema, is not the subject's religious experience but rather an acceptance of the collective nature of Islamic life and an individual devotion to the cause. In other words, the Islamic community as a political entity and its goal of bringing justice and equality to everyone are at the center of this vision of society. Islamic culture is used to unify and empower the marginalized majority, the poor, the disadvantaged, the dispossessed, the weak, the disempowered, and the inferior (the mostaz'af), against the rich, the powerful, the superior (the mostakbar). The nationalist cultural version of revivalism hopes to protect itself from the criticism that it concerns only "the privileged few."

The fourth element is the construction of a militant notion of Islam, based on the polarization of Allah (God) and *taghut* (idolatry), which mobilizes jihad. Fundamentalist discourse, like nationalist discourse, depends on the concept of otherness to organize an ideological "we."

Here the subject emerges, in a Hegelian sense, to recognize an unhappy consciousness resulting from subordination and oppression. This is a masculinist notion, since it finds meaning in an ethical world of masculine responsibility.[14] In contrast to the modern, Cartesian conception of selfhood, which rejects the idea of the divided subject in favor of a unified rational self, Islamic fundamentalist discourse recognizes the inner division of the subject and connects it to an exterior separation. An awareness of the inner and outer division of the self and its regulation makes possible a subject position that challenges dominant regimes of subject formation. In the fundamentalist view, jihad is not only a revolt against the ruler but also against oneself as defined by the notion of *jihad-e nafs,* or worldly asceticism. Ayatollah Khomeini refers to these two forms of jihad as *jihad-e akbar* (major jihad) and *jihad-e asghar* (minor jihad), or holy war against *taghut* (idolatry) (1980, 52). Khomeini's reference to *jihad-e nafs* as *akbar,* or grand, underscores the importance and difficulty of a holy war waged against one's individual needs; the self is sacrificed to the will of Allah. The polarization of Allah and *taghut,* God and idolatry, in the *jihad-e nafs* opens the way for an enduring cultural and psychological rejection of non-Islamic values and for the internalization of Islamic values. In order to become a member of Allah's community, one must reject *taghut* before proclaiming a new adherence to Allah.[15]

The fifth element is the conceptualization of the Islamic ummat as a material, historical, and actual entity, with a purpose and a direction. The idea of progress is central to modernity and the Enlightenment. This idea presumes that history has a path and a direction that promise control over human destiny, moving toward a society free of injustice and cruelty. The Islamic notion of ummat becomes an entity that undertakes the idea of progress in its linear movement toward a just society in the future. In his advocacy of an Islamic republic, Khomeini criticizes imperialist powers for preventing industrialization in Iran through control of natural resources (including oil), control of the government through the establishment of puppet governments, and control of the market through the transformation of Iran into a large consumer market for the West (1981a, 39). The idea of progress is central to the reconstruction of the Islamic ummat, since none of the versions of Islamic nationalism and fundamentalism claims a regressive movement toward the past; rather the past is used to give meaning to the future. Ayatollah Khomeini states that what constitutes the backwardness of Islamic nations is the belief in the racial superiority of the West in general and of the United States in particular (1984, 175). In fact, all versions of Islamic nationalism and fundamentalism assert the compatibility of materialist progress and Islam. *Harekat* and *tagiir,* meaning movement and change, are borrowed from Islamic discourse to pronounce an evolutionary schema of progress (Gafari 1979, 15–17).

The sixth necessary element for the formation of an Islamic community is the rule of law. In this case, the rule of law becomes subservient to the rule of God and the hegemonic leadership of a juridico-clerical Islam. The blending of Islam with modern forms of sovereignty and governmentality creates the possibility for the materialization of an Islamic republic and the forging of the Guardianship of the Islamic Legal Authority *(Velayat-e Faqih).* This is a key concept in the constitution of the Islamic Republic and refers to the leadership of the supreme religious leader.[16] The main responsibility of the Islamic Legal Authority, which is independent from the government, is to make sure that society does not deviate from Islamic principles.

As a fictive entity, the fundamentalist ummat is a site of contradiction and tension, since it contains both those subjects legitimated by the power of the nation-state's sovereignty—by definition a desacralized community—and those subjects subordinated to power subjects within a sacred community. Here a double process of sacralization/desacralization is at work in the legitimation of power by the force of a non-negotiable God, as well as in the notion of community as a collection of atomized individuals who serve as a source of legitimation and subordination. Any attempt to create a sovereign state prompts the question of who has the right to rule, engendering a crisis of legitimation. In fundamentalism, the individuals making up the fictively unified entity of the "people" cede sovereignty to God and become its source of legitimation. Such legitimacy is contradictory and inconsistent with any particular group's attempt (as a particular lived community) to incarnate this impossible entity, which is based on the joining of the rule of God and the rule of the people.

The process by which fundamentalism creates communities constructs a direct relationship between God and the individual. I am arguing that, like his modern counterpart, fundamentalist man achieves a self-conscious identity through a process of remasculation that allows him to become a legitimate citizen of the local and global community. This process does not apply, however, to the case of women because of their domestication through voluntary submission to the religious community.

Not a Class War but a War of Position:
The Mostaz'af and the Mostakbar

> Hail, Muslims of the world and the mostaz'afan under the
> rule of the oppressors. Rise and unite and defend Islam and
> your destinies, and don't be afraid of the tumult of those in
> power because, with the will of God, this century is the
> century of the victory of the mostaz'afan over the
> mostakbaran and justice over falsehood.
>
> Ayatollah Khomeini (1984, 116)

> Formal, organized political activity, even if clandestine and
> revolutionary, is typically the preserve of the middle class
> and the intelligentsia.
>
> James C. Scott (1985, xv)

It is in the name of mostaz'af that Khomeini led the revolution. While the revolutionary period can be characterized by the intensive negotiation of contesting political forces, certain ideas, such as mostaz'af, enabled the renegotiation of hegemony by reconstructing a central consensus through which revolutionary reality could be filtered. The concept of hegemony and a war of position is borrowed from the work of Antonio Gramsci. By hegemony I refer to both the competing social and ideological forces and those forms of representation that are the major sources of domination.[17] I also use the war of position to emphasize ideological struggles over the building of hegemonic alliances between classes and the direction of the Islamic movement of opposition to the state during the revolution. The power of mostaz'af is located not only in its polysemy and its capacity to bring together different experiences and identities, as well as popular and high culture, but also in the ways in which it can bring together the local and the global. In addition, the concept of mostaz'af brought all fractions of the movement together with masses of people in their opposition to the state as the incarnation of a powerful ruling class. On a number of occasions related to his call for the end of idolatry wherever it existed, Ayatollah Khomeini called for all Muslims of the world to unify with the disempowered mostaz'afan of the world (1984).

I am investigating here the notion of mostaz'af that emerged in the context of the Iranian revolution of 1979 and that was used to mobilize the people, specifically in the shah's "White Revolution" and the Islamic Republic's cultural revolution. Such revolutions rely less on people as active participants in the revolutionary process than on what is good for people and should be done for them. Mostaz'af is important for two reasons: its relationship to the pluralized moment of the revolution and its importance as an emblem of the new sign system, which changed a religious system into a militaristic system. Turning the Quran into a militant text, Khomeini argues,

If you study the Quran, you see that there are a number of verses on war, ordering war. War against who[m]? Against the powerful. . . . The Quran is an invigorating book, a book that motivated Arabs who did not know that much to overturn some of the most oppressive and brutal empires of the day. If the Quran and Islamic teaching functioned as an opium, they would have not been able to expand universally, and it would have been impossible for them to disturb empires. (1991, 18–19)

The mostaz'af provided space for the formation of a unified, religious, nationalist oppositional subject. This concept unifies those who have been disempowered nationally and internationally. It also bridges the public and the private, since mostaz'af incorporates the notion of *za'if*, which refers to the weak. Traditionally, the word *za'ifeh*, which derives from *za'if*, has been associated with femininity and was used to refer to a woman living under the protection of a man. As a concept, mostaz'af has the power to mobilize both the protectors and the protected under the banner of Islam. In the case of men, the word has the power to mobilize those who have been emasculated in the process of colonization and modernization. During the revolution, mostaz'af was used to include women because of their disempowerment and objectification by consumer capitalism and to invoke their need for mobilization. Thus, mostaz'af brought together various classes and ethnic groups, as well as men and women, to create a religious nationalist community, an Islamic ummat, the invocation of which created space for a revolutionary position, which addressed the deterritorialization of the nation-state and located subalternity both inside and outside of the nation.[18]

The concept imbricated power relations in cultural, political, and economic spheres. It had the potential, therefore, to speak for those subjects in multiple positions of powerlessness.[19] Because of this, religious meanings provided a linguistic expression for the militancy of the mostaz'af and for opposition to the mostakbar. Both positions were seen as illegitimate, since they represented either a surplus or a deficit of power, wealth, and privilege. However, the nationalist effort, in its cultural and religious drive to give the mostaz'af a voice and the construction of the voice of the mostaz'af as the voice of authenticity were central to what Foucault calls the "authentification of the revolution" (1994b, 759).

It should be noted that mostaz'af functioned as an indigenous concept, distinguished from the modern and imported concepts of the left, such as *proletariat, ranjbaran* (laborers), *karegaran* (workers), and *dehaghanan* (peasants), which were used to invoke the most disenfranchised groups, those who were victimized by the exploitative nature of the shah's regime. Ayatollah Khomeini also used the concept of mostaz'af to marginalize competing nationalist, Marxist, and socialist groups. Far from forming an avant-garde group, the mostaz'af included all those who were disempowered locally as well as globally. As a concept and as a signifier, it linked the local and the global not in a class war but in a war of position, creating links through its identification of power as both a temporal and a spatial relation.[20] In this process, culture became the main locus of power; the cultural nationalist framework of an Islamic vision placed the mostaz'af in polar opposition to the mostakbar. It was used to undermine the diversity and particularities of the revolutionary struggles from the general strike of oil workers to the participation of masses of women, from the demands of ethnic and religious minorities to peasant revolts. It also blurred differences between urban and rural classes.

While multiple sites of contestation were the order of the day during the revolution, the working of hegemony made it possible for the discourse of revolution to become invested in power by winning the consent of those who participated in the revolution. Revolutionary discourse engaged with particular images and signifiers in order to enable unification and to ease the transmission of power from one state elite to another. Such unification was important for bringing together the various groups participating in the revolution and for reconciling their contradictory demands in order to create an oppositional framework that worked effectively to put an end to the shah's reign. This unification enabled a positioning beyond the modernist categories of worker, laborer, and proletariat, and created space for fluidity, multiplicity, and the inclusion of various classes and groups. In addition, this category allowed the disempowered to be addressed not as an abstract category but as people located in particular cultural and religious traditions. As a result, it enabled the Islamic movement to distinguish itself from the humanist subject of the modernist revolutionary discourses of secular nationalists and other groups on the left. The notion of class-based and classless societies, which was used extensively in the context of Iranian oppositional movements, remained abstract in Iranian society. What was referred to as class in Iran remained an ambiguous concept, since neither class divisions nor class culture and class mobility could be defined rigidly in Iran. In addition, class structure, especially in the rural and tribal parts of Iran, was not based on class antagonism but was modeled after family relations, specifically paternalism, communal welfare, and family care.

Ayatollah Khomeini used the Quranic word *mostaz'af* to incorporate such ambiguity and respond to the application of class antagonism and a classless society in the discourse of the Islamic guerrilla movement and the younger generation of Islamic students who were intrigued by this vocabulary. Ayatollah Khomeini challenged the idea of the "classless human" proposed by a student *(talabeh)* of Islam: "These groups of people, who have emerged and are from a religious background, are likeable but they are mistaken. . . . They think Islam has come to make a classless human . . . meaning that they all have to live in the same way in this world and there should be one state to support them. They all have to pay taxes to the state and serve it at the same time" (1994, 12). The idea of a classless society entered Iranian revolutionary discourse via the Marxist-Leninist left and was coded by Islamist groups as *jame'eh-e bi tabage-he towhidi* (classless monotheistic society). In his attempt to claim an indigenous discursive space—*na sharghi, na gharbi, jomhouri-e eslami* (neither west nor east but an Islamic Republic)—Khomeini interrupted such discursive continuity between religious and secular notions of a classless society. In the postrevolutionary era, numerous groups who participated in the revolution—from the oil workers, whose strike immobilized the machinery of the shah's economy, to peasants to women's resistance movements—were suppressed and rendered abject in the name of the revolution. Those who achieved hegemony then became the protectors of revolutionary values, along with their conflicts and contradictions.

The massive participation of women in demonstrations against imposed veiling in Tehran was condemned by factions of the revolutionary movement, both secular and religious, as an act of collaboration with the Westernized elite of the ancien régime and its ignorant victims, such as entertainers and prostitutes. The participation of prostitutes and women entertainers in the demonstrations was used as proof of the misbehavior of "good revolutionary" women. Women were blamed for betraying revolutionary ideals through intentional and unintentional collaboration with counterrevolutionary forces and for distracting the revolution from its primary concerns. By blurring the boundaries of respectability separating pure women from impure ones and by transgressing the revolutionary/counterrevolutionary border, women became the first targets of disciplining and containment within the terms of revolutionary discourse.

The epithets *mostakbar* (powerful) and *mostaz'af* (disempowered) were applied as markers of the boundary between those who had access to representational power (even though their power was illegitimate, since it was associated with the contaminated spheres of the ancien régime and the West) and those who did not. As a result of a particular sign system that emphasized a constant antagonism between the mostakbar and the mostaz'af as signifiers of revolutionary and counterrevolutionary subjectivities, militant religious and cultural meanings became the main focus of the regulatory forces of the new state elite in the postrevolutionary era.

Through the production of gendered bodies and Muslim bodies as the surface for the inscription of an Islamic nation and the idea of the mostaz'af, which was positioned in opposition to the mostakbar, cultural and religious nationalists were able to write their meanings onto the events of the revolution. However, *mostaz'af* is now a category in crisis in postrevolutionary Iran as a result of the narration of the Islamic nation in the territorial space of the nation-state and in the diaspora, where the nation has left its territorial boundaries, which are divided by gender, sexuality, class, and ethnicity.[21]

Veils, Blood, and Revolution

> Shehadat is a blissful state that is achieved by men of God.
> Let's talk whenever we become men.
>
> Ali Ghorbani, a warrior in the
> Iran-Iraq war (Fahimi 2000, 155)

The revolution of 1979 disrupted gender identities that were based on Westernized and modernized models of femininity and masculinity, which were produced in the context of an Iranian modernity relying on a racialized notion of a pre-Islamic Persian superiority, Islam's "otherness," mimicking the "West," and the heterosexist class culture of a modernized local elite. As I argued in chapter 3, such dominant views were countered by various forms of oppositional gender and class identifications—from Islamic to Marxist and socialist. Islamic fundamentalist discourse also used a particular conceptualization of masculinity and femininity to oppose the ancien régime and its Western allies and to construct gendered citizenship in the establishment of a postrevolutionary Islamic republic. Throughout the pre- and postrevolutionary period, gendered performance tropes were an important site of everyday boundary construction. While the main obligation of both men and women became *jihad-e nafs* (worldly asceticism), different but complementary gender identities were established to create homogenized national and transnational communities. Through the newly created sign system of a God-based community, the figures of the warrior brother and veiled sister emerged, evoking persistent militancy, political awareness, and ethno-religious pride.

Martyrdom entered into the symbolic language of gender identity as a site of agency and remasculinization. Martyrs' blood resacralized public spaces, streets, avenues, and alleys and marked them with the names and memories of *shohada* (martyrs). Martyrdom had become an important point of reference in prerevolutionary Iran; more martyrs had meant a bigger share of truth. Martyrdom reflected the will to die for revolutionary ideas and the ideals of a just society. The blood of martyrs was a sign that life was worth living, since martyrs' altruism could only benefit those who were alive. While martyrdom gained new significance with the revolution, it was the reactivation of Shia historical memory that provided space for the massive performance and reception of martyrdom. The popular forms of martyrdom were found in the myth of the Hussein, revitalized through Shari'ati's distinction between Alavi's Shiism and Safavi's Shiism. In the context of the Iranian revolution, martyred men took back the public sphere once dominated by the ancien régime.

In the postrevolutionary era and during the Iran-Iraq war, "the culture of the battlefield" (as it was named by the Islamic state) became an important site for the representation of martyrdom, masculinity, and citizenship. At the time of the breach of the boundaries of family, state, and nation in the revolutionary and postrevolutionary era and their collapse into an Islamic ummat, women were offered subjectivity in a complementary communal role through an emphasized femininity symbolized by "the veiled woman."

The collaborative force of the warrior brother and veiled sister, under the rule of God the Father and the state, materialized and channeled the

collective will-to-peoplehood. The representation of blood/martyr-
dom and the veil—the main sites of subjectivity—assigned radically different yet complementary positions to men and women. The civic body
became the site of gender performance by veiled women and warrior/
martyred men. Indeed, during the revolutionary period, the will to die
for the revolution was neither uniquely gendered nor based on adherence to the Islamic religion. It was rather a matter of oppositional subjectivity for men and women, Muslims and non-Muslims. For example,
when the shah's troops fired on a crowd in Zhaleh Square in Tehran on
Black Friday—Sharivar 1978, a turning point in the revolution—a large
number of women, some obviously pregnant, were massacred.[22] The
significance of Black Friday as an event lay in the fact that it began as a
gathering of heterogeneous groups not identified with any one particular political organization. The participation of ordinary people and the
substantial number of female dead marked the history of the Iranian
revolution.

The slogan "Khaharam hijab-e to koubandeh tar az khoon-e man ast
[My sister, your veil is more assertive than my blood]" was one of the
most popular among Islamic fundamentalist groups in Iran.[23] It appeared repeatedly on the walls of Tehran and on banners in fundamentalist demonstrations during and after the revolution of 1979. The
metaphors of blood and veil signify the reconstruction of a hegemonic
masculinity and an emphasized femininity in a community of brothers
and sisters. Both tropes refer to Muslim men and women deeply committed to their community and to its militancy against local and global
taghut (idolatry).[24] Discursively, both blood and the black chador carried symbolic local and global meanings.[25] Locally, these symbols transcended all differences of class, religion, and ethno-national origin;
globally, they created a transnational Muslim femininity and masculinity that stood in opposition to the West through their complicity with
the ummat in a cultural war of representation.

In the symbolization of hijab as the site of discovery of a true self
and the place of the Islamic embodiment of divine womanhood, the
ethno-religious community of Allah stood in opposition to the Westernized local elite and a global order (Rahnavard 1990, 17, 25). Through
hijab, women's revolt was traced to "Khadijah, the first Muslim
woman, who sacrificed herself for the prosperity of Islam," in the idiom
of Rahnavard, an Iranian Muslim activist who was a fundamentalist
woman and scholar (23). The old self, fashioned by family and politi-
cal-economic powers and inherited tribal customs, was rejected and

replaced with a new self, enlightened by Islamic teachings. Freedom was thus articulated in terms of an identitarian recognition of being Muslim. It was the responsibility of the woman to cover herself in a black chador. The black chador became a "weapon," according to Rahnavard (9).[26] The veil signified an Islamic femininity that policed feminine bodily comportment and generated a restricted spatiality. Furthermore, the violation of the body, its opening to the veil and to death, was eroticized through an Islamic femininity and a complementary masculinity, reinforcing heteronormativity as central to the practices of citizenship.

By sacrificing his life for the community and showing his commitment and responsibility, the "warrior brother" remasculated the Muslim man.[27] The self-piercing Muslim man had to free himself from dependency upon material trappings, such as wealth, family, women, and children (Gafari 1979, 34). The Muslim man had to reject his humanity in order to regain it. As a process of remasculinization, martyrdom entered the symbolic language of gender identity. Public spaces (the streets, avenues, and alleys) in every city and town were reappropriated by the names and memories of *shohada* (martyrs).[28] Their pictures, omnipresent in the urban spaces of contemporary Iran as symbolic models of masculinity, seized the sphere of representation and citizenship. Interestingly, however, no women's names were used in the renaming of public spaces. The red bandana was used to refer to martyrdom as a signifier for Muslim masculinity, while such meanings excluded women in the revolutionary and postrevolutionary era.

This hegemonic masculinity was complemented by an emphasized femininity, symbolized by the veiled woman. These concepts did not mean that fundamentalist women did not (and do not) give their blood, but blood does not symbolize women's contribution. While devotion to the political community of God was essential in the construction of a will to peoplehood, blood and veil as the main signifiers of subjection assigned radically different yet complementary positions to men and women. Indeed, during the revolutionary period, the will to die for the revolution was neither uniquely gendered nor linked to an adherence to Islamic religion, but rather was a site of oppositional revolutionary subjectivity for both men and women, Muslim and non-Muslim, as in the example of Black Friday, when the shah's troops fired upon a crowd in Zhaleh Square in Tehran and killed a spectacular number of women. After Black Friday, people unofficially changed the name of Zhaleh Square to "the square of martyrs."

Men gained the ultimate subject position through martyrdom, to become *ghalb-e tarikh* martyrs, who are "history's heart" (another popular slogan). In order to become a historical subject, one had to be "in the body." Grosz echoes Foucault in making the point that "the body is not outside history, but produced through and in history" (1994, 148). Furthermore, relations of power produce the body and harness the energies and potential for subversion that power has constructed. In Iran, the formation of a revolutionary subject is related to two concomitant processes: the transgression of the boundaries of regulatory forces, which requires an understanding of what can be interrupted, and the exercise of power through the construction and legitimization of a particular knowledge that is closed to the control of the West and the Westernized local elite.

It was through the maintenance of the body's boundaries in veiling that woman—according to Rahnavard—"could transcend her physical and sensual attributes to become the essence of divine womanhood, an essence that endows her with the power to be a mother, a sister and the sweetheart of her husband" (1990, 9). Women and men entered the sphere of cultural representation, intervening in the symbolic realm by way of competing masculinities and femininities in constant conflict over power, self-realization, and self-expression. The cultural imagination of an emerging Islamic ummat created space for the interpellation of new gendered subject positions and also facilitated social intervention in the revolutionary moment to reorder the chaos resulting from the prerevolutionary breakdown of the national imaginary.

These symbols spoke to individuals, reminding them of their responsibility and commitment to the Islamic ummat, calling them to give up their individuality to the communal will and the laws of political citizenship in the sacred community of God. It is a mistake to read women's acceptance of the fundamentalist encouragement to wear the black chador as a sign of either passivity or religiosity. Women perceived it rather as a gendered invitation to political participation and as a sign of membership, belonging, and complicity.[29]

In postrevolutionary Iran and during the Iran-Iraq war, the transformation of Islamic fundamentalism from an oppositional movement to state power, along with the marginalization and suppression of social movements of diverse political ideologies, brought a sharper gender division into the realm of militancy and war. While the taking up of arms by urban women during the revolution remained alive in the spheres of representation and popular, social memory and influenced women's notions of political participation, the Islamic state officially institution-alized the role of warrior only for men, who were supposed to fight on the battlefield. Women were expected to perform a variety of tasks, from raising future martyrs to nursing, cooking, and cleaning "behind the battlefield" *(posht-e jebheh)*. In this case, even though women continued to undergo military training, the attribution of "offense" to men and "defense" to women displaced earlier gender-neutral revolutionary no-tions, such as the people's army, and established a division of labor within institutions like the Guardians of the Revolution.

The Voice of Martyrs:
Death, Feminization, and Remasculinization

> Karbala is not a ground but a background.
>
> Abolgassem Hosseinjani (1998, 18)

> The tragic action, in its deepest sense, is not the confirmation of disorder, but its experience, its compensation and its resolution. In our own time this action is general, and its common name is revolution. We have to see the evil and the suffering, in the factual disorder that makes revolution necessary, and in the disordered struggle against the disorder.
>
> Raymond Williams (1979, 83)

Death and its representation are central to Islamic fundamentalist ide-ology in Iran. Indeed, awakening consciousness of the body as an in-strument of power is part of an effort to reconstruct and remap the body in a counterhegemonic movement. Martyrdom allows for death to make human will and power both possible and impossible. Martyr-dom is a site of representation where death is given not only a voice but also a life. Bonyad-e Shahid (the Martyrs' Foundation) is one of the most important state-regulated institutions in Iran.[30] Being the mother of a martyr confers high status in the new fundamentalist state, and mar-tyrdom is constantly evoked by the media, in reports directed to both global and local audiences. Death is suffused with masculinity, because death, power, and political representation are closely intertwined.[31] In the context of political oppression, death becomes a dramatized scene of subjectivity and empowerment. The boundaries between life and death, between past and present, between living and dead bodies, are blurred and reproduced in the reconstruction of social memory through mythical concepts and forms, moving constantly from semiology to ideology.[32]

Shiite myths have a great deal of influence in the daily life of Iranians. They are of great importance not only to the understanding of forms of communalization, but also to the way women enter history. In the "Karbala Parable," which relates the martyrdom of the third imam, Mohammed's grandson Hussein stands with his family in opposition to the oppressive tyranny and corruption of the Umayyad caliph, who for Shiites is a usurper of the legitimate leadership of the Islamic ummat and the destroyer of its promise of social justice. Watching the existential tragedy of the war between good and evil and the victory of the forces of evil over the forces of good as they are played by local performers during the month of Muharam, the audience learns to identify with the extreme pain and suffering that Hussein and his family experienced in Karbala.[33]

Through the symbolic order of martyrdom, men's bodies are constructed as omnipotent and transcendental. In the case of women, however, even as veiling constructs an Islamic femininity beyond geographical and temporal location, it binds them to a transhistorical, biological female body. Through the process of martyrdom, the body is rejected for higher values, while through veiling, the body becomes desired yet objectified, forbidden, and alienated. However, it is through the otherness of femininity and its domestication that men gain subjectivity and agency in the scene of martyrdom. There are at least three places where women's domestication precludes the exchange of individuation and subjectivity for objectification and submission: first, their representation in the reconstruction of the past; second, their domesticated role in the drama of martyrdom; and third, the veiling and reterritorialization of their bodies.

Karbala is not only a key episode in Shiite history, but also a symbol of self-sacrifice and resistance. In Karbala, women and men demonstrate bravery in different ways. Men are the warriors, and women the guardians of family ties and kinship. Women are, therefore, the main agents of social continuity; mothers, sisters, wives, and daughters are role models for the community. The double embrace of this world and the other world in Karbala has been effectively used to mobilize the disempowered Muslim masses. As Derrida argues,

And hence only in so far as it mourns, becoming itself in the labor of infinite mourning, in the indemnification of a spectrality without limit. It is sacred, holy, infinitely respectable only in the name of what is worth more than it and what is not restricted to the naturalness of bio-zoological (sarificeable)—although true sacrifice ought to sacrifice not only "natural" life, called "animal" or "biological," but also that which is worth more than so-called natural life. (1998, 50–51)

Shehadat (martyrdom) becomes the culmination of the realization of the impossible. Women always enter the fundamentalist reconstruction of the past as wives, mothers, and daughters and not as individuals. The imposition of veiling contributes significantly to the domestication of their martyrdom.

Surveyors and Surveyed: Women in the Drama of Martyrdom

The veil, then, is highly pertinent to our understanding of the relationship between subjectivity and objectification in fundamentalist discourse. Indeed, both martyrdom and veiling have an enormous capacity for narrative containment. In the case of martyrdom, two elements are used to domesticate the experience of women. One is the fact that women enter the sphere of martyrdom as family members—sisters, mothers, or daughters—rather than as independent individuals. Thus, their predetermined social roles constitute their relationship to God. The fundamentalist position on unmediated relationships between the individual and God—that is, prioritizing a subject position tied to a conscience or self-knowledge before God—is nullified in the case of women. Indeed, women have to become dependent on men and community before becoming independent individuals before God. Any sense of agency depends upon the acknowledgment and validation of such social roles. The work of mothers, sisters, wives, and daughters is the only work validated and encouraged for women. In this sense, women are reskilled and given an identity, but their subjectivity and agency is based on domestication. Even at such a radical site of subjectivity, where it is impossible to die for the other—in the sense of "to die in his place" (Derrida 1993, 25)—martyrdom cannot create agency for women because of the mediation of domesticity. Death becomes a site of subjectivity and cultural identification. Indeed, death is always culturally contextualized.[34]

Veiling plays an important part in this domestication, racialization, and genderization of fundamentalist ideology. It racializes women by establishing a sense of inclusion/exclusion. It sexualizes them through signs of femininity and creates subjectivity by casting them as both surveyor and surveyed, as objects of others' gazes and subjects of their own submission. As a system of symbolic and material marking, veiling disciplines and homogenizes all Muslim women into a single category. It distinguishes them from non-Muslims and renders invisible local, national, ethnic, class, and age differences, as well as all the ways of being a Muslim woman. It thereby consolidates Muslim femininity. Islamic womanhood becomes a site of transnationality, feminine subjectivity, and citizenship in the community of God by creating a participatory process of becoming that is guaranteed by deepening knowledge of Islamic traditions and laws.

What if, however, the veil, which is portrayed as a site of activity and agency, is nothing but an empty signifier, a means to insert the body into the world of consumer capitalism? Or, conversely, what if the veil, which is depicted in the West as an ultimate signifier of passivity and victimhood, is instead an expression of the desire to hide from the panoptical gaze of modern regimes of power and knowledge? What if the veil is nothing but an occasion for passing, a ruse, a mask, or a site of action by a performing and willing subject? What if the martyrdom and the tragic memory of Karbala are also a commemoration of the homoerotic love banned by modern regimes of power and knowledge? What if the pressure to be warriors is the condition for men to become legitimate citizens of the modern nation-state?

The (Homo) Eroticization of War: "Vesal-e Hussein" in the Land of Karbala

> Often times when a warrior lies down, with the earth as his bed and the sky blanketing him, he is showered with affection by the other warriors. If he rests his head on the feet of one of his peers, the other will move the warrior's head and rest it on his chest to show that the warrior's place is in the other's heart. Sometimes they each lean their heads on the chest of the warrior next to them in a group of up to fifteen people, relaxing for hours in this affectionate embrace.
>
> Mehdi Fahimi, *Culture of the War Front* (1998, 103–4)

> I am in love, in love with your eyesight, Hussein.
>
> Ali Biglari, a warrior in the Iran-Iraq war (Fahimi 2000, 89)

The meaning of eroticism escapes anyone who cannot see its
religious meaning!

Georges Bataille (1989, 70)

The Iranian revolution challenged the discourses of modernity in many
ways. It moved beyond and in opposition to the division between mind,
emotion, and body by exploiting all the senses—textual, visual, and au-
ditory—to mobilize and lead the people. It challenged the cultural
order of modernity by integrating high and popular culture. Through
its reference to the hybridity of Iranian culture, it questioned the dichotomy between the secular and the religious, based on the separation
of pre-Islamic and Islamic Iran. Finally, it mobilized a premodern male
homoerotic and homosocial world of meaning, throwing into crisis the
heteronormative world of modernity.

The visual and textual representation of the battlefield in the context of the Iran-Iraq war illustrates the subversion of homoerotic and
homosocial views of male desire already present in both Persian and
Islamic premodern traditions.[35] In conclusion, I wish to turn to "the
literature of the battlefield" published by the Islamic Republic's Department of War Propaganda each anniversary of the Iran-Iraq war, a
war that lasted for eight years. I will focus on a collection of photography, prose, and poetry published to honor the third anniversary of
the war, *Talashi dar tassvir-e jebheh* (Iran-Iraq war: An effort to portray the battlefield).

The book depicts mainly male warriors in the war zones; the few pictures of women portray them as mothers and wives saying goodbye to
their sons and husbands as they depart for the battlefield. Most of the
images are from Karbala, the southern part of Iran that was occupied by
Iraqi forces and later liberated by Iran. In the book, men, both old and
young, go about their daily lives—playing, exercising, reading, talking,
strategizing, hugging, sleeping, bathing—on a battlefield that is both a
real and an imaginary landscape. The war zone is a place between death
and life, a land without women, enabling the expression of homoerotic
desire. In this homosocial world, men live in proximity to each other
and take care of each other. Women do not exist; this is a city of men of
different generations living in harmonious contiguity. Contingent upon
but parallel to the "real" world, the battlefield is a space where men are
left alone.

In the introduction, the "daily temporality of ordinary life" is opposed to "battlefield temporality"—a quest for an eroticized notion of

suffering that is distinguished from a boring quest for consolation and material life. One type of temporality is attained through risk taking and death; the other is a comfort zone. As an allegory for Karbala, every battlefield has a tragic subtext: death by the forces of evil.[36] However, in the lingering moment between life and death, there exists a possibility of erotic love.

Male warriors wearing red headbands bearing the slogan "Hal man nasr men Allah" mediate between the realm of the nation-state and the arena of myth. In both temporalities, male subjectivity is defined by the inevitability of a tragic death; it is only in the "in-between" space of the battlefield that the tragedy is deferred and replaced by the sensuality of a tangible and erotic connection between self and other. The entrance to the land of Karbala requires care of the body and the ritual of purification performed by Muslims before prayers. One of the first images in the book is that of a sentence written on a welcome sign: "Enter while you are purified *[ba vosou vared shavid]* because this soil is perfumed with the blood of martyrs" (7–8). The poetic and romantic dialogue of the lovers (Raz and Niyas) invigorates the sensual use of the smell of blood as perfume.

The book has ten sections, each of which starts with a sensual poem containing words such as *asheq* (passionate love), *yar* (friend or lover), and *asheganeh* (amorously). The book begins with a salutation borrowed from Imam Khomeini to "those warriors who perfumed the battlefield with their prayer and their *raz va niyaz* [dialogue] with the lover *[mahboob]*." The abstraction of the lover and its ambiguity have a long history in the homoerotic tradition of Persian poetry, especially in the composition of *ghazal* (a lyric genre of poetry usually celebrating love) and in the famous poetry of Hafiz and Rumi. The poetry of the battlefield describes a longing for the scent and the sight of the lover and promises the union of the martyr with the lover at the end of the path where the lover awaits. The motif of romanticized and eroticized longing in the poetic space of the battlefield continues in the union with Hussein: "All *yaran* [comrades], we passionately join Hussein. *Vesal-e Hussein* [union with Hussein]. The union with Hussein is approaching" (108). Ironically, tragedy is transformed into the homoerotic union of men, and the homoerotic union of men into tragedy.

The convergence of popular cultural practices grounded in Shia mythology, modern nationalism, and premodern and modern views of gender and sexuality creates a homosocial and homoerotic world for warrior men to establish a community of brothers who recognize themselves through the concomitant processes of othering and domesticating women. Here, the concept of community, or a religious community of brothers and sisters, is related to both the state and the family, resolving the tension that arises from the separation of the private and the public in Iranian modernity. The concept of Islamic ummat replaces the nation, which resolves two problems: the tension between particularism and universalism, which is deeply rooted in modern secular nationalism, and the tension between family and the state, which is rooted in the gender constructions of the nation-state. Such convergence juxtaposes two desires: the desire to conform to modern notions of masculinity (to have a place in the gender hierarchy and to be a warrior, a guardian, a protector of the women, children, and community members) and the desire to be relieved from the pressure of a heteronormative masculinity by taking refuge in a homosocial world that is open to the expression of male homoerotic desire at the expense of women's abjectification and domestication. The discourse of sexuality is central to the invention of a postmodern Islamic nation, which is able to mobilize modern notions of gender identities and subjectivities, yet unsettle them by opening space for the staging of men's ambivalence toward heteronormative gender performance. In this context, the affective experience of bodies in proximity disrupts the framework of the established order within which the historical subject rises above himself.

CHAPTER 4

The Sacralization of Politics and the Desacralization of Religion

> We should no longer reflect exclusively on the meaning,
> historically and in the present, of religion—of faith and belief
> and their supposed opposites such as knowledge and
> technology—but concentrate on the significance of the
> processes of mediation and mediatization without and outside
> of which no religion would be able to manifest or reveal itself
> in the first place.
>
> Hent de Vries (2001, 28)

> But to relate a sacred history is equivalent to revealing
> a mystery.
>
> Mircea Eliade (1987, 95)

Islamic transnationalism and nationalism function as ideological frames of meaning within the context of a global world. While Islamic nationalism has become the ideology of an Islamic republic defined by particular territorial boundaries, Islamic transnationalism has moved beyond the boundaries of the nation in its dispersal around the globe. Islamic transnationalism has to grapple with the simultaneity of claims to unify the nation while generating a transnational Islamic ethnicity. The creation of an Islamic ethnicity is as much the work of Orientalism and Western representational practices as it is the result of negotiations and contestations of Islamic nationalism and fundamentalism. However, contradictions and disjunctions have arisen from the convergence of Islamic nationalism and transnationalism. While Islamic nationalism has brought religion up against its conceptual limits by creating a centralized modern nation-state that rules, as I argued in earlier chapters, in the name of an Islamic ummat, Islamic transnationalism relies increasingly on a global consumer society in order to bring the ideas of state and nation into crisis. In this sense, Islamic nationalism and transnationalism are products of modernity and postmodernity rather than of religious or cultural traditions as such.

Transnational Islam uses the media and representational tropes familiar in the West to talk about subjectivity, identity, and power. It is interested in power and the rule of power. It is political and deploys tropes that are substantially gendered. Membership in transnational Islam is based not on religiosity but on the adoption of a particular view of Islam (both from the outside and inside) and the willingness to (dis)identify with it, to fight for or against it. What I call Islamic transnational fundamentalism is thus a coproduction of the conditions of consumer capitalism and new regimes of governmentality. Gender and racial tropes are an important part of this form of Islamic identity. Transnational Islamic identity relies on modern foundational and fundamentalist figures to create a unified community of Allah. It uses new communication technologies, the global circulation of images and capital, and popular culture and its identitarian claims, which are transmitted by the media and consumer culture. Moreover, transnational Islam has created circuits of production, marketing, and consumption for an Islamic-based global entrepreneurship.

The production of Islamic fashions demonstrates not only Islamic entrepreneurship, but also Islam's position as a product of the dynamic forces that shape any consumer market. A good example of this form of entrepreneurship is found in fashion companies that produce dress and various forms of veiling for the global Islamic market. Navaro-Yashin's (2002) monograph on fashion companies, such as Tekbir in Turkey, explores this mode of consumerist practice in order to demonstrate its diversity. These studies indicate that the veil remains the dominant signifier of Islamic femininity. In Iran, window displays of fashionable veils appeal to a particular type of femininity—in this case, upper-class Islamic femininity—which is produced and reproduced in the market. Veiling as the privileged signifier of Islamic femininity also surfaces in certain diasporic fashion designers, such as Bijan in Los Angeles, where the spectacle of the veiled woman in advertisements is a sign of difference intended to stimulate male consumers. In other words, a diasporic designer like Bijan successfully reaches a cosmopolitan market by co-opting difference into the global regimes of multicultural capitalism. The compression of time and space, which some scholars refer to as the politics of mobility and the unequal control over mobility and communication (Massey 1994, 151), makes it possible for the national and the transnational to reproduce each other. It also brings together different worlds of commodity, concealing all traces of history, the very processes that produced them, and the social relations implicated in their production.

Just as the disjunction between Islamic nationalism and transnationalism has come to characterize political and cultural spheres in Iran, transnationally unified notions of Islam and Muslim women have become a very important component of political militancy and war in the Islamic world. The racialized notion of a Muslim other is indispensable for the militant claims of Islamic fundamentalists who present Islam as transnational, unified, and defined by very particular regimes of representation. However, the ensuing contradictions have brought contestations both nationally and transnationally. In the specific case of Iran, we can identify two disjunctive moments in nationalist and transnationalist Islam that are characterized by the conflicts between the cultural politics of citizenship and the cultural politics of gender. The very concept of the collective will of the Islamic ummat, however, is undermined by the cultural and political reality of the subjects subsumed into this phantasmic whole, a reality that is fragmented by the conflicting desires and expressions of subjects marked by gender, class, and different religious beliefs.

Political and Cultural Citizenship: The Making and Unmaking of the Nation

The convergence of the state and religion in postrevolutionary Iran has inspired a call to save Islam, or what is called religion, from the state. Those who defend the notion of the Islamic intellectual advocate opening up religious discourse to reflect current changes in global relations and claim space for an Islamic plural society that could intervene in the construction and reconstruction of a political will.[1] A wide spectrum of positions are at play in this debate about the role of Islamic intellectuals—those educated Muslims who intervene in the interpretation of Islamic knowledge—from the position of fundamentalists *(bonyadgarayan)* who take a foundational approach to Islam (such as Ayatollah

Khomeini) to the positions of those who, in Akbar Ganji's terms, identify with a fascist perception of religion, and those of reformists *(Eslah talaban)* who argue for the redefinition of gender issues.[2]

The Iranian form of Islamic government is radically different from that of other Islamic countries, such as Saudi Arabia, Afghanistan, and Pakistan, since a pluralistic conception of Islam and Islamic government has emerged in Iran as a vital part of the civil society. These political and cultural aspects of Iranian Islamic government include a wide spectrum of ideas and ideologies regarding what is meant by Islamic governmentality, the relationship between the state and religion, and the role of Islamic justice and democracy. In Iran, political logic has surpassed religious logic and put the Islamic state in crisis. These debates have created a secular space, which is not antireligious, but where, as Olivier Roy notes, religion defines the secular, and Islamic norms are simply either not relevant or no longer pertinent (1999, 12–15). These debates have divided the political and intellectual elite of the national clergy and the outside religious establishment into numerous ideological positions from the far right to the far left of the spectrum. What is referred to in Iran as the reform movement includes a variety of positions that are pressuring the conservative segments of the state to reform government policies and procedure.

Islamic feminists and women activists have been crucial in giving voice to women's problems within the realms of religion, jurisprudence, and the state, as they work for positions of political leadership, legal equality, and further recognition of their needs and desires. In 2001, the Persian-language women's magazine *Zanan,* popular among educated urban women and famous for its focus on gender issues, initiated a discussion concerning whether religious intellectualism recognized "the women question" *(masaleh zanan)* as a problem to be addressed and whether religious intellectuals had a solution for it. This formulation provoked a response from a number of reformist male intellectuals, who, as a result, have recently begun to focus on issues affecting women.

An examination of this debate reveals three recurring topics: first, a revisiting of the work of prominent religious intellectuals who wrote on women's issues and contributed to the creation of a discursive space for the formation of Muslim women as political subjects and participants in the construction of an Islamic nationalist movement during the prerevolutionary era;[3] second, a recognition that, while this discursive formation went beyond the dichotomy of tradition and modernity to enable women's participation in the Islamic nationalist movement, it was not able to address women's issues in the postrevolutionary era because of its inability to create space for the formation of women's political agency; and third, a concern for the identification of the issues crucial to a discussion of women's rights within the Islamic Republic.

In a reexamination of Ali Shari'ati's famous *Fatima Is Fatima*, Mohamad Javad Gholamreza Kashi (*Zanan* 70, 1) argues that Shari'ati moves beyond the modernity/tradition split to defend an in-between position, investigating the colonizing effects of modernity and tradition on women and inventing an ideal model of femininity by revisiting the significance of Fatima, the wife of Ali and daughter of Muhammad. However, Kashi argues that Shari'ati's views did not help women move beyond a masculinist view of the public good. He suggests that, while women were eager to participate in political life, they were not able to ask for their share of the revolutionary agenda. While Kashi's views have opened up space for a rereading of Shari'ati and an engagement with women's issues, he does not explain what is problematic in the masculinist view of the public good, which includes women as political participants in the Islamic community while excluding them as subjects with their own will and desire. While there is a moment of openness in Kashi's recognition that Shari'ati positions Fatima as an ideal model of femininity because of her status as the daughter of Muhammad and the wife of Ali, Kashi nonetheless accepts religious nationalists' appeal to the family as the foundation of the nation. As a result, he falls into the modernist naturalization of the nation as a source of legitimacy for the state.

Ali Reza Alavi, another contributor to the series of special issues *Zanan* dedicated to the woman question, examines the views of another important prerevolutionary religious figure, Ayatollah Motahari, famous for his writings on women's issues. Alavi argues that, in contrast to fundamentalist notions of Islam, Motahari had a dynamic, historical view of Islam and Muslim women (*Zanan* 75, 3). Alavi quotes Motahari's statement that "inertia *[jamid]* is used by the old, which hates the new. . . . Inertia *[jamid]* calls everything that is new a deviation" (*Nezam-e Hoghouge zan dar Islam* 1978, 118; *Zanan* 75, 3). He maintains that Motahari was able to recognize differences between men and women without accepting the notion of women's inferiority. He further argues that Motahari imagined a future social order that was neither feminine nor masculine but *mazanass* (mixed). Alavi's reading of Motahari makes it possible for history to revisit the present in a way that is inclusive of both men's and women's experiences; nevertheless, his view is limited because, like Motahari, he takes existing gender categories for granted and fails to go beyond Motahari's concept of "equality within difference."

The Islamic subject of postrevolutionary Iran, while in dialogue, as it were, with the liberal subject of modernity, has caused a crisis for both religion and modernity. While modernity's discourse of equality requires a rereading of Islamic law vis-à-vis women, Islamic particularism—and its universalist claim to power—positions modernity's self-representation as the ultimate form of universalism in crisis by bringing to the surface its own particularistic impulses.[4] The sacralization of politics is not, of course, limited to Iran or to Muslim countries; religious discourse has remained an important part of political discourse in modernity.[5] What I mean by sacralization is the convergence of religious and political agendas. In the case of Iran, the amalgamation of religion and citizenship has made participation in the modern nation-state the sacred duty of all citizens. Indeed, desacralizing and resacralizing in the context of modernity have created a tension between the religious and the secular, which brings both religion and secularism up against their conceptual limits. Modernity has in no way led to the disappearance of religion; instead it has paved the way for postmodernity to become a space for a dynamic engagement with religion. However, without an examination of the power underlying the sign of modernity as it defines the relationship between individuals and collectivities, it is impossible to understand this process. Any analysis of what has been characterized as religion in modernity requires an analysis of the sacralization of the political sphere and its desacralization within the context of power relations. A dynamic engagement with religion requires an analysis that goes beyond the dichotomy of the sacred and the profane. As Asad notes, the definition of the sacred cannot be separated from the European encounter with the non-European world and the construction of religion and nature as universal categories (2003, 33). It is essential, though, to investigate the ways in which the power attributed to the sacred becomes an integral part of the modern, secular state, and to understand sacralization and desacralization as domains where the convergence of the religious and the secular creates legitimate power for the regulation and disciplining of the citizens/subjects.

The creation of a religious realm that is distinct from the political, the cultural, and the economic is, of course, a project and a product of the Enlightenment and its particular way of thinking, which are invested in what Caputo calls "moderns' rigorous sense of boundaries, limits, and proper domains" (2001, 46). Locating religion beyond the messiness of everyday life and its political and cultural meanings might seem exotic to moderns, but it is no different from other forms of exoticizing. Taking refuge in subjectivities defined by, for example, religious pietism, goddess spirituality, nature worship, or other modes of mysticism is inevitably a form of longing for a premodern, exotic, and irrational spiritual space. An analysis of the sacred through a dynamic, nonlinear examination of the process of sacralization-desacralization-resacralization is a necessary point of departure for dealing with a postsecular global world. The breakdown of all fundamentalisms in postmodernity and the abandonment of the very idea of a foundation as part of this process have created a desire, in Vattimo's terms, for an "authentic condition that can only be understood as a resting in the essentials" (1998, 81). Vattimo argues that, in advanced societies, the fear of losing the meaning of existence goes along with the boredom of consumerism (1998, 80).

Disjunctive Temporalities of an Islamic Nationalism and Transnationalism

Homogenizing notions of Muslim womanhood contradict the complex reality of actual Muslim women, women who identify with various interpretations of Islam not only in relation to the male elite but also in relation to each other. Nevertheless, the fabrication of a transnational Muslim femininity manages to transcend such negotiations and construct a global Islamic womanhood as a site of universalization. Transnational femininity is instrumental in the commodification of Islamic identity politics in the late capitalist global market. Transnational Islamic womanhood—in its reliance on the binary opposition of Islam and the West—occludes the contradictory lives of Iranian women, many of whom live in the Iranian diaspora. In the context of the Islamic republic, women negotiate a gendered citizenship around the issues of legal rights and equal political participation. Islamic political and legal discourses are structured on presupposed views of gender that create untenable situations for women struggling for political rights.

Islamic nationalism and fundamentalism are attempting to grapple with the fragmented moment of postmodernity by articulating a hegemonic will, which is in conflict with the West as a transnational reality.

However, since the time of the Iranian revolution, Islamic nationalism and transnationalism have created contradictions for each other in Iran. The most palpable tension is not experienced in the space of formal or electoral politics, but at the level of popular culture, where political citizenship dissolves into a cultural citizenship, which is defined by transnational institutions and regimes of governmentality.

Three instances of disjunction have led to a revision of the narrative of national identity. The first disjunction occurs between a unified notion of Islam (which, since the Iranian revolution, has been available to represent the poor, the disempowered, and the subaltern) and the everyday reality of life in the Islamic Republic. A second disjunction exists between the gendered national narratives, based on visibility and identity, and passing as a site of ambiguity. The third disjunction arises between the ways in which Muslim women are construed discursively and the reality of their lived lives. To explore the first two types of disjunction, I will examine the medium of film. To elaborate the third instance, I will examine the articulation of a plural and fragmented will by Iranian women, both inside and outside of Iran, to analyze how it undermines the unified will to power of the Islamic ummat. While there are a number of films relevant to my discussion, the particular examples I have chosen are unique in depicting subjects—including women, children, clergymen, and the transgendered—who fail to reflect the position of the unified Islamic gendered subject by displaying subject positions that are incomplete, disintegrated, or divided. I build on Michael Fischer's argument that filmic space has become an alternative site of cultural struggles by facilitating critical reflection on social issues (2001, 463).[6]

Mediatization, Visual Technology, and Filmic Reflection

In Iran, the apparatus of film production, once engulfed in the fires of revolution, has now become a major site for socializing, negotiating cultural issues, and staging everyday life. Visual media, popular and mass-mediated, have been important channels for the articulation of a collective revolutionary will and continue to spatialize modernity through the representation of alterity. However, this staging of difference relies on local forms of abjectification and displays of absence, opening in return the spatial notions of difference to the temporal narratives of the nation. In other words, the local should not be seen as a romantic space characterized by the absence of power relations. Indeed, the writing of space into time and of the local into the national discloses the relation between what is representable and what is unrepresentable. However, several questions remain to be asked, including: Who writes the local into the global? Whose body is at stake and how? Who are the viewers? And how do they read these films?

Furthermore, the collision of temporalities—the cyclicity of myth, the linearity of modernity, and the repetitive time of prime-time television, for example—has brought Islamic nationalism and fundamentalism up against their limits by staging an Islamic subjectivity that is incomplete, plural, and fragmented. While the time of religious myth is in the realm of the sacred, which transcends the temporal duration that precedes or follows it (Eliade 1957/1987, 71), the time of modernity has been constructed as developmental and universal time. Prime-time television conversely has transformed the "world into a spectacle" (Slatman 2001, 222). In Iran, prime time has moved beyond the dichotomy of high and low culture; audiences are not religious experts but consumers, and religious stories are constructed and programmed by media companies and studio executives. The rigid narratives of nation and religion have also been thrown into crisis by cinematic commentaries and what Fischer calls "filmic critique" (2001). Film narrative disrupts the political order by binding audiences to stories that are open to interpretation. In this way, films have become a crucial space for political negotiations.

In 1996, for example, the television screening of a series called *Imam Ali* by the screenwriter and producer Davoud Mirbaqeri sparked an intense controversy across Iran. The controversy expanded beyond this particular series to include the ramifications of films that depict the life of sacred Islamic figures. This series, which, according to the film magazine *Donyay-e tassvir,* brought together "alem va ami [the literate and the illiterate]" (Moallem and Rowhani 1997, 48), is an instance of this filmic intervention, since it retells the story of one of the most important and sacred Shia figures and his family. The legitimacy of such cinematic interventions—namely, the retelling of the religious past—was called into question in media discussions of the controversy, since these interventions combined local popular performances of religious stories with a centralized, mostly state-regulated mode of representation. In Mirbaqeri's view, even though the series alternated between the disappearance of the historical into the dramatic and the dramatic into the historical, it was important because of its historical relevance to the present time (50). The similarity of certain characters in the series to current political figures in Iran opened up space for audiences to criticize the government and the Islamic political elite.

Another popular television series, entitled *Velayat-e Ishq* (The Empire of Love) and written and directed by Mehdi Fakhim Zadeh, is a historical recounting of the life of Imam Reza. Imam Reza, the eighth imam of Shia Muslims, is an extremely important figure in Iran. His tomb in Mashhad (in Khorasan province in northeastern Iran) is a sacred site, a shrine that attracts thousands of pilgrims every year. Imam Reza is famous for being highly educated and for his debates on scientific and theological matters. A number of museums and libraries surround his shrine. Imam Reza is believed to have been poisoned by Mamoun, the Abbasid caliph and son of Haroon El Rashid. He was martyred in Khorasan. Imam Reza's mother and wife were non-Arab noblewomen taken captive by Muslims. His sister's Masumeh Shrine in Qum is another important holy place. Many people go to Imam Reza's shrine to ask for miracles, especially for the healing of those with health problems. Imam Reza's charity receives a considerable amount in donations and gifts every year.[7]

Both series depict the lives of the imams through the lens of Iranian Shia nationalist historiography. Poetry, music, and songs reflect the population's love for these imams. The series use modern Iranian pop music combined with religious lyrics and poetry to create an affective and emotional ambiance. They maintain the mythical quality of Imam Ali and Imam Reza by refusing to show their faces and by keeping a halo of light around them, depicting them as otherworldly. Politically, the imams are famous for having strong ties with Persians. The series focus on the racial distinction between Arabs and Ajams (Persians) and the ways in which this distinction created political antagonisms and alliances. The series depict the imams as deeply involved in the political life of their era, yet always reluctant to be fully assimilated into the ruling classes because of their commitment to social justice and to the poor. The Imam Reza series proposes a reading of Shia history that depicts Imam Reza's leadership as relying on peaceful negotiations, education, refusal of warfare, and outreach through debate and open discussion, as well as the example of an ethical life that maintains a connection to the least privileged members of the community. While Imam Reza is famous for having been raised in a noble household during the rise of Islamic sciences, he is depicted as remaining faithful to a simple life connected to the poor, the foreign, and the weak.

Gender is an important component of both series, which demand a careful reading of their depiction of gender and ethnic relations. Women's decisions to support the imams despite resistance from their husbands and fathers mark crucial turning points in both series. In addition, non-Arab ethnic groups, and non-Arab women in particular, are depicted as distinct from the Arab majority. Women, especially those from Iranian noble families, are depicted as brave and trained in horsemanship and warfare. Historical women are depicted as coming to their own understanding of social justice regardless of their connection to the male figures (fathers, brothers, husbands, sons). However, the power to rule the community is shown as belonging to the male elite. A shift from history to memory occurs in the series when the two Shia imams take on mythological status as leaders who foresee their martyrdom yet consciously choose to lead the Shia community in a struggle against oppression and injustice. The shift from historical memory to mythical forms of remembering in both series invokes two important notions of power: the power of governing the community and the ruse of power in the world. The juxtaposition of these two forms of power, while legitimizing the role of religion in the state, also creates a space for the critique of religion, where the manipulation of religion is possible, where, historically, power is used and abused by the Muslim ruling elite, a gesture that allows the audiences to judge and to read the present critically.

This textualization of religious narratives opens up space not only for the reconstruction of such narratives by the filmic gaze, but also for the participation of women as producers and performers and for audiences to be able to rewrite the stories via their participation in such moments. In this case also, prime-time television has become an important site of the desacralization of some of the foundational myths of the Islamic nation. While the sacred Shia myths—for instance, the tragedy of Karbala—have been instrumental in the politicization and militancy of the masses in Iran, their reconstruction through television has created space for renarrativization and reinterpretation. The production, circulation, and consumption of religious stories by television audiences are distinct, in important ways, from those of passion plays enacted by local performers and from their oral recitation in religious speeches. In the case of the passion play, men perform women's roles and each locality produces its own version of the play, whereas in the television series, women perform the female roles.

From audio- and videocassettes to cinema and television, modern information technologies played an important role in the success of the

Iranian revolution, and they remain a crucial site of cultural and political negotiation in Iran. With the displacement of written culture by visual culture and the expansion of civil society into the transnational realm, cinema has become an important space for national transgressions and transnational encounters. The boundaries of the nation are blurred by visual media and cyberspace, where cultural products target audiences both within and beyond the borders of the nation-state. While the nation-state is still the main regulatory agent of what can or cannot be produced or circulated, the demands of national and diasporic audiences have been equally important in media production. The transnational market of consumers with their taste for Iranian cinema has pressured the Islamic state to relax its censorship of cinema. "Banned in Iran" seems to be a good marketing strategy rather than necessarily an indication of the limits and problems of state control of the arts. Iranian film production, located at the intersection of the national and the transnational, has, however, forced civil society to include diasporic Iranian communities all over the world and to reach out to larger audiences, thereby allowing for critical exposure and the possibility of cross-cultural exchange.

Both in terms of the application of a politics of de-Westernization and the promotion of indigenous media production, the postrevolutionary reorganization of national media production has created space for the participation of a new generation of filmmakers, producers, and performers who are less concerned about mimicking Western narratives and filmic representations and who focus more on national and local cultural negotiations. By looking inward rather than outward, the Iranian film industry has been able to respond creatively to the demands of the national market without needing to compete with Western films. At the same time, it has been able to submit Iranian films to international film festivals and markets as a national product. In its obligation to create the nation visually, Iranian cinema has also participated in the undoing of the nation by challenging the idea of an Islamic ummat as unified and homogenous, disturbing the revolutionary harmony of the nation of mostaz'afan in its war against the *estekbar-e jahani* (world powers).

Since the Iranian revolution of 1979, a number of movies have challenged the status of religion. Changes in financing practices have allowed for greater private investment in cinema, which in turn has weakened state control of the film industry. After the revolution, the Islamic state took an active role in sponsoring film production to promote the

Islamic notions of art and culture. The state established the notion of *hoseh-e honari* (the artistic realm) within the *Sazeman-e tablighat-e eslami* (Islamic propaganda unit) to fulfill such a purpose. To this day, the state continues to offer low-interest bank loans for movies. While most films are now supported by private donors and investors, including the filmmakers and producers themselves, in order to be screened publicly in Iran, all films must presented at the Vezarat'e Ershad-e Eslami (the Ministry of Islamic Guidance).

Even though the state has a central role in the regulation of the film production, the transnational network for the production, distribution, and reception of Iranian movies is crucial to the vitality of the film industry. Seeking to find their own form within Iranian society, democratic movements rely on film to expose forms of totalitarianism, oppression, and exploitation. The media plays an important role by dislocating and fragmenting the body and its civic construction from both national and transnational regimes of governmentality. The experience of watching film is mediated by a fragmentation of the phantasm of the national body and its manipulation in filmic space. However, the desire to return the body to its unity under the sign of one nation, religion, or culture is also an effect of the medium. While many of these Iranian movies undo the idea of the nation, they create the nation for Iranian communities across the globe through their transnational circulation and consumption. They also create either a nostalgic body—one which was at some point united with the national body but is now dislocated and exiled— or else an imaginary body (a literal body) to be united with the nation at some point in the future. In either case, the nostalgic or imaginary conceptions of a national homeland (Iran) become the foundation for recognition of a gendered body subjected to either secular or religious disciplinary practices.

Both film and television have provided space for challenging and interrupting nationalist and fundamentalist notions of religion and gender. By taking an ambiguous position vis-à-vis both Islamic narratives of gender, nation, and religion and modernity's foundational myths of subjectivity and identity, they have managed to create space for filmic reflection. However, they accomplish different political goals. Television series, which are mostly regulated by the government, have reached out to numerous households in urban and rural areas, mediating between religious narratives and audiences. While the mythological component of such religious narratives in television series legitimizes the Islamic government as well as the commodification of religion,[8] their historical character reveals uses and abuses of power within the community of ummat. In this context, television series play an important role in promoting particular consumer objects, clothing, and travel associated with religious stories. Also, the repetition of prime-time television series has created space for everyday discussions of governmental policies and politics. During the screening of the Imam Ali and Imam Reza series, many viewers associated characters in the series with living political figures. Television series are mostly produced for national consumption, although the Imam Ali and Imam Reza series have been distributed to networks in the Persian Gulf region. Unlike television series, films are consumed by mostly urban populations that are able to go to the movie theaters. The target audience for films is more often the educated urban classes, with a number of films reaching global audiences.

Zir-e Noor-e Maah:
What Is Intolerable under the Moonlight

> Faced with all this misconduct, injustice and lawbreaking, how much longer will there be benightedness, ignorance and indulgence? Now that the shah and the United States are not dominating this country, how can we make them responsible for all our problems and difficulties? Why don't they listen to sympathetic critiques? Why don't they use their talents and minds?
>
> Ayatollah Taheri, letter of resignation from his position of Friday prayer Imamat of Isfahan, addressed to the people

Under the Moonlight (2001), directed by the young filmmaker Reza Mir-Karimi, is the first film in the history of Iranian cinema to critique religious education and expose it to critical intervention and mediatic commentary. The film tells the story of Seyyed Hassan, a country boy (*shahrestani*) who chooses to pursue a religious education in order to become a clergyman. Throughout his education, he is haunted by the idea of having to wear religious garb after he graduates from school. His anxiety about donning clergyman's dress is a metaphor for his self-doubt. For Seyyed Hassan, the visibility of religious garb creates a risky distance from and an ironic intimacy with the community. The film directly addresses long-standing popular skepticism about the role of the clergy, sometimes pejoratively called *akhound* or *mollah* to imply that the robe and turban conceal hypocrisy, self-interest, and immorality. The religious garb takes on a double meaning for Hassan: it represents both a new way of connecting with his community and, at the same time, a barrier protecting him from real life. Ambivalent and confused, he finally overcomes his self-doubt and hesitation and decides to wear religious garb the day of his graduation from the seminary.

The film exposes the contradictions between two notions of religion, one focused on the centralization of Islamic knowledge production and the other invested in the politics of daily struggles, politics, and issues of social justice. In the first case, the film refers to the ways in which globalization and new information technologies make such centralization possible. For instance, cell phones enable seminary teachers to be in contact with other teachers and government officials. Such a possibility of constant connection breaks through the isolation of seminary teachers in particular localities by increasing the potential for centralization of religious knowledge and networks. *Under the Moonlight* is a direct discussion of the politicization of religion. The filmic gaze penetrates the space of the seminary, a homosocial male space where differences of class, ethnicity, and locality are finessed by the status of membership—there is a significant social hierarchy in the seminary—which distinguishes the seminary from civil life. Hassan finds the thought of returning home and leaving the homogenous space of the seminary disturbing, since his clerical dress might indicate to his fellow villagers a prioritization of Islamic knowledge over everyday life. Religious status radically distinguishes seminary students from members of civil society, marking a radical difference between cleric and ordinary man.

Hassan's encounter with a young boy, a street hustler who eventually steals the fabric for Hassan's ordination robe and turban, leads him to a group of homeless people who live under a bridge. They are portrayed in the film as marginal outlaws who have, despite everything, created a caring community. The group includes two entertainers who lost their business during the revolution, a woman prostitute, a jobless man who cannot pay alimony to support his ex-wife, the young hustler, and a musician. The city of Tehran is represented neither as a pure urban space nor as an impure one, but rather as a "veiled city," whose surfaces—new highways, modern bridges, the hegemonic pictorial Islamic style—are inhabited by an underworld whose members consist of the abject, the marginal, and the deviant. The allusion to a community that lives without shelter "under the moonlight" evokes the underworld of poverty and marginalization. The poverty that previously characterized south Tehran (well known in prerevolutionary times for its slums and its poor neighborhoods) has shifted and is now largely hidden from the popular gaze.

The film alludes to the ways in which the homosocial space of the seminary can be isolating, disconnecting the religious elite from the poor, men from women. The impossibility of communication with women or other community members jeopardizes Hassan's relationship to the divine by making him risk leaving the homosocial world of religious masculinity. When Hassan discovers that the hustler stole the material for his graduation robe, he goes after him and discovers the group of homeless people living under the bridge. Waiting for the boy to return, he decides to spend the night with the social outlaws and is able to listen to their stories and find out about life under the bridge. Hassan's tolerance of difference is measured by his acceptance of the outlaw and his refusal to participate in Islamic disciplinary jurisprudence, not only by refusing to give them a moral lesson or turn the outlaw over to the Islamic judicial groups, but also by actively helping them. That night, when a young prostitute who lives under the bridge tries to commit suicide, Hassan takes her to the hospital and identifies himself as her brother to speed up her treatment. The search for social justice requires a rupture with both a national and transnational Islamic ummat in exchange for reconnecting with the abject, the marginal, and the outlaw. The film represents clerical robes as trafficked objects, since Hassan's ordination robe is made from contraband.

Hassan's relations with the clergy exemplify the situation of the Islamic elite in Iran and in so doing introduce the viewer to a number of complex issues. First, the film reveals the lost connection between clerical Islam, which has gradually become a scriptural Islam, confined to the masculine and privileged space of the state or the seminary, and the socially disadvantaged—the poor, the female, the deviant, and the homeless. Second, the film explores the conflict between two readings of religion, one based solely on an orthodox mode of recitation of religious texts and the other an interpretation of the text mediated by the connection between the religious elite and the people. Hassan and his friend laugh at a new student who does nothing but recite the Quran over and over without paying any attention to its meaning. They call him a *khar Mazhab* (one who follows religion like a donkey). Hassan obviously distances himself from such views of religion by investigating the relationship between his religious education and the needs of the community outside the seminary. Hassan's curiosity in following the boy demonstrates his desire to investigate the meaning of religion for the social outlaw and the least privileged.

It is in this encounter with the community living under the bridge that the viewer is invited to reject a universalist, fundamentalist morality and instead recognize marginalized communities, a notion that is by definition antifoundationalist and antifundamentalist, as well as at odds with modernity in its desire to prioritize politics over religion and needs over laws. In the moment of crisis when the prostitute tries to commit suicide, Hassan takes her to the hospital and passes for her brother. By choosing to pass for what he is not, Hassan dissolves the boundaries separating the Islamic from the non-Islamic, the pure from the impure, the contaminated from the uncontaminated, the good from the bad, the outlaw from the law-abiding, and the male from the female and replaces them with a new sense of community, a contingent community defined by an ethic of care and responsibility.

Once he has crossed these boundaries, Hassan feels less resentful about wearing clerical robes. After he is ordained, he becomes involved in the life of the young hustler, who has been put into a rehabilitation center. In order for Hassan to become a religious leader, the film makes him pass as a brother of the prostitute and a friend to the thief and the entertainer. It is not solely through his identification with clerical Islam and its educational institutions, but through a reconnection with the abject city—the city under the bridge—that religion becomes important in Hassan's life. In this context, the convergence of politics and religion is more than the hyphenation between the nation and the state; it reveals the tension between the ummat as an Islamic imagined community and the community living under the bridge.

By its nature, film challenges the idea that religion is confined to the world of text and the space of religious education. *Under the Moonlight* shows the clergy using cell phones, which suggests the possibility of an institution removed from the urban underworld of crime, prostitution, and homelessness, and one potentially connected to popular culture by new technology. Urban space is portrayed as a veiled space that divides the perverse netherworld of entertainers, prostitutes, and the morally exiled elements of Islamic society from the official moral regime of the Islamic republic. However, a state ruling in the name of religion requires religion to concern itself with the well-being of all citizens.

In this context, Islam as a religion is asked to take on a new role, that of a religion able to tolerate difference in the name of its responsibility for the welfare of all citizens. This new role changes the responsibilities of religious students, who are now required not only to become knowledgeable in Islamic teachings but also to understand and politically intervene in social issues. Under these circumstances, absolutist notions of religion have to be put aside; religion is transformed by the reality of everyday politics. This new tolerance of difference, attached to the idea of Islamic citizenship, puts fundamentalist Islam in a bind because of its absolutist prioritization of morality over politics, of reason over the body, and of a transcendental over an embodied Islam.[9] However, despite its critical treatment of religious themes, the film nevertheless remains trapped in masculinist notions of politics and religion, where needs are defined only in terms of particular representations that focus on survival and victimization, and not pleasure and desire.

Unintegrated Subjects of *Do Zan* and the Revolution That Did Not Take Place

> I believe that to be able to lead a healthy social life, we have to be able to criticize ourselves by looking at our past. Once I said we have to plow our past to see what happened and I was ridiculed in the media. In the history of the last twenty-two years there has been a horrible silence, and generally history and the revolution have been distorted and defined one-sidedly. It is important for us to look back and see what happened to us. When the revolution took place, my generation was eighteen years old. We were like a traveler who boarded a ship that was struck by a storm or blown up and destroyed. Consider my generation: they are either refugees, or died in prison, or were executed, or died in the war, since the war started one year after the revolution. They lost their lives in the war, or got stuck at home. They are all my generation and this generation was judged very harshly, they were treated with cruelty, bad decisions were made about them. In other words, none of the ideals that we imagined materialized.
>
> Tahmineh Milani (2001, 6)

Iranian filmmakers have focused extensively on the theme of women and children, not only as passive objects in a masculine world but as subjects and agents in the making and the unmaking of the nation. While in many cases women and children are represented as the markers of national boundaries and the uniqueness of the Iranian Islamic nation, some films have used them as models of subversive subjectivity. Both women and children are portrayed as fragmented, unintegrated subjects who signify the impossibility of the completion of the nationalist cultural project. The representation of children necessarily deals with the period of subject formation, of becoming a gendered, sexualized, classed, and nationalized subject.

These themes are evident in a recent film, *The Day I Became a Woman* (2001), a triptych of connected stories directed by Marzieh Meshkini. To avoid the scrutiny of the Islamic republic, the filmmaker made three short films and put them together later, since short films do not require approval by the Ministry of Guidance before screening. Through the character of Hava, children are shown to encounter culture and politics as "subjects in formation," which undermines the taken-for-granted undertone of gender identity in various forms of nationalism. In the film, Hava's transition into adulthood at the age of nine is marked by her sexualization and genderization, when she is asked not to play with boys anymore and to recognize and conform to dominant models of femininity. The girl undergoes "nationalization" and is asked to wear the veil as a marker of her citizenship in an Islamic nation. However, the protagonists in the three stories—the young girl (Hava), a married woman (Ahoo), and an older woman (Houra)— refuse to be unitary, complicit subjects because of their need to fulfill their own desires. Representing three passages in a woman's life, the characters fail to comply with the mores of gendered, national forms of subjectivity and respectability. The two older women can be seen as a continuation of the younger character. Hava takes pleasure in a sexual transgression by sharing the oral pleasure of sucking the same lollipop with her male friend Hassan in the last hours before she becomes a woman. Ahoo, a young woman, escapes her marriage and her family's pressure to conform by taking a competitive bicycle ride along the coast with other young women. Houra, an older woman, uses an inherited legacy to buy all the domestic goods she has coveted in her lifetime and takes them along with her on a seaside adventure. Houra goes on a boat ride, a forbidden gender transgression that she desires.

Do Zan is a 1999 film by Tahmineh Milani, a prominent female director in Iran. The film is another challenge to the nationalist narrative of the revolution, since it explores the significance of gender and class differences. *Do Zan* is about the ways in which the revolution excluded women and suppressed gender issues by marginalizing them in the spheres of family and community. The film demonstrates that whereas women's issues were relegated to the private domain, class position in fact enabled women to negotiate their gender position. Here again, the notion of mostaz'af (the disempowered) and the revolt of the powerless against the powerful are thrown into crisis by the renarrativization of the revolution and the deromanticization of the idea that it brought change for women. The film focuses on a brilliant and energetic woman student of architecture, Fereshteh, who develops a friendship with another woman, Roya, a mediocre student who needs tutoring to get through the university. The two come from different class backgrounds: Roya is from an upper-middle-class Tehrani family, while Fereshteh is from a lower-class family from the countryside. The story takes place during and after the revolution of 1979, when the worlds of Fereshteh and Roya are filled with anxieties and concerns that parallel the unfolding revolution. Yet regardless of revolutionary ideals, the revolution remains incidental to the lives of the two women, who continue to deal with the same social issues during and after revolution.

The revolution has no impact on Fereshteh's life because her destiny continues to be determined by her lack of economic power. While the revolution goes on, Fereshteh deals with an obsessive young man named Hassan who has fallen in love with her, expects her to love and marry him, and threatens to throw acid in her face if she does not.[10] With the support of Roya, Fereshteh manages to cope with the man and his advances, until the day the stalker throws a bottle of acid at Fereshteh that hits her male cousin, whom he has mistaken for her boyfriend. Blaming her for bringing disgrace upon the family, Fereshteh's father forces her to return home after the student strikes and the shutdown of the universities. The stalker follows Fereshteh to her hometown and confronts her when she sneaks away from her house to make a phone call to Roya. When Fereshteh rushes back to her car to escape from him, Hassan follows on his motorcycle, hysterically shouting that he will find her wherever she goes. Fereshteh drives into a narrow street where a couple of children are playing and hits one of them with her car. Hassan follows her on his motorcycle and hits another child. Both Fereshteh and Hassan are arrested and sent to jail. In the Islamic court of justice, the stalker, accused of child homicide and the harassment of Fereshteh, is sentenced to thirteen years in prison and the payment of blood money. Fereshteh is accused of breaking the highway code and injuring a child. Hassan is sent to jail, but Fereshteh is given the possibility of release from jail, contingent upon the consent of the child's parents and payment of blood money. Her family, frustrated and angry because of her imprisonment and the dishonor she has brought upon them, is unable to pay the blood money to free her from prison. Ahmad, a family friend who is interested in Fereshteh, settles the payment and saves the family reputation. While Tehran burns in the fires of revolution, Fereshteh is forced to save her family's honor by marrying Ahmad.

The issues central to the discourse of cultural nationalists—including Islamic identity, veiling, and opposition to the West—seem irrelevant to Fereshteh and Roya's lives. The pressure of patriarchal relations and the criminalization of women who resist the norms of respectability are at the center of Fereshteh and Roya's preoccupations during the revolution. While the well-off Roya manages to finish school, marry the man she chooses, and find a job as an architect, Fereshteh continues to be harassed by the stalker after his release from prison. She tries to keep alive her intellectual interest in reading, but her husband becomes obsessively concerned about her developing an identity that might threaten her role as a loyal wife. Struggling against the stalker, her family, and her husband, Fereshteh is not, however, portrayed as a passive victim, but rather as a woman who actively resists her circumstances. She continues to acquire and read books, secretly manages to maintain her friendship with Roya, and hopes one day to reconcile her desires with the material conditions of her life.

After her husband discovers her secrets, he makes Fereshteh a virtual prisoner. In the absence of any public institutions to support her, Fereshteh is forced to take refuge in the family, which leads her into a new web of oppressive relations. After the dramatic death of her husband when he attacks the stalker, who is about to kill Fereshteh, she is left with the responsibility of raising two children as a single mother. She faces a life of struggle, untouched by the events of the revolution. The film ends with Fereshteh anxiously realizing how much is left for her to do and wondering how she is going to cope with it all.

The film looks away from the political, urban tensions of the revolution to deal with the complexity of what the revolution might have meant for the protagonist, a woman subjected to the crimes of passion of an obsessive man, the pressures of her family, gender norms of respectability, and the criminalization of women who resist gender oppression. Because the film turns away from the drama of revolutionary events, it is able to foreground gender conflicts that remain unresolved by the revolution, gender conflicts where no alliance can ever be formed between the aggressor and the aggressed. The renarrativization of revolution as an absence in the life of the two women reveals the untenability of mostaz'af as a unitary category.

The stalker's life and his masculinity are pertinent to the gender critique made by the film. The film portrays the stalker as an unemployed young man with a motorcycle who fixates obsessively on his love object as a way of dealing with unemployment and a lack of education. The film cannot avoid evoking the image of the young men who found a place for themselves in the *Basiji* organization and the revolutionary guards and who were charged with disciplining women.[11] The postrevolutionary state legitimized, channeled, and institutionalized violence against women by transforming women from singular love objects into the love object of a whole nation of men. While revolutionary models of femininity broke with the notion of family honor and transgressed the boundaries of gender respectability for the revolutionary cause, the tragic compromises that Fereshteh makes reveal the incompleteness of the revolution: it is a revolution that did not take place.

Subjects in Becoming: *Children of Heaven* and Postmodern Consumer Capitalism

Children of Heaven, written and directed by Majid Majidi in 1997, depicts the story of Ali, a young boy who loses his sneakers on the way to the cobbler to have them repaired. He arranges to share his sister Zahra's sneakers, so that he can continue to go to school. Ali and Zahra are able to share a single pair of shoes because the school has two shifts a day, one for girls and the other for boys. In this way they manage to avoid shaming the family as it struggles to survive. Ali feels responsibility for the family's financial difficulties—his sick mother needs expensive medication and his father, like masses of migrant workers in southern Tehran, has to search for seasonal jobs. Ali, Zahra, and their parents share a single room, which makes impossible adherence to modern middle-class notions of separate domestic spaces, as well as spheres of individual responsibility. The lack of separate space exposes the children to the realities of adult life in a way that prevents childhood from being a period of prolonged innocence, problematizing the very idea of childhood and adulthood as generalized defining categories in modern societies. Everyone in the family is exposed to the daily struggle for survival and must take an active role. Sleeping, eating, talking, homework—all take place within the boundaries of the family's home/room. Like Zahra and Ali, the audience witnesses the conversations of the parents as they strategize survival. The film radically challenges the mainstream, homogenizing notion of Iranian youths as consumers of MTV and Western fashion. The filmmaker Majid Majidi (1999), who was himself raised in a working-class family, has spoken about a generation of Iranian youths who have become not consumers of a service-based society but rather participants in its economic survival, a generation that, on account of its material conditions rather than its belonging to the imagined community of the ummat, is able to experience life in the process of becoming.

The film opens in southern Tehran, where there is a concentration of rural immigrants and seasonal workers, and then moves to northern Tehran, where the middle and upper classes live. The poverty of Ali's family and their struggle to survive are portrayed neither in terms of a loss of dignity and solidarity nor as moral decadence. Class hierarchy is not depicted as the antagonistic encounter of rich and poor. Rather, in its representation of poverty and class differences, the film refuses to invoke modernist notions of poverty as the result of a lack of nobility or moral judgment by showing a rich culture of family and community support among poverty-stricken people. However, the film avoids sentimentality through its frank depiction of the spatial segregation between the classes and the gap between rich and poor. It thus challenges any ideologically inclusive notion of mostaz'af.

The sneaker stands for the whole adult world of consumer capitalism into which the child is initiated regardless of need or desire. A race organized by the school becomes a potential solution for Ali because the third-place prize is a new pair of sneakers. The first- and second-place prizes—the opportunity to attend a modern youth camp on the Caspian Sea offering activities from swimming to painting to sports—are of no interest to Ali. Children from all classes, some with fancy clothing and some barely equipped for the race, participate in the race, which becomes a spectacular representation of children's formation as consumer subjects. Ali's desire for the new sneakers is ironically thwarted when he takes first place. The audience is thus left to contemplate the ways in which capitalism doesn't meet his needs, but rather offers extravagant pleasures that do nothing to mitigate the poverty of his life. The reality of class differences and the dismantling of the nationalistic narrative to resist capitalism undermine a cultural nationalist construal of mostaz'af.

Adam Barfi: "Passing" and the Dis-order of Things

Adam Barfi (The Snowman), directed by Davoud Mirbagheri and released in 1999, concerns a displaced Iranian man in Turkey who cross-dresses to obtain a visa to migrate to the West, but who stops short of wearing a hijab.[12] The portrayal of a woman without a hijab (even in an act of cross-dressing) created a great deal of controversy in the media in Iran. Adam Barfi was immediately banned by the Ministry of Culture because it transgressed the Islamic code of hijab. Despite and probably because of the banning, the film circulated widely in video format between 1996 and 1999. Regardless of the efforts by the government to remove videotape copies from circulation, it continued to be widely distributed on the black market and became one of the most popular movies in Iran. After its release in 1999, it became the best-selling movie that year.

The film satirizes government rules and regulations about gender and passing in its depiction of the Iranian diaspora in Turkey, a diaspora composed of people who live a life of hardship while they wait to migrate to Europe or North America. It also depicts the network of entrepreneurs, middlemen, and smugglers who ruthlessly exploit them while they wait to make the journey to the country of their destination. It is the story of a dislocated man, Abbass, who infiltrates the hypermasculine network of the Iranian mafia in Turkey to find a way to emigrate. They ask Abbass to leave Turkey disguised as a woman. Portrayed as a sensitive man who refuses to fight with the thugs, Abbass is intrigued by femininity and develops an intimate friendship with Donya, another diasporic Iranian trying to find her way out of Turkey; Abbass soon falls in love with her. Donya does not know that Abbass is a man. Adam Barfi ends when Abbass and Donya abandon their plans to emigrate and return to Iran to marry. The film portrays some of the difficulties facing dislocated Iranians.

This film depicts cross-dressing as something that happens away from home, in the space of diaspora, where people are dislocated culturally, economically, and emotionally. The return to Iran or to the homeland thus becomes a return to (hetero)normativity. Those who return to Iran are supposed to conform to hegemonic rules and regulations. Passing permits the male protagonist to temporarily loosen the constraints of his masculinity, which require him to be tough and aggressive, follow moral codes, protect his country, fight for the Islamic republic, and control women. This moment of rupture, which pulls the subject of masculinity away from himself, fails at the level of both the national and diasporic reproduction of the nation.

Abbass's ambiguous masculinity simultaneously renders visible object and subject positions for the viewer, creating multiple points of identification. The spectator moves back and forth between identifying with the object to be gazed upon and the subject of the gaze. The displacement of gender, together with the strategic use of masculinity and femininity, creates fluidity in gender identification. While Iranianness becomes a taken-for-granted location established through essentialized gender identities, the self-made gender identity revealed through passing problematizes national belonging and gendered citizenship.

The need for identification with the imposition of coded gender rules by the state on an unwilling populace—their transgression notwithstanding—has been an important feature of postrevolutionary Iran. For example, the escape from Iran of two male political leaders, Rajavi and Bani Sadre, one representing the hypermasculinity of an Islamic guerrilla group *(Mojahedin-e Khalq)* and the other from the nationalist elite, and their passing as women in order to cross the border remain a vivid folk-memory in the postrevolutionary revision of masculinity.[13] In this case, a contradictory process is at work: on the one hand, the subject seeks identification with the coded gender rules to protect himself or herself, and, on the other hand, this identification extends the possibility of social and political regulation of citizenship.

Adam Barfi examines the vulnerability of the masculine subject in diaspora, beyond the protective borders of a homeland. It shows how only certain kinds of masculinity survive in diaspora; for the others, passing from the space of the nation to the space of diaspora is to find oneself in the sphere of femininity. In *Adam Barfi* the possibility of agency is created through the protagonist's relationship with hegemonic and subordinated masculinities, including the hypermasculinity of the diasporic underworld. The process of gender identification, although supervised and controlled by men, is reinvented through the process of passing. The return to heteronormative identity for the protagonist is a return to the order of national respectability. However, this masculinity is transformed through its exposure to dislocation and, at the same time, attachment, care, and emotionality. Since values attached to femininity are denied to men in Iran, what the protagonist of *Adam Barfi* gains from the process of passing is a reconnection with the "feminine other." The film resolves the issue of passing by inventing a brother for Abbass's passing character, who returns after the female-passing character is sacrificed figuratively and announced as dead to Donya. The female-passing character dies so that Abbass may assume his masculinity before returning to the homeland. In this scenario, after being given an occasion to identify with the fragmented body of the protagonist, viewers are invited to feel the security brought by the return to Iran, a return to heteronormative masculinity and to the body before its fragmentation. The medium of film becomes the site of the deconstruction of national gender identity by functioning as a democratizing force, but at the same time it is also a site of the naturalization of gender and the nation. The culture produced by exiles gets exported back to the homeland, where it expands its subversive and oppositional role with respect to the ideology of national identity.

Hamid Naficy has argued that exiles produce a popular subculture as a means for the expression of resistive, subversive, and oppositional ideas within mainstream American culture (1993; 1996). I would argue that such expression is not exclusive to the exilic culture, but is available as an option for those located within the nation thanks to the global expansion of the media and communication technologies. The imaginary space of diaspora is indeed a place where those living in exile can express ambiguity and ambivalence vis-à-vis the nation left behind. In addition, hybridity is the collective condition of diaspora created by new forms of globalization providing space for a reflexive battleground in the realm of culture as a field of meaning-making and contestation. I argue that such representational practices take place in an imaginary cultural space where notions of self, other, place, displacement, and so on are articulated in complicated and contradictory ways. Most of these cultural representations rely on naturalization of the nation through a chain of representational practices that depict the nation as the natural site for the regulation of bodies. I am making a case here for the usefulness of recourse to gender identity and family relations in efforts to contain the contradictions and discontinuities that emerge between economic exploitation and cultural domination. Creating continuity between the nation as a physical territory and the nation as a transnational, affective space subordinates cultural citizenship to political citizenship.

Dokhtaran-e Korshid: Dis/identification and Departure from the Body

Passing is the theme of another contemporary Iranian film, *Dokhtaran-e Khorshid* (Daughters of the Sun), directed by the Iranian woman film-maker Maryam Shahriar in 2000. This time it is under the gaze of a diasporic director who lives in Italy that the concept of passing comes to film. The film has been shown at a number of film festivals outside Iran as well as in professional circles in Iran, but has not been officially released for public screening. The film is unique in Iranian cinema in its depiction of passing from femininity into masculinity.[14]

The film tells the story of Amangol, a village girl who is sent by her father to a village far away from home to work in a carpet-weaving workshop. As in *Adam Barfi*, the subject's dislocation is the condition that makes passing possible. In this film, it is Amangol's parents who decide on her cross-dressing. Her father shaves her head and sends her to live and work in the workshop. Amangol is a skilled carpet-weaver but cannot be sent to the workshop because girls are not allowed to live on site. The film depicts the exploitation of young girls and boys in rural Iran by their parents and the harsh conditions in the carpet-weaving sweatshops run by middlemen entrepreneurs who mediate between the families and the carpet industry. In this case, the owner of the shop promises to remit Amangol's wages to her parents. The workshop is represented as a feminized space, where most of the daily workers are young women. Only one person—Amangol, now passing as Aman—lives in the shop.

As in *Adam Barfi*, passing is a survival strategy. However, while *Adam Barfi* ends with the protagonist's return to his masculinity, Aman's return to femininity in *Dokhtaran-e Khorshid* is another form of passing, one that conceals deviance and criminality. For her, passing has two uses: as a survival strategy and as a way of avoiding the consequences of acts of resistance. The film portrays passing not as natural or essential but as a process of self-creation by means of transgressive gender acts. *Dokhtaran-e Khorshid* goes against fundamentalist constructions of femininity and womanhood. It speaks to the reality of many young women who escape from their family, shave their heads, and live on the streets as homeless boys.[15] Some filmmakers have touched on this subject in recent years, including the prominent Iranian woman director Rakhshan-e Bani Etemad in her feature film *Banuy-e Ordibehesht* (Ordibehesht [the second month of the year in the Iranian calendar]

Lady) and the London-based Iranian anthropologist and filmmaker Ziba Mir Hosseini in her documentary *Doghtaran-e Farari* (Girls on the Run).[16] These films portray self-creation as constituted not only by the strategic use of the dress code (still enforced by the Islamic state, since it is the main signifier of belonging to the Islamic ummat) but also by the possibility of reflection on the multiplicity of the self and its fragmentation.

The movement, or passing, from femininity to masculinity creates the opportunity for the protagonist to find a job, which enables her to live and work in the carpet-weaving atelier. At the same time it exposes her to the exploitative conditions of young male workers. In this case, masculinity is portrayed not as a natural locus of power but as a place where power is distributed unequally among men. Masculinity is characterized by a division of labor, a hierarchy of power, alienation, and physical violence. The young women share the exploitative situation, but gender boundaries protect them from direct physical abuse. Moreover, working in carpet-weaving shops is not thought of as a permanent situation for women. A female carpet-weaver who falls in love with Amangol (Aman) is on the verge of marriage, which she speaks of as a way out of exploitative working conditions. The film does not romanticize marriage, but rather portrays it as yet another institution regulating the life of young women in the villages.

There are four key motifs in the film. These key motifs reveal the institutional power of both private and public patriarchy not only over the subject's labor but also over her body. While private patriarchy legitimizes the appropriation of women's bodies by men (fathers, husbands), public patriarchy legitimizes male violence toward other men. Both forms of patriarchy separate the subject from its body and dispossess her of the power to act through the body with its passions or desires. As a result, the subject's rebellion and resistance require a new consciousness of the body and its passions.

The first motif is the theme of male violence toward other men, which is justified in terms of a work hierarchy that sanctions the exercise of power over other men. Amangol's beating by the boss when s/he tries to protest the working conditions reveals the strict and arbitrary rules concerning imposed silence on the job, work breaks, sick leave, and surveillance, measures designed to prevent workers from creating any form of solidarity, support, and care. The second motif relates to passing, as it represents the possibility of action for the protagonist as a female subject. Both the display of and the return to an ambiguous self are characterized as an ingression to the world of action, revenge, and self-disciplining. The third key motif, of love's transgressive momentum, concerns a love affair between the protagonist and one of the young female coworkers. The young woman is just about to say yes to a suitor but falls in love with the protagonist and expresses her will to reject her suitor. In the exchange of looks between the two female lovers, the protagonist becomes both the object of the cinematic gaze and its subject. She sees herself as a subject once the other woman identifies her as a subject; s/he is recognized as a subject through her own recognition by the subject who falls in love with her. The young woman's attraction to Amangol is not depicted in terms of masculine seduction but as the attractiveness of emotionality, affection, and gentleness. Gender passing here allows women to fall in love with each other. The film exposes the ruse of the dress code and gender performance by exposing the radical possibility of gender transgression within the dominant regime of heteronormativity. The fourth motif concerns Amangol's flight from the sweatshop at the end of the film. After being beaten and locked up by the owner, Amangol decides to take revenge by setting the workshop on fire. In the very last sequence, when the shop is shown aflame, Amangol wears her long floral robe and runs away from the work site to a green meadow. Here, her return to femininity is a strategic act to conceal criminality, since it is in the role of Aman, the male-passing character, that Amangol takes action against the exploitative and violent working conditions. Femininity becomes a hiding place, a refuge from the criminal system of modern Iran, in which the Islamic state, like any other modern state, relies on labor exploitation and the legal system fails to protect the most vulnerable members of the society regardless of their gender. In this case the destructive reaction of Amangol to the conditions of carpet-weaving is not considered an act of rebellion by the criminal system, but rather an act that disrupts the institutional mechanism controlling the labor force. As a result, both class and gender hierarchies offer subject positions that guarantee the exploitation of women. Both as a woman and as a worker, Amangol not only does not own her labor force, but she does not control her body. In the context of the patriarchal family, Amangol's body is first appropriated by her father and then rented to the owner of the carpet-weaving workshop. The film refuses to romanticize the family, revealing its complicity with other institutions in benefiting from exploitative labor.

In *Daughters of the Sun,* the female protagonist moves in and out of femininity and masculinity, and so invites the viewer to become aware of the self as plural and gender as an artifact. However, it is through passing that she has an opportunity to construct her identity as a subject. By moving into a subject position, which enables her to confuse and fool the viewer, the protagonist resists becoming an object of the gaze; rather she is a subject able to control her identity by exposing it to or concealing it from the viewer. While in *Adam Barfi* movement in and out of masculinity is constantly kept under surveillance by the other characters in the film, in *Daughters of the Sun* Amangol escapes surveillance by playing with ambiguities and eroticizing silence. In this way she is able to display a subversive love, keeping open the possibility of strategic shifts of identity. But here, since the subject not only transgresses gender borders but also becomes an outlaw who passes in order to conceal her criminality, the audience is left with an even greater sense of the potential ambiguity of cross-dressing.

Both films show how identity, rather than being some kind of essence, is performed through religious, scientific, legal, and medical discourses. This idea is, to be sure, a profound challenge to the hegemonic notions of womanhood under Islamic nationalism, which rely heavily on essentialized notions of gender and sexuality. Passing, masquerade, and disguise therefore create spaces for subjects to resist fixity. It would, in this light, be quite possible to develop a new perspective on the Islamic *hijab* by seeing it as a form of passing from the overt identity of "Westernized and modernized emphasized femininity" to a resistant subject position. However, Western representational practices, along with Islamic nationalism and fundamentalism, as well as global consumer capitalism, have made veiling into yet another fixed subject position. Both passing and *hijab* can be seen as ways of "transcending the body" through which female identity is fixed. However, fundamentalist and nationalist encoding of the body serves to create yet another abstract body, an Islamic body, whose representation circulates both nationally and transnationally. The veiled woman is the signifier that creates the possibility of a female subject position, which begs the question of the subject position of the unveiled woman—who continues to exist, although not in public. In addition, the veiled woman is abstracted to a transcendental body. This civic body, as I have called it elsewhere, which is disconnected from lived experience, is a site of gendered subjectification. It is indeed a movement from the semiotic to the experiential that passes as the fundamentalist vision of Zahra Rahnavard and her "essence of womanhood."

Both *Adam Barfi* and *Daughters of the Sun* reveal values denied to femininity and masculinity in Iran by exploring what is gained and what is lost through passing. The breaching of boundaries seriously challenges stereotypical notions of Islamic gender segregation as purely oppressive and, I have argued, opens up space for an investigation of the gender tropes behind the workings of power and authority. In addition, the transgendered hero(ine) of these films, by staging antinormative erotic desire, permits fantasizing about and promotion of alternative sexualities. Through silence, eye contact, gestures, and dress codes, an erotically ambivalent situation is set up that allows a display of sexual deviance. The queering of the gendered citizens of the Islamic republic and the cinematic display of bodies that are ambiguous with respect to gender mean that *Adam Barfi* and *Daughters of the Sun* transgress the boundaries of citizenship and subvert veiling as a disciplinary tool.

Muslim Womanhood: The Will and the Law

> Dear Sister: I don't have any special advice regarding your *hijab* since I know that you have chosen it consciously. You know that your *hijab* is our ummat's flag of independence and your invincible umbrella; you are holding the flag of this resistance, resistance against the Satan of carnal *desire* and the Great Satan.
>
> Letter from the front during the Iran/Iraq war,
> written by a *basiji* (volunteer combatant),
> *Zan dar Ayeneh defa'e Moggadas* (1990, 74)

> Government authorities, wherever they are and whatever their responsibilities are, propagation, legislation and judiciary, must act in a way that all forms of inequality between men and women will be eliminated. They should work to gain women's trust. Although equality between women and men does not mean sameness of rights, discrimination between men and women must not be tolerated since if the authorities do not challenge discrimination, women themselves will combat it.
>
> "Have Iranian Women Tried to Obtain Their Rights?"
> reprinted in Taleghani 1991 (58–66)

As I have argued, the construction of a collective political will during the revolutionary era relied on imagining a community—the ummat—

unified in its opposition to the West and to the *mostakbaran-e jahani* (the powerful of the world). The imagined community of ummat has also created space for gender agency and the ensuing negotiations resulting from the diversity of those subjects now cast as willing participants in the ummat as a community. Such gender relations are not predetermined, but are contingent on their ability to interrupt the will to power of the nationalist and fundamentalist elites. Various dichotomies—religious versus secular, Muslim versus Western, traditional versus modern, and so on—are at work, both domestically and in the Iranian diaspora, to place women on one side or the other of these binary oppositions. However, the articulation of a plural and fragmented will by Iranian women in varying locations undermines the unified will to power. To put it another way, although the emergence of women's agency in the making of an Islamic ummat and an Islamic collective will has been crucial to the formation of Muslim women as willing subjects of the new republic, nevertheless the nation-state's collective will is interrupted by "the incomplete repetitions of codes and rules" (Butler cited by Smith 2000, 25). The process of emergence of women's agency and the formation of an Islamic female subject have been informed both by a demand for representations of an Islamic femininity positioned in opposition to hegemonic Westernized models of femininity and by the active participation of women willing to identify with such an oppositional model of femininity.

In Iran, women and men, as they enter the space of citizenship, use Islamic values to negotiate power and authority. As Najmabadi has noted, the current political democratization in Iran is no longer an exclusively male preserve by virtue of the fact that women's needs are topics of discussion and women have become public commentators on canonical and legal texts (2000, 31). Moreover, the Islamic dress code has functioned as a form of symbolic capital enabling women in the villages and countryside to enter the nation and to become politically active locally. In Sudan, according to Bernal, the association between power and nationalism was forged through Islamic dress (under Numeri in the early 1980s) and symbolic public acts (1992, 10). Bernal argues that women are seen as embodying tradition and as ignorant and backward: "By juxtaposing 'correct' Islam to life as lived by ordinary Muslims, fundamentalists actually are helping to effect a break between life and faith" (11). In Iran, through the sacralization of politics and the collapse of the categories of believer and citizen, both religion and nationalism have lost their credibility. Citizens and believers alike are faced with the limits of the modernizing state functioning as an agent of a unified "religious or national culture."[17]

One could argue that, under Reza Shah, bourgeois culture and taste, which rely on hegemony rather than absolutism and on persuasion rather than coercion, were presented as a modernist strategy. However, the Islamic revolution, with its reliance on style to signify Islamic morality, was able to make the work of hegemony effective. The Islamic dress code was not always adopted by decree but often was preferred out of a desire to be more Islamic and to have an Islamic lifestyle. As stated by Mackie, "Successful incorporation into bourgeois social order involves not a person's subjugation of his own will to that of the 'law' but the absence of any distance between that will and the law" (1997, 21). While Islamic culture represents any incorporation of bourgeois culture as a transgression of law and a deep form of self-violation, oppositional modernism gains strength from the construction of a secular subject who feels profoundly connected to modernist lifestyle and fashion, which are opposed to Islamic values.

Consumerism has been creating a connection between the national and the transnational by marketing desire for religious versus secular styles of dress around self-fashioning in religious and secular terms. The creation of and emotional attachment to taste and style have been a crucial part of social regulation and control in modernity. As Mackie (1997) argues, fashion serves as a way of thinking about social reform, but often the transformations offered by fashion are symptomatic of normative repetition and conformity rather than difference and change. Echoing Roland Barthes, we can read veiling as a recursive reflection of itself. Paradoxically, veiling in postrevolutionary Iran plugged the bodies of Iranian women into consumer culture and announced acceptance rather than challenge or revision of what the modernized culture of the shah and the West had to offer.

However, the sexual division of labor instituted by consumerism directs men and women to compete with members of their own sex while disguising ethnic and class differences between men as male solidarity. In the context of a modern Islamic republic, contact with the liberal rights discourse of equality has opened up a discussion of gender inequalities; nevertheless, the sexual division of labor continues to persist in the economic sphere. The Islamic discourse of gender difference, including the case for gender segregation, has legitimized gender inequalities in the political sphere even as it creates economic opportunities for women in the labor market.[18] The outcome of this interplay between equality and difference is unpredictable because it is a potential threat to both liberalism and Islamism. However, the consumerist moment of capitalism and the incorporation of transnational notions of an Islamic femininity—in terms of who women are and what they consume—have made possible the perpetuation of a gender division of labor in the production, circulation, and consumption of femininity. Again, there may well be unforeseen consequences in terms of who is able to be a consumer of Islamic values, who is not, and why. As a result, there may be space for what is suppressed in the presence of the consumerism of a transnational Islamic womanhood.

Contradictions between subject formation and agency have created unsustainable tensions that threaten the coherency of the idea of the unified will of the Islamic ummat. As it encounters the liberal subject of modernity, the Islamic subject of postrevolutionary Iran creates a crisis for both religion and modernity because the discourse of equality—that is, the will to rule in the name of the people and under the rubric of "men as equal by nature"—challenges the Islamic concept of ummat, which is based on the inequality of men and women. In the domain of legal and judiciary practices, for example, what are called personal status laws (the laws governing marriage, divorce, and child custody) have been the subject of intense political negotiations. In addition, a critique of women's ignorance regarding their legal and judicial rights has led a number of Iranian gender activists to initiate educational and media campaigns on the topic. For Ashraf Geramizadegan, the editor of the monthly magazine *Houqouq-e Zanan* (Women's Legal Rights), which started in 1998, women's legal security is central to the society's sense of security and justice (Ardalan 2001, 10–12). As Kar and Hoodfar note, both secular feminists and Islamic women activists have questioned the conceptualization of Islamic justice by flooding the media with stories of injustice done to them as women, wives, and mothers (1996, 35). However, as Kar specifies, conservative women tend to view the most contested articles of Iran's civil laws reflecting gender inequality (e.g., a husband's right to divorce whenever he likes, or the custody rights of fathers) as divinely inspired and unobjectionable (2001b, 180–83).

Conversely, the discourse of difference claimed by Islamic fundamentalist women puts pressure on the liberal discourse of equality. The claim to a distinct Islamic cultural identity has led to an internal cultural debate, at the forefront of which is the woman question. Islamic fundamentalist women, far from being merely victims or followers of the Islamic male elite, have been able to articulate their own will to power through the discourse of difference. This discourse has brought the issue of Islamic cultural meanings to the forefront of social, political, and legal negotiations. In fact, reliance on the discourse of difference has facilitated the creation of a legitimate discursive field within which women's concerns are being articulated. This discursive field includes discussions of topics ranging from Islamic law to women role models, drawing on published biographies of major female Islamic figures, letters to newspaper editors, and interviews with workers, peasants, and schoolteachers,[19] as well as comparisons fostered by international gatherings between Iranian Muslim women and women from other Muslim nations.[20] The fact that Muslim fundamentalist women prioritize the Islamic ummat over any other notion of community suggests that further investigation is required to understand the historical conditions of belonging within which subject positions are claimed.[21]

CHAPTER 5

Transnationalism, Feminism, and Fundamentalism

They say women will be crushed under people's heads and hands, do they think we are ants?

> Interview with a woman soccer fan, *Zanan*,
> Year 6, Azar 1376 (1997)

Only the dominant self can be problematic; the self of the Other is authentic without a problem, naturally available to all kinds of complications. This is very frightening.

> Gayatri Chakravorty Spivak (1990, 66)

The surge [*déferlement*] of "Islam" will be neither understood nor answered as long as the exterior and interior of this borderline place have not been called into question; as long as one settles for an internal explanation (interior to the history of faith, of religion, of languages or cultures as such), as long as one does not define the passageway between this interior and all the apparently exterior dimensions (technoscientific, tele-biotechnological, which is to say also political and socioeconomic, etc.).

> Jacques Derrida (1998, 20)

Globalization and the expansion of new forms of print and visual media, along with the erosion of the nation-state, have generated a crisis in modernity, rationality, and identity. This crisis of identity correlates with the expansion of global culture in the aftermath of decolonization (Hall 1991a). The outcome has been a war over representation and position between dominant and dominated ethnicities as well as hegemonic masculinities and emphasized femininities. These crises have generated a series of questions concerning group identification and individual selves, globalism and nativism, and center and periphery—questions such as: Who are we?[1] What is our relationship to others? How do we relate to our own selves? What is particular about us? Who has the authority to control us? In the name of what and for whom?

The global conditions of our postcoloniality can be depicted as a moment of crisis. I understand crisis in the way that Spivak does, as "the moment at which you feel that your presuppositions [about] an enterprise are disapproved by the enterprise itself" (1990, 139). Islamic religious nationalism and transnationalism are increasingly strong forces that respond to the global and local crises of rationality and masculinity in postmodern consumerist capitalism. Central to this crisis is the question of the subject. The return of feminine, religious, and cultural others, once contained in the realm of the "irrational," has challenged the foundational myths of modern politics, leading to a crisis of what Foucault calls "the governmentalization of the state."[2] The modern concept of a universal rationality based on a transcendental subject is meant to be, as Asad points out, one of the faces of power (1993, 232). Such crises are generated in three arenas of social reality—cognition, coercion, and production—and significantly impact the nation and the state as the main sites of subject formation in modernity.

The crisis of cognition, by which I mean ways of perceiving oneself, is characterized by a moment of fragmentation that interrupts the dominant, unified notions of the self in modernity and sometimes replaces them with new spaces of subject formation. These new spaces involve what Poster has called an insistence upon modernist forms of subjectivity and their desire for a lost unity, which coincides with a colder postmodern subject construed as bundles of data.[3] The crisis of cognition fuels modern subject formations of race, class, gender, and sexuality. The effects of continuously overlapping and conflicting subject positions in the context of new forms of globalization have taken to their limit modern notions of the subject as always capable of recognizing itself as such.[4]

The crisis of cognition coincides with the crisis of coercion or authority to rule. The crisis of coercion is characterized by the erosion of the nation-state and the emergence of new forms of governmentality and citizenship in what could be called a transnational civil society (Appadurai 1996; Ong 1999). These conditions have the effect of mobilizing various forms of cultural and religious nationalism defined neither by territoriality nor by the attachment of power to a particular government or rule of law, but rather by the transnational politics of identity.

As Foucault argues, modern regimes of governmentality are based on the triangle of sovereignty, government, and discipline, with populations as the primary target of the governmentalization of the state and the apparatuses of security (policing, border surveillance, military action, etc.) as their essential mechanism. In this context, the task of knowing about populations, as well as what some postcolonial scholars have called the self-knowledge of the populations as particular subjects, has been essential to the endurance of modern forms of governmentality. What Foucault calls "le savoir," or the constitution of knowledge of the population to regulate territory, wealth, and property, has been central to the governmentalization of the state, the process by which the state is created as a form of government. In this context, the expansion of mass-mediated spaces and information technologies, as well as the massive dislocation of people, has caused a rupture in the coercive and cognitive regulation of citizenry as a core component of the governmentality of the state. These crises have created general anxiety as well as a new focus on security measures. The modern textualization of political citizenship is gradually being challenged by new notions of the self as fragmented and connected to multiple locations. Displaying multiple sites of identification, such a fragmented subject challenges the modern division between the public and the private, a division that is no longer limited to a territorial mapping but rather located in a minimum of two nation-states, and creates discord within the nation-state, which is no longer a well-orchestrated entity, since membership in the nation does not necessarily mean membership in the state or vice versa.

In the sphere of production of goods and services, the restructuring of time and space in the context of technological change has created a greater reliance on mediatization and consumption, since they create new cycles of accumulation of wealth and knowledge and new consumer subjects. The boundaries between domestic and nondomestic as the major defining gendered spatial markers of work and nonwork in modernity have been distorted. In the context of a growing multicultural capitalism, or of a "multiculture of capitalism," in Appelbaum's terms, the decentralization of production and of subcontracting have led to the commodification of domestic space wherever there is a massive presence of Third World and diasporic women (1996, 309). Recourse to gender identity and family values in the discourse of cultural nationalism and religious fundamentalism becomes useful in containing the contradictions and discontinuities that emerge between economic exploitation and cultural domination. Gender issues and gender identities are at the heart of these shifting cultural and economic systems of meaning. The large-scale intrusion of women into labor markets, the shift of power relations between women and men, the visible presence of women in institutions of knowledge, and especially their access to print, scripture, and visual media have all helped bring gender to center stage. The possibility of storing, organizing, and transmitting words and images via transnational networks and institutions is as fundamental as the production and storage of wealth.[5] These changes have left behind unresolved issues, such as the separation between the private and public realms, between domestic and nondomestic production, and between an ethic of care based on the invisible emotional labor of women and an ethic of responsibility based on a notion of abstract, rational citizenship. Such changes have intensified gender identification across class, race, and ethnic lines, as well as the significance of identity politics.

Feminisms and fundamentalisms are among the growing forces attempting to deal with global and local identities on both the individual and collective levels. Fundamentalists and feminists are waging war over the means to control the mechanisms of cultural representation. Both are major players responsible for and responding to the "crisis of rationality," as well as the "crisis of masculinity."[6] Both arose inside the problematic of modernity, as reflections of relations between men and women with respect to the universal and the particular, the public and the private, the family and the state, and the individual and the community. Islamic fundamentalism and what may be called Western "egalitarian feminism" have become important sites for the construction of new forms of global oppositions perpetuating old colonial divisions between a barbaric, oppressive, and patriarchal Muslim world and a civilized, tolerant, and liberated West. While I am limiting my discussion to Western egalitarian feminism's opposition to Islamic fundamentalism, other forms of Western feminism, including versions of Third World feminism and women of color "womanism," share the problematic of egalitarian feminism in their opposition to Islamic fundamentalism. Although this chapter does not systematically address other versions of Western feminism, I do provide examples of the convergences between egalitarian feminism and other forms of feminism, which suggest a similarity in their political agendas.

I have passed over a number of different and sometimes antagonistic strands of feminism to address one particular aspect of Western egalitarian feminism, which emerged in the context of Euro-American modernity, which was itself generated in various places and contains a range of positions on women's social subordination. I am focusing on Western egalitarian feminism because of its hegemony over other forms of feminism and its centrality in the modern Western liberal political structures. In my treatment of Islamic fundamentalism in chapters 2 and 3, I address the particular interpretation of Shia Islam prevalent in the pre- and post-1979 revolutionary era in Iran. In addition, I give examples from fundamentalism in other religious traditions. In this section, I deconstruct the dichotomization of Western egalitarian feminism and Islamic fundamentalism as unitary transhistorical formations representing good and evil, freedom and lack of freedom, civilization and fanaticism, and modernity and tradition.[7] My discussion focuses on four sociological matters: first, the contemporary ground upon which feminist and fundamentalist discourses encounter one another; second, the cognate issues that both feminist and fundamentalist discourses address; third, the discursive spaces where feminism and fundamentalism find themselves radically at odds; and fourth, the notion of Islamic feminism in Iran, not as a conceptual impossibility but as a site of cross-fertilization between fundamentalism and feminism that has opened up space for further examination of modern patriarchal hegemonies and issues of cultural difference.

Feminism, Fundamentalism, and the "Spectacle of the Other Woman"

Before I get to a discussion of feminism and fundamentalism, I would like to elaborate on the visual and discursive tropes in which Western egalitarian feminism and Islamic fundamentalism have found space to claim identity. In other words, I would like to investigate the paradoxical presence of feminism in fundamentalism and fundamentalism in feminism through deconstruction and an examination of modern regimes of visibility and the representation of difference in the "spectacle of the other woman."[8] Derridean notions of deconstruction are essential for my analysis in this chapter, since a "revolutionary change of mind," in Spivak's (1980) terms is needed for developing theoretical strategies to think about both feminism and fundamentalism. Using the insights of deconstructive thinking, I criticize the ways in which both feminists and fundamentalists create discursive enclosures by claiming to have the truth and interrogate the ways in which the truth is produced historically. A deconstructive interrogation of the privileging of certain ideas and concepts in both egalitarian feminism and Islamic fundamentalism is necessary, since the conceptual binary oppositions that are taken to stabilize the meaning of feminism and fundamentalism at this particular conjuncture are a by-product of precisely such discursive practices.

I also use the insights of feminist postcolonial and transnational theories to understand this relationship, since there is a well-known body of transnational and postcolonial feminist scholarship that has investigated feminist discourses and their historic conditions of possibility.[9] I am borrowing Stuart Hall's (1997) notion of the spectacle to emphasize the importance of thinking in terms of the spectacle in the age of global media, which locates the feminine Other at center stage. I argue that the spectacle of the other woman has been crucial in containing the modern crisis of the nation-state, by participating in the "militarization of the gaze," by which I mean the legitimization of military occupation[10] and the renationalization of the states.[11] I refer to renationalization to talk about two phenomena: first, the erosion of the nation-state and the crisis of modern governmentality, and second, the ways in which, through the spectacle of the other woman, a particular notion of the subject as belonging to a unified "we-ness" emerges as a conceptual necessity to draw together the nation and the state. In other words, renationalization refers to the importance of nationalism as it glues together the hyphenated categories of the nation and the state and new forms of political mobilization in a transnational context.

I find Hall's notion of the spectacle valuable to a transnational feminist cultural studies perspective for a number of reasons: first, its analytical potential in addressing the relationship among gender, modernity, and visibility, which have become central components of popular culture and the global media; second, its ability to create space for an examination of the visual images, symbols, metaphors, and representations that help to create the body as a site of political performance in modern nation-states, as well as nationalist and fundamentalist movements;[12] third, its helpfulness in understanding the materials circulated through visual media, popular culture, and consumer capitalism, materials that have become a crucial site for the circulation of gendered, sexual, racial, and national tropes; fourth, its usefulness in investigating new forms of Orientalism articulated around staging the bodies of Muslim and Arab women; and finally, its capacity to create a space where hybrid and transnational subjectivities become impossible.[13]

A number of examples are illustrative of such spectacles in our global world. For example, since September 11, 2001, the depiction of Afghani women as the ultimate victims of the Taliban, as being in need of protection from their barbaric fundamentalist men, has mobilized various feminist groups and organizations in the United States. Cultural essentialism and racism are of course major players here, distinguishing between barbaric and civilized nations. The tropes of the Muslim woman in general and the Afghani woman in particular as the ultimate victims of a timeless patriarchy defined by the barbarism of Islamic religion and in need of civilizing have become very important components of Western regimes of power and knowledge. That is why the need to engage with gendered Orientalism is no longer a flourish of postcolonial criticism but a sine qua non, since it is under the sign of a veiled woman that we increasingly come to recognize ourselves not only as gendered and heteronormative subjects but also as located in the free West, where women are not imprisoned. These images are still used to justify a civilizing mission that began in the age of colonial modernity and continues to give meaning to our contemporary world. In the post–September 11 period, there is an abundance of examples showing the persistence of civilizational thinking in the representation of the other in the hegemonic moment of the articulation of an American multicultural nationalism, which relies heavily on Orientalism and Eurocentrism.[14] What I mean by civilizational thinking is a powerful modern discourse influenced by the Enlightenment and the idea of progress dividing the civility of the "West" from the barbarism of the "Rest." As Hall notes, the Other that was dependent on the discursive figures of the noble and the ignoble savage and of crude and refined nations was cast as the opposite or the negation of everything that the West represented in the discourse of civilization (1996, 221). In chapter 1, I showed how historically this discourse constructed Persia as the other of Europe. I invoke civilizational thinking to signal the reappearance of this discourse at the center of our current regimes of representation. Western egalitarian feminists are not exempt from the latest forms of civilizational thinking. In the recent case of Afghanistan, through the call for sisterhood with the victimized Afghani women and protection of these women from their barbaric men, Western egalitarian feminists participated in the discourse of civilizational thinking. In this conjuncture, sisterhood is defined by women's relationship to patriarchy rather than deeper, cultural relationships. In this case, sisterhood emerges in the taken-for-granted spaces of civilized nations defined by the cultural superiority of the West.[15] Here, it is through the convergence of the state of population with the state of civilization that the nation-state is able to renationalize to avert its erosion. The feminist imagining of the other woman takes place within historical formations of cultural and national belonging that are divided by the historical formation of peoplehood within a particular location/nation-state, concealing exclusions and violences of the nation-state.

It is crucial to investigate the feminist staging of difference in the spectacle of the other woman and its role in the intensification of the demand for renationalization.[16] The spectacle of the feminine other has been crucial in creating space for the emergence of a unified notion of womanhood for Muslim fundamentalist women. It has also been crucial in effacing the hybrid nature of Islamic nationalism and fundamentalism as by-products of modernity. However, in the last few years, hybrid notions of Islamic feminism have brought unified notions of the Islamic nation into crisis, while the spectacle of the feminine other, depicting Muslim women as the veiled object of barbaric patriarchies defined by the religion of Islam, has served to make and remake the nation for Muslim and Western feminists alike. Through the spectacle of the feminine other, discourses of global sisterhood and acceptance of women's participation in national struggles are finding a "home" in the heteronormative and fraternal communities of brothers. Nationalism in feminism has indeed become an important part of an attempt to contain the crisis of nation-states, taking part in the renationalization of the state. The spectacle of the other woman—feminine others—enables the relocation of nationalism and fundamentalism in feminism. It promotes a particular notion of feminism, which claims solidarity with a global community of sisters yet is primarily defined by its cultural belonging to modern fraternal communities of a nation in crisis.

I have chosen to compare and contrast Western egalitarian feminism and Islamic fundamentalism for a number of reasons. First of all, the spectacle of the other woman, or the visual regime in place at this particular historical conjuncture, is focused on Islamic fundamentalist women as the other of Western egalitarian feminists. Second, through representational practices, both discourses have created subject positions that are exclusive because of their own fragmentation and hybridity. In a postcolonial world of unequal power relations, both discourses conceal the power relations among women, who are located unevenly in the social hierarchies of class, race, sexuality, nation, and culture. As a result, both discourses are now at center stage of a new global order that is being represented in terms of the dichotomy of Western egalitarian feminism and Islamic fundamentalism at war with each other, one in its effort to liberate women and the other to force them back into the dark world of tradition. This new form of dichotomization is not about free-floating signifiers circulating around the world; rather it is defined by neocolonial and imperial global forces that are justifying war, militarism, and social injustice. Western egalitarian feminism is invested in and complicit with unifying notions of the West as free, secular, democratic, and modern. Islamic fundamentalism has become "the name" for a unified Islamic world, which is unfree, religious, oppressed, and traditional.

The signifier of "woman" remains central in both discourses, defining the boundaries of modern/traditional, secular/religious, free/unfree, and civilized/barbaric. This dichotomous logic has disastrous consequences both in the West and in the Islamic world. First of all, the association of fundamentalism with Islam undermines the powerful presence of various forms of fundamentalism in the West and disguises their relationship with liberal, democratic political orders. Secondly, by defining the West as secular and the Islamic world as religious, Western modernity claims hegemony over other forms of modernity, as it represents itself as a bounded entity containing its own conflicting principles. Thirdly, while both Western egalitarian feminism and Islamic fundamentalism are sites of debate and dissent, such dichotomous discursive performances are part of the modern cultural imaginary and political reality of the binary production of the West and the non-West, justifying the global hegemony of the West. Indeed, a number of postcolonial and transnational feminist scholars have produced substantial critiques of the Eurocentric notions of those Western feminists who conceive of the women's liberation movement as a purely West European and North American phenomenon. These scholars have challenged the hegemonic power of the West in representing its others and called for an understanding of geopolitical inequalities (Grewal and Kaplan 1994, 1996; Minh-ha 1989; Mohanty 1991a and 1991b; and Spivak 1988a and 1988b). Mainstream feminist literature, however, is still dominated by egalitarian feminist notions of freedom and liberation. Finally, there is an urgent need for critical feminist intervention in the discursive and political practices that claim a version of history based on the fraternal conception of time and space. As I explained in the introduction, while in recent years feminist scholars have contributed to an understanding of nationalism, feminism, and fundamentalism, the response of numerous feminists and womanists to such events as September 11, the war in Afghanistan, and the military occupation of Iraq shows the extent to which both nation and territorial nationalism are still taken for granted as sites of identification for Western feminism. The mobilization of antifeminist Christian fundamentalist groups who have now established missionary schools to protect, educate, and civilize Afghani or Iraqi women is the most worrisome consequence of this situation.

Global Cultural Encounters with Feminism and Fundamentalism

Moving beyond the dichotomization of feminism and fundamentalism as two separate and antagonistic positions, I define both Western egalitarian feminism and Islamic fundamentalism as regimes of truth that are inconsistent in their desire for change and closure. I argue that for both of them a desire to question what is intolerable in modernity merges with a desire to construct new absolutes, postponing the question of ethical responsibility in determining interdependence and autonomy for others. As I explained in the introduction, I am critical of hegemonic definitions of fundamentalism as either uniquely Islamic or defined only by religion. I do not see fundamentalism as an archaic, traditional, or antimodern phenomenon. I agree with scholars such as Butalia who insist that we need to explore the many layers of sedimented ideologies that lie within us, including ways in which we talk about groups such as the "Hindu right" as distant and distinct from secularists or the liberal intelligentsia (1995, 61). I am arguing that feminism and fundamentalism are neither uniquely secular nor uniquely religious phenomena.[17] They include a plurality of discourses and practices. Whereas egalitarian feminism emerges from a discourse of universalism (a discourse marked by latent masculinism) aimed at achieving human equality worldwide, Islamic fundamentalist discourse prioritizes its own difference, insists on its cultural uniqueness, and opposes any assimilation of modernity, modernization, and Westernization. Thus, the equality/difference pairing of modernity becomes indeterminate in both feminist and fundamentalist discourses.[18]

Neither feminism nor fundamentalism is exclusively located in the West or in the Middle East.[19] They oppose transnational worldviews, located in the "West" and the "East." Both are located within and beyond the borders of the nation-state. Both have found a place within different religious systems of meaning and their secularist counterparts.[20] Both are matrices within which a constant process of subject formation takes place.

Feminism and fundamentalism have cross-fertilized each other to create hybrids, that is, a feminism with fundamentalist elements and a fundamentalism with feminist elements. Even though for some critics any interpenetration between feminism and fundamentalism is a conceptual scandal, hybrid varieties exist. Many fundamentalist women renegotiate their place in society within a fundamentalist discourse by using mainstream feminist concepts such as patriarchy and male chauvinism.[21] Likewise, many feminists assume culturalist positions that are informed by fundamentalism and depend on the idea of an essentialized, nurturing femininity, often associated with a glorious matriarchal past. Consider, for example, the notions of goddess worship as "a symbol of the affirmation of the legitimacy and beauty of female control" (Christ 1979, 278; Starhawk 1989); "Womanspirit" (Christ and Plaskow 1979); and "mother-child love" as "passionate, sensual and personal love" (Starhawk 1979, 264). For these kinds of feminism and fundamentalism, a nonnegotiable fictive past determines the vision of the future.

Certain white feminists also rely on an essentialist notion of the category "woman," which leads to rigidification of gender categories.[22] It should be noted that an oppositional form of feminist work, which has emerged in the wake of critiques by women of color or Third World feminists in the United States, converges sometimes with fundamentalism in its critique of the equality paradigm and the fetishization of womanhood and sometimes with egalitarian feminism in its universalistic notions of woman. For example, Alice Walker, in her definition of *womanist* as opposed to *feminist*, essentializes woman as being "emotionally flexible and traditionally universalist" (1990, 370). While the literature of women of color has challenged the modernist idea of the unified self through its discussion of racial difference, the continued investment in the concept of woman as foundational to subject formation perpetuates a fundamentalist logic.

Both feminist fundamentalists and fundamentalist feminists are constrained in their negotiation of women's issues and complicit in perpetuating existing power relations, either by sustaining the boundaries of a totalistic ideology (as in the case of fundamentalist feminists) or by creating restricted boundaries through a replacement of patriarchy with matriarchy or limiting women's issues to only one set of social relations (male/female relationships) and thus putting an end to any constructive sociological discussion.[23] In this context I want to problematize not only fundamentalism for—among other things—the construction of a false totality, but also feminism for its tendency to construct rigidified categories.

The Paradoxes Haunting
Feminism and Fundamentalism

In their attempts to address contemporary crises of identity, Western egalitarian feminism and Islamic fundamentalism begin from a similar critique of a global, rationalist, and universalistic order.[24] Both question the sexual objectification and commodification of women in a modernized, global patriarchy; both support women's control of their own bodies; both renounce the separation of private and public and attempt to create a direct relationship between individuals and the political community; both claim transnationalism in their attempt to reach people beyond the boundaries of the nation-state; and both acknowledge women's subjectivity and call for women's political participation. Accordingly, in this chapter, I explore the paradoxical, ambiguous nature of the relationship between feminism and fundamentalism to show how they sometimes function as rivals and antagonists, and sometimes as complicit forces. Feminists and fundamentalists alike insist on the value of the domestic and emotional work of women, yet come to very different conclusions about its place in society. Fundamentalists see women as the natural, inevitable providers of such work and perceive care of the home as the basis of social respectability and virtuousness for women and as intrinsic to their complementary role in the institution of heterosexuality. For example, Islamic fundamentalist women's demand for wages for housework in Iran recognizes the value of women's housework yet naturalizes housework as the responsibility of women and an extension of their femaleness. Feminists, to the contrary, problematize the social forces acting to produce the sexual division of labor. They question the discourse and practice of domestic work and caregiving, and they challenge the institution of domesticity that contains them.[25] However, while feminists have challenged the naturalness of domestic work, an examination of the impact of the sexual division of labor on women's political rights has not been a priority for many Western egalitarian feminists.[26]

There is a paradox in feminist and fundamentalist claims to the institutions of knowledge, however. The desire to know is influenced by the will to power, which both feminism and fundamentalism overtly reject. Feminists' access to the institutions of knowledge has created new sites for the interpretation and reinterpretation of various texts. Fundamentalists also endorse access to knowledge for all individuals—men and women—but minimize the possibility of interpretation. For example, in Iran, fundamentalist women (*hezbullahi*, or those belonging to the party of God) have been able to successfully lobby the Islamic state for women's participation in rituals such as the recitation of Quranic verses and *Mufatieh-el jenin* (Shia book of prayer) and for women's preaching gatherings (*rowzeh-e zananeh*) and communal religious performances led by local female Islamic experts.[27] However, fundamentalist women's commitment to Islamic nationalism and the ideology of gender complementarity has prevented them from breaking with the male-dominated interpretation of textual and clerical Islam.[28]

These challenges to modern dichotomies—material/spiritual, natural/cultural, secular/religious, public/private—aim at a holistic reading of gender relations. In creating an abstract, all-encompassing notion of "woman" or "women," both feminists and fundamentalists are complicit in constructing a discursive site for the consolidation of universals and particulars. While fundamentalist challenges to modern dichotomies find expression in the notion of an essentialized woman as a universal particular (who is universally defined by her cultural particularity), feminist claims to particular universals (women exist as particulars but function as a universal category), through notions such as "global sisterhood," become a site of struggle against a universalized patriarchy. For example, Rahnavard blames a corrupt system of Western capitalism for making woman "a sex object, a brainless doll, a mistress" (1990, 15). For Rahnavard, it is "the divine essence of womanhood as an infinite source of goodness" that is the source of gender identity (17). Such reference to womanhood as an essence is not far from the notion of global sisterhood in the universalizing discourse of Western global feminism. Global feminists' concept of women as a unified category victimized by a transhistorical and transcultural patriarchy is no less problematic than its fundamentalist counterpart. In this literature, metaphors of pain and suffering identify a victimized body of women, who are cast as oppressed regardless of their place within complicated networks of power relations. It is through the compassionate and voyeuristic gaze of Western feminists at the suffering body of "the other"—the mutilated body of the African woman, the burning body of suttee, the veiled body of the Muslim woman, and the constrained body of the Chinese woman—that the need for a global sisterhood is created. This position is not peculiar to second-wave feminism (Daly 1978; Dworkin 1974) but persists as a privileged site of feminist imperialism.[29]

A transnational feminist critical intervention, with respect to gender constructions within the Islamic nation and to the Western civilizing narratives of Muslim women as the ultimate victim and the "other" of free, Western women, can reveal how cultural perceptions of identity remain complicit with modern racial and sexual perceptions of subjectivity. Modern views of community, which rely on nationalization and transnationalization as processes that bring together a community of brothers and sisters to give meaning to a unified "we," depend on the friend/foe logic. Ideas of sisterhood, both in its local and global expressions, mask the reality of power relations and the ways in which power is invested in these categories to legitimize various forms of governmentality. The recognition of the heterogeneity of women and the historical specificity of their subjectivity is crucial to a feminist transnational perspective. However, sisterhood as a site for the transnational unification of women in relation to men is a trap where gender identity becomes fixed and then defined through the naturalization of fundamentalist and nationalist notions of we-ness. If sisterhood stands in opposition to fraternity, to the regime of brothers under the rule of the father, it still does not represent a break with either the state or the nation, because sisterhood, even its global configuration, is framed by what Derrida calls "a schematic of filiation" and a tacit relationship to some preexisting fraternal community (1997, viii). A schematic of filiation does make it possible for feminists to undermine their own complicity as sisters in the community of brothers before claiming a "global sisterhood." However, once located within the framework of the we-ness, even as oppositional, willing sisters, a sorority is bound to the claims of blood and soil, those central signifiers of national filiations. The language of filial kinship is by no means unique to Islamic nationalism and fundamentalism; it also underlies modernity and its regimes of governmentality. Islamic fundamentalism and modernity can function together to construct "willing subjects" capable of self-regulation and self-disciplining, regardless of whether their loyalty is to a transnational community of sisters or to a national community of brothers and sisters.

The sexual objectification of women's bodies by a global, rationalist, patriarchal order is an object of criticism for feminists and fundamentalists alike, since both groups are concerned with the body as a bearer of culture, religion, values, and morality.[30] For example, in the introduction to a well-known book on the Iranian constitution, respect for family and motherhood is mandated in an effort to eradicate the objectification and exploitation of women by valuing their contribution as mothers in raising ideological (*maktabi*, following the Islamic doctrine) human beings (*Qavanin va Moqarrat-e vijeh zanan* [Specific Law and Regulation on Women in the Islamic Republic of Iran] 1999, 15). This line of thinking reflects the position of many fundamentalist women who participated in the revolution and actively supported the Islamic Constitution. They believe that they will gain subjecthood by being recognized as equal to but different from men.

Fundamentalists reappropriate women's bodies and impose on them a particular form of femininity that dictates their communal duties and responsibilities in exchange for the social gratification of maternity and motherhood. Egalitarian feminists' notion of an abstract and universal female body—biologically determined and socially subordinate through its reproductive capacity—converges with the fundamentalist position, yet seeks to overcome such restrictions through new technologies or changes in power relations. Whereas fundamentalists call for women's control of women's bodies and their reproductive capacities, feminists question the patriarchal construction of the female body in order to dismantle the machinery that turns a female body into a feminine one. If for fundamentalists the body is a stable site of gender identity, for feminists the body is a site of femaleness opposing the patriarchal construction of femininity. Although egalitarian feminists' idea of the body as a site of true femaleness or maleness converges with its fundamentalist counterpart, feminism's concern about the patriarchal construction of normative femininity provides space for a rethinking of gendered bodies. For social constructionist feminists and deconstructive feminists, this critique becomes a site of theorizing. Foucault's (1979a) notion of disciplinary practices producing "docile bodies," in particular the notion of "gendered embodiment," has flourished in feminist literature. For example, Grosz argues that the body or bodies are not ahistorical, precultural, and natural objects but are produced by various historical and cultural representations and inscriptions (1994, x and xi). Sandra Lee Bartky uses the Foucauldian notion of the docile body to examine "those disciplinary practices that produce a body which in gesture and appearance is recognizably feminine" (1990, 65).

Both feminists and fundamentalists draw upon historical memory, theological texts, legal practices, cultural spaces, and the symbolism of the body to control, define, and negotiate sexualized and gendered bodies, as well as to create discursive sites around motherhood, sexual identity, femininity, and masculinity. Fundamentalists deploy history to reinforce the sovereignty of the sexual binary and the naturalness of heterosexuality in the face of the anomalies of homosexuality, bisexuality, and transsexuality; feminists use history to trace the social disciplinary practices involved in the symbolic and material marking of bodies in the process of genderization and sexualization. Female bodies are particularly important in both feminist and fundamentalist discourses because of the issue of control of reproductive forces. Fundamentalist and nationalist ideologies in defense of a "right to life" speak of the fetus as a human being and of "threats against the nation"; they consider the female body an incubator for children and the object of collective surveillance. Western egalitarian feminists advocate technological innovation or ideological equalization to facilitate women's control of their bodies.[31]

As feminism and fundamentalism move beyond the boundaries of the nation-state, they envision two radically opposed notions of transnationalism. Feminists embrace the idea of a global oppositional discourse of all women directed against patriarchy. In this view, women are the other of the nation—an "otherness" within the "we-ness"—and seek solidarity under the sign of alterity (this otherness). Fundamentalist transnationalism transcends the political boundaries of the nation-state to invoke a particularistic form of community, namely "the community of God." In this sense, fundamentalist transnationalism fails to break with nationalism vis-à-vis the control of women. Nationalist fundamentalists regard women as an important force for group cohesion and continuity and encourage women to transmit group values to their children. Thus, a group can share its identity through the conduit of women's bodies and women's powers of social reproduction.[32]

The nation-state, that important site of modernity, has been at the core of legal constructions of what is permitted and prohibited for men and women alike. Both feminism and fundamentalism contribute to the crisis of legitimation, which Bhabha calls "the unbearable ordeal of the collapse of certainty" at this historical conjuncture (1994, 149). For both groups (feminists and fundamentalists), citizenship depends on how individuals stand not only before the law but before the common good, the moral, and the ethical. While egalitarian feminists have sided with the absolutist universalism of modernity, their universalistic impulse has been questioned by fundamentalists who assert the relativity of values as the condition for the perception of the intolerable and hence moral action.[33] This fundamentalist criticism of modern universalist absolutism is in fact predicated on a particularistic absolutism. An ethic of responsibility and an ethic of care are no sooner articulated by societies than these ethics are surrendered to God-given categories. For example, the idea of mothering as woman's God-given responsibility disguises the ways in which women's care is social work, thus preventing it from becoming the ethical responsibility of all citizens, which in turn perpetuates gender division of labor as well as gender domination. Egalitarian feminists criticize the modern universalistic discourse of human rights for its exclusion of women, yet they contain women under the same kind of universalist rubric in the exclusion of geopolitical and cultural differences from their arguments. Complicit with modernity, the two groups uphold absolute values and generate a transcendental ethic in a social world that produces moral subjects by forming, packaging, and protecting them. Subjects that are produced in this process by a particular regime of knowledge are considered and assumed to be coherent and recognizable.

For feminism and fundamentalism, ethical issues are political. Fundamentalists base ethical standards in moral authority and agency in a faith that demands self-sacrifice. They assert, therefore, the priority of morality over politics. Feminist consciousness, on the contrary, has been marked by the experience of ethical ambiguity and a form of moral agency based on historical specificity, singularity, alienation, and reflexivity.[34] There is nevertheless a convergence between fundamentalist and feminist responses to the contemporary crisis of morality in that both address the moral questions that surround "caring activities."[35] The modern subordination of the private sphere and the family to the public sphere and the state is intolerable for the two positions. However, fundamentalism becomes complicit with modernity in its refusal to call for the emergence of an ethic of male responsibility toward women to correspond to an ethic of female care of men, because it would separate gender roles from gender ideologies. It justifies caring as the essentialized, God-given role of motherhood and wifehood, leaving masculinity unchallenged.

Fundamentalist women build on the idea that women and men are created differently and, as a result, should be assigned different positions in society. According to Vakili, it is through a return to this nature, which is by definition the result of divine creation, that women are able to find their true value and status in society (1991, 9–11). This argument does not, of course, preclude the possibility or existence of patriarchy as an oppressive system imposed on women, but it does state that Islam as a religion is by definition antipatriarchal (Vakili 1991, 10). This position relies extensively on the things said or the pronouncements made about women by the male Muslim elite. Almost all the references listed in the literature associated with this position are based on what Mernissi calls a "sexist Muslim memory" that is found in the Islam of the middle classes, the *ulamas* (religious savants) of the cities, and town dwellers for whom women have no right to equality (1996, 79–80). Men stand outside the sphere of caring, while women's citizenship becomes domesticated. Fundamentalists work to revitalize "women's morality" by insisting on the primacy of morality over politics, while feminists prioritize politics over morality in their elaboration of an "ethic of care" and the private as the domain of "political life."

Feminism valorizes women's subjectivity and political participation as individuals in an emancipatory process marked by change and uncertainty, while the fundamentalist understanding of subjectivity is tied to social prescriptions narrowly prescribed by a faith that offers certainty. The First International Congress of Women and Islamic Revolution in 1987 (17 Bahman 1366) generated a twelve-section declaration, which included an important passage:

We, the Muslim women, consider Islam and the holy Quran as the most completed guideline for humans to free themselves from oppression and exploitation. Learning the Quranic sciences is the most important thing on the agenda for Muslim women of the world as the educators of the future generations. We question all Western and Eastern patterns for women, since they are produced by superpowers and heretic orders, and recognize Hazrat-e Fatima, the prophet's daughter, as the role model of all women of the world, and we use her life as a practical guide to our personal and social development. We emphasize the preservation of Islamic virtue, chastity, and *Hijab* for all Muslim women, and we see the development of Islamic society as conditioned upon women's chastity and *hijab*. We condemn those oppressive and unjust countries that prevent women from entering scientific and cultural centers because of the Islamic veiling, which is the symbol of resistance against blasphemy and arrogance, and urge them to respect all human and Islamic rights of women. (*Namah-I inqilab-I Islami* 8, no. 45, 1366 [1988])

In this passage, women are invited to actively participate in the political, social, and cultural life of the Muslim communities. However, this participation is conditioned upon their acceptance of women's chastity and *hijab* as the most important components of Muslim identity. The subject that emerges in this context requires a quite particular interrogation: Why are these two particular values extracted from the holy Quran as universal values for women? Who decides what is women's most important responsibility in preserving Islamic virtue? Which forces are involved in this process? And what if such definitions of Islamic feminine virtue are produced historically by a male-dominated culture?

Fundamentalists and feminists share preoccupations characteristic of modernity—the insistence on man's participation in the political community, the importance of its categories of consciousness, agency, responsibility, and choice, and the inclusion of women as equal participants in the political sphere. In this sense both grapple with problems of modernity, one by attempting to create absolute values and the other by trying to resolve the tension between equality and difference.

The Spectrum of Equality versus Difference

> I would say that the future of a philosophy that is no longer anti-feminist is being performed somewhere in the direction of Brechtian drama, which . . . produces unfinished plays which always have a missing act and are consequently left wide open to history.
>
> Michele Le Doeuff (1977, 8)

Western egalitarian feminism and Islamic fundamentalism are not unmediated discursive spaces. They are haunted by the phantoms and monsters of modernity. They each have their own horizons and contradictions. Feminism and fundamentalism are ideologically positioned discourses that serve to destabilize modernity and at the same time contain the chaotic situation arising from the basic contradictions of modernity. Within the spectrum of equality, the category of difference emerges to put feminism in crisis; within the fundamentalist spectrum of difference, the category of equality emerges to create a crisis.

While both discourses reject a feminine ideal characterized by passivity and powerlessness, Western egalitarian feminism and Islamic fundamentalism adopt diametrically opposed views of women's subjectivity. Fundamentalism invites women to adopt a religious sense of identity and to enter a predetermined realm of identification, whereas Western egalitarian feminists have a conception of subjectivity based on an understanding of women as free, rational, and self-determining subjects. Both positions encourage women to take steps to transform their outlook and consciousness for the better in order to lead happy lives. In feminism, the goal of the process is to become an individual; in fundamentalism, to gain membership in a God-given community. Feminist and fundamentalist views of subjectivity are complicit with modern Western epistemological ideas of subjectivity in transforming "a happy consciousness" into "a joyous consciousness," in the Hegelian sense[36]—that is, a consciousness that turns a "fact" into a "contradiction" (Bartky 1990). However, this consciousness remains constrained in not recognizing its own contradictory social location as both victim and victimizer.[37] While Islamic fundamentalists offer women subject positions as devoted agents in the consolidation of a God-given community, egalitarian feminists affirm individuality as the site of subjectivity.

In this play of mirrors reflecting a gendered conceptualization of modernity, the supposition of a transnational Islamic womanhood underpinned by religious community emerges to join the egalitarian feminist notion of global sisterhood. However, the idea of a transnational womanhood with a logic of equality (in feminism) or difference (in fundamentalism) lacks an understanding of the very discourses in which such subject positions are constructed. In the last decade, hegemonic Western feminism has been challenged by the critical writing of antiracist, anti-imperialist, postcolonial, and postmodernist feminisms. The constant effort to deconstruct "woman" as a category by underlining white Western women's complicity in the formation of an ethnocentric and imperialist order is part of the contemporary feminist identity crisis.[38] In Iran, the transition of Islamic fundamentalism from an oppositional social movement to a hegemonic state ideology has created fragmentation and contradictions in fundamentalist transnationalism. Over the last few years, Iranian Islamic fundamentalists have had serious difficulty reconciling their transnationalist claims of Islamic particularity and unity with the demands of a class- and gender-based nation-state.

Feminism and fundamentalism cannot avoid mirroring each other in their challenges to sexual objectification: feminists denounce femininity as a site of objectification, and fundamentalists retreat into the gratification of womanhood. The separation between the ontological as a site of fundamentalist recognition of the feminine self and the epistemological as a site of feminist consciousness has culminated in mutually exclusive forms of subjectivity.[39] Feminism's conscious effort to resist domesticity is matched by the position of domesticity as a site of subjectivity in fundamentalism. In fact, feminism's critique produces the valorization of the object of the critique in fundamentalism, that is, the promise of a new pleasure in motherhood and domesticity. In this sense, fundamentalism has become subversive in relation to its feminism because it allows women to take pleasure in what is prohibited to them in feminism. But while signifiers of domesticity are at the center of feminist and fundamentalist discourses and practices, the importance of such signifiers in the symbolic unconscious is left undisturbed. Both feminists and fundamentalists undermine the complexity of women's desire by emphasizing their political vision and by imposing an ideal order based on consciousness-raising and intentionality.

It is important to recognize the interplay of dominated and subordinated masculinities and femininities in the new forms of globalization and in the encounter between feminism and fundamentalism. Fundamentalists depend on the mobilization of the subordinated masculinity of colonized or emasculated men (in this case Muslim men) to counter the hegemonic masculinity of colonial modernity—white, European, and Christian—and overcome the challenge of equality from the feminist subject position by making female subjectivity disappear. However, the speaking subject of feminism cannot escape the unconscious mechanisms of culture, nation, class, and sexuality, or its own momentary relationship to socio-economic conditions and their concomitant effects in lived experience. Facing the inequality of modernity, the speaking subject of feminism can be reconciled with fundamentalism as it attempts to line up a fixed subject position for every single situation. Feminism is haunted by subject positions that are components of the radical singularity of a lived life in the symbolic unconscious, by subject positions that are always conflicted, complicit, and contradictory. I am not referring to the unconscious as a repertoire of repressed content that can simply be manipulated and regulated by a rationalized subject, but rather to the complex relation between the subject/individual and its socio-historical constitution and epistemological instability.

At the Intersection of History and Memory

I am calling for transnational feminist theories and practices to be based on historicity, subjectivity, and the linkage between a macro- and micro-political and relational articulation of nation, race, gender, class, and sexuality. Layoun's concept of "theoretical narratological competence" is useful for such an analysis:

Narratives are internally and externally conflictual whatever their medium. There are no foregone and conclusive master narratives though there are, clearly, dominant or hegemonic narratives. Internally, narratives attempt to contain their constituent elements—actors, actions, story past, and present, narrative space—within "an orderly" and "naturally" self-justifying framework. But they are also spoken or written or played out from multiple perspectives, not all of which are equal, or equally convincing. . . . The workings of narrative and narratological competence are learned, socially shaped, and always partial; they are interjected, articulated, and acted out or practiced in various ways. The competence in question is not simply chosen and "performed" individually from an unlimited array of possibilities but is discursively and practically constructed— and theorized—in speaking, thinking, and acting. (1992, 413–14, 412)

The identitarian claims of fundamentalism and feminism do not necessarily disrupt the logic of capital or of the nation-state, with its exclusionary notions of citizenship, as long as the subject does not discern its own complicity in its suppression of alterity, its own noncontradictoriness. Such a subject position remains imprisoned and self-contained because it is cut off from the historical and the geopolitical.[40]

The survival of fundamentalism is conditional upon a communitarianism based on the exclusion of women as individuals and their inclusion as "selfless others." The survival of feminism, on the contrary, depends upon its ability to embrace a transnationalism rooted in the recognition of the intersecting social relationships of nation, race, ethnicity, class, gender, and sexuality and the positionality of the self. In this global war of representation, in order for feminism to subvert fundamentalism, it has to recognize, understand, criticize, and disrupt sites where it is itself liable to complicitous, fundamentalist rigidification.

Islamic particularistic fundamentalism and Western universalizing feminism are undercut by multiple forms of transnational subjectivities and resistance to the new forms of subjugation. The fetishization of the unitary individual and the universalization and rigidification of totalizing categories potentially lead feminism to a fundamentalist politics of closure and a simple inversion of the moral superiority of feminism, thereby leaving space for a fundamentalist, hegemonic community to rule. For example, the Western feminist claims to the simplistic formulas of a universal category of women undermine the particular historical disciplinary practices that produce feminine bodies in different geopolitical locations and open up space for the particularistic display of cultural difference as a spectacle of agency and subjectivity. Fundamentalist women's self-imposition of inegalitarian disciplinary practices becomes a place where the social construction of the feminine body at the intersection of history and memory is concealed, thus serving the interest of patriarchal domination.

Whose Sister? Whose Brother? What Subject?

> In my opinion, the reconciliation of feminism and Islam at this particular conjuncture is important. Even until recently, "feminist" was an insult in Iran, but we have tried to discuss feminism in our magazine without taking sides, by opening up the discussion about the various tendencies active today in order to familiarize our people with this issue. Also, we should know what kind of feminism we are talking about and which interpretation of Islam we are referring to. I do not believe that feminism is only a Western phenomenon. Feminism is growing in Islamic countries. In every region of the world there has emerged an indigenous feminism, and women in various countries are not forced to identify with a Western woman's experience and to consume a prefabricated remedy.
>
> Shahla Sherkat, chief editor of *Zanan* magazine
> (Berlin, April 2000)

The plurality of positions articulated by Muslim women contradicts the supposition that Muslim women's participation in Iranian political and cultural life is unified and consistent with official interpretations of Islam. One of the most interesting aspects of the Iranian situation has been the emergence of Islamic feminism. The phrase *Islamic feminism* is a contradiction in terms for both Islamic fundamentalists and secular feminists, because a convergence of Islam and feminism is a conceptual impossibility that each characterizes as an "invasion." Bringing Islam and feminism into the same frame of reference has caused a predictably hysterical reaction from Iranian modernists as well from anti-West fundamentalists. As a result of such convergence, the modern dichotomies of secular/religious, tradition/modernity, and Islam/West have come up against their own conceptual limits. As Najmabadi argues, a consciously formulated, tactical concession in resisting the urge to draw a line between what constitutes the Islamic and the un-Islamic has been indeed in the interest of activists working for social change in Iran (2000, 32). In this context, the notions of Islam and feminism as predetermined, unified systems of meaning have been strained by everyday discourses that challenge patriarchal masculinist interpretations of religion and culture.

I do not wish to engage either with those secularist feminists who promote a fundamentalist reading of Islam by viewing it as a closed meaning system or, by the same token, with those Islamic fundamentalists who take their own interpretation of Islam as the truth. What I will address in this section, albeit briefly, are those feminist positions that refuse to engage with the cultural constructions of race, gender, sexuality, and class in modernity either by separating the world of ideas and discourses from the material world of political economy or by not investigating the genealogy of dichotomies at work in colonial modernity. For example, an Iranian feminist scholar, Haideh Moghissi, states in her analysis of Islamic feminism that it has invaded the secular intellectual agenda and reflects a profound defeatism, which presumes the end of secularist liberal and socialist projects in Islamic societies (1999, 10). For her, any convergence between feminism and Islam puts an end to modern social formations, such as feminism, secularism, and socialism. While she echoes the critique of the universalizing tendencies in feminism, she ignores the ways in which the secular liberal and the socialist projects to which she refers unproblematically have been defined by the modernist opposition drawn between religion and secularism, not to mention that between religion and culture. Indeed, the dichotomy of religion and nonreligion has provided a speaking position for fundamentalism and, at the same time, produced religious subjects. Indeed, the taken-for-granted conceptualization of secularism that many Iranian feminists refer to needs a careful historical examination in the context of Iranian modernity and cannot be extracted from its Western forms. The word *ghair-e mazahabi*, or nonreligious, does not adequately address the issue; and the word *secularism*, which is used without translation in Farsi these days, does not reflect the history of the nation-state in Iran.[41]

There is an urgent need for Iranian feminists and gender activists to deconstruct the hegemony of modernist paradigms and their regimes of visibility, including the myth of progress and the dichotomies of secular and religious and tradition and modernity. In addition, while some Iranian feminists have been able to create collaborative networks between Iranian feminists who live in Iran and those who live in the diaspora, the power relations of such exchanges remain unexamined. Transnational feminist theories and practices require recognition of these power relations and their impact on representational practices. A number of Iranian feminist networks, both in Iran and in the diaspora, have gone beyond the dichotomy of the homeland and the diaspora in their analysis of gender and women's issues. These networks, however, are prone to become new comfort zones either for the celebration of identity or the supposition of feminist unity. Such practices have become new sites of transnational nationalization by supporting notions of sisterhood that are based on ideological alliances and coalition-building rather than recognition of conflicts and unequal access to power.[42]

As I mentioned, the transition of Islamic groups in Iran from oppositional social movements to the power behind a hegemonic state ideology has created fragmentation and contradictions in Islamic cultural nationalism and transnationalism. The Islamic state has had serious difficulty reconciling the transnationalist claims of Islamic particularity and unity with the demands of a class-, ethnic-, and gender-based nation-state. The election of March 1997, when the massive participation of women allowed for the election of President Khatami, who was known to be more open to a hermeneutic reading of Islam, is a reflection of this crisis. In an interview in the Japanese daily *Asahi Shimbun*, Faezeh Hashemi states: "Men have always been those who interpreted Islamic law; they were the main Islamic scholars, and they were the ones who implemented these interpretations, and, therefore, they manipulated Islamic law" (Feb. 6, 1997). The idea of "with veil but active in all spheres of society" has facilitated women's presence in public (Kadivar 1996, 226). Interestingly enough, although Iranian women require permission from their fathers and husbands to leave the country under the Islamic Republic, nine women were able to apply for the presidency. The Council of Guardians must approve all presidential candidates, and the women were rejected by all male members of the council.[43] By exhibiting a willingness to lead the country and by provoking men's hostility to their participation in politics, Iranian women have succeeded in bringing to the public's attention the contradictory claims of the Islamic state that women are equal participants in the political structure of the Islamic state.

Islamic feminists in Iran join numerous women's movements in the Middle East, South Asia, and elsewhere in their desire to bring together Islam and feminism as a site of feminist political intervention. Emerging out of Islamic fundamentalism and its call for an informed agency and militant activism, Islamic feminism distances itself from the antifeminist agenda of fundamentalism by its contestation of both Islam and feminism. Calling for the "reconciliation of feminism and Islam" and the articulation of an indigenous Islamic feminism, Iranian women have been able to negotiate various cultural, legal, and economic expressions of patriarchy. A number of Iranian feminists and gender activists have refused to use the spectacle of the other woman (in this case, Western women) to represent gender and women's issues in Iran. A careful examination of such positions requires ethnographic research about the various agents, as well as the political and representational strategies they deploy.

In the Islamic Republic, women now negotiate gendered notions of citizenship in the political sphere. Issues of legal rights and equal political participation are at the center of these negotiations. While women's particularity and difference are presupposed in the dominant political sphere, Islamic political and legal discourses have brought into focus the intolerable gendered frames of meaning and have been countered by the Islamic state.

Homogenizing conceptions of Muslim women must be reconciled with the reality of women who identify with different interpretations of Islam. The two major questions at the center of these negotiations concern equality before Islamic law and leadership. With the inclusion of women in the traditional religious schools and the political sphere, exclusionary gender practices in the realm of political and religious leadership have been challenged. A number of Muslim women writers, scholars, jurists, and political activists have offered alternative, egalitarian interpretations regarding the position of women in Islam. Two strategies are used in such discussions; one highlights the contradictory statements in Islamic discourse and questions the biases of the male elite, while the other publicizes the point of view of those religious leaders, in Iran or elsewhere in the Muslim world, who have argued for a more egalitarian vision of Islam vis-à-vis women (Kadivar 1996; Kar 2000b, 1997; Ebadi 1994). For example, by juxtaposing human rights and the Islamic Republic's constitutional laws, Shirin Ebadi, an Iranian lawyer and legal scholar, foregrounds the inconsistencies of the Iranian constitutional and civic laws in confronting sexism (1994). Feminist legal scholar Mehranghiz-e Kar also elaborates on the limits of the Islamic republic civic laws in her discussion of the political rights of Iranian women (1997). Popular women's magazines, including *Zanan, Payam-e Hajar,* and *Payam-e zan,* have exposed their readers to a more egalitarian view of Islam in their interviews, articles, and editorials. Interviews with religious scholars and clergy, such as Hojat ol-Eslam Sa'idzadeh, editor-in-chief of *Payam-e zan*,[44] who is well known among women activists for his writings on women's issues, his knowledge of feminism, and his refutation of Islamic jurisprudence that opposes the principle of equality, provide examples of the efforts to open up fundamentalist notions of religion to alternative interpretations.[45]

Clerical Islam has established itself in postrevolutionary Iran through the construction of a cultural, nationalist revolutionary will to rule in the name of Islam, a will that both includes and excludes women. Inclusion of women as gendered subjects or sisters in a community of brothers enables religion to protect itself from the masses of young, educated women who read, interpret, produce, and consume religion in many different ways. By assigning gender-specific roles to women and by mediating between Islamic texts and women, clerics continue to privilege their own interpretation of religion, which has a significant impact on the realms of politics, law, and economics. Knowledge is the key to admittance to the realm of power, and thus control of the channels of knowledge is crucial for future gender negotiations. While certain male clerics, such as those who contribute to *Payam-e zan* magazine, challenge inegalitarian interpretations of Islamic law and Islamic jurisprudence, women have not yet been able to participate significantly in these negotiations, since they were only able to enter the Jame'at al-Zahra and Zahra Theological College in 1986. The outcome of women's theological scholarship and their perspectives on theological and legal issues will need careful examination. The determination of the role of the "knower" or religious savant is still controlled by the religious male elite, which has guaranteed itself a modern role by juxtaposing religion and politics under the hegemonic leadership of *marja'e taghlid*. However, such control of knowledge has been challenged by the recent idea of the "religious intellectual." As a concept, religious intellectualism has provided space for the intervention in the construction of a political will of an educated and knowledgeable group of men and women who have not been trained by the religious schools yet are able to articulate their religious views in civil society. Rhetorically, gender and women's issues have found a place within this discourse, which has opened up the fundamentalist reading of religion to historically contingent and plural willing subjects.

The pressure on intellectuals to take a position on women's issues has created space for a productive discussion of gender issues in the Islamic regime. This intellectual trend, which is also called "innovative religious thinking," is based on the advocacy of a thoughtful relation to religion that takes into consideration the recognition of human reason and experience as well as the recognition of interaction between religion and the realities of everyday experience (interview with Mohamad Javad-e Kashi, *Zanan*, no. 61, 2001, 1).

An early instance of the public discussion of women's issues can be found in one of the first editorials in the magazine *Zanan* (Sherkat 1991). The editor-in-chief, Shahla Sherkat, writes: "We believe that the key to the resolution of women's problems is in the four following fields: religion, culture, law, and education" (2–3). While Sherkat points out that until very recently the term "feminist" was considered an insult in Iran, I believe that it is time to reconcile feminism with Islam (Sherkat 2000, 127). Discursive juxtaposition is the key here, since the discourse on Islamic rights has entered the same frame as the discourse on human rights (vis-à-vis women). By this very fact, a space is created for the legal temporalization of Islam. According to Gorgi and Ebtekar, while the Quran is a source of absolute consensus among the various schools of Islam, its laws and decrees take a generalized form and are subjected to interpretation (1994, 146).

The wide-ranging positions expressed on women's issues by prominent male scholars and leaders of religious intellectualism have created debate in the cultural sphere. This intellectual current recognizes the plurality of positions in the Islamic world. According to Ali Reza Alavi Tabar, three major hermeneutic currents characterize the contemporary Islamic world: fundamentalism, traditionalism, and innovationism (*Zanan*, no. 65 [2001], 1). While Islamic fundamentalism has been successful in reinforcing the inequality of men and women, religious intellectuals have begun to challenge fundamentalism. In Alavi Tabar's view, this process has created new forms of political and cultural alliances between members of the Islamic clergy (*Rohaniyat*) and Islamic intellectuals as they claim a political position that is supportive of the current reform movement in Iran.[46]

Although fundamentalist interpretations of Islam persistently resist compromise and claim to represent the "true Islam," which is not subject to interpretative practices, the incessant activism of Iranian women has had a great impact in creating space for discussions about political citizenship. In addition to political and legal negotiations, women have tried to enhance their knowledge of their civil and Islamic rights in relation to marriage, divorce, alimony, mutual responsibilities, and custody, as in, for example, the series of booklets produced by the Group for the Study of Women's Issues. These booklets are prepared in an accessible language to introduce women to their rights under Islamic law. In addition, frequent interviews on women's rights in Islam with various religious leaders have been crucial in showing the diversity of views and interpretations of women's rights in Islam. For example, according to Ayatollah Bojnourdi, a prominent scholar of Islamic law, Fo-qaha or Shia scholars have had different viewpoints, and this is due to their independent interpretation of the holy Quran ("Figh and Women's Human Rights" 1997, 41).

Islamic feminism is itself a product of the modern temporalization of nationalism, liberalism, and humanism. Islamic feminism has the potential to go off in new directions or to bind itself securely with other systems of meaning. Nevertheless, transnational Muslim femininity transcends such negotiations and constructs global Islamic womanhood as a site of universalization. Such transnational femininity is instrumental in the commodification of Islamic identity politics in a late capitalist global market. Transnational Islamic womanhood—in its reliance on the binarism of Islam and the West—occludes the varied existences of Iranian women, both in Iran and in the Iranian diaspora.

The feminine body continues to be disciplined within the order of the gaze, which determines the normalization of an essentialized body by functioning outside the register of sight of particular bodies, splitting off both the national and the transnational from what Lowe calls "the unrepresentable histories of situated embodiment that contradict the abstract form of citizenship" (1996, 2).[47] In Iran, through the retelling of the Shia past, Fatima's mourning gives continuity to the community of God, since she witnesses the immortality and eternity of Imam Hussein, who gives himself the "gift of death."[48] Thus, access to an ethic of responsibility and citizenship is legitimized for previously emasculated Muslim men within and beyond the borders of the nation-state.[49] By blocking the emergence of an ethic of responsibility for women and by leaving men out of the sphere of caring, the Islamic ummat becomes complicit with modernity and its gender division of labor within and beyond the borders of the nation-states.

Although it has become the site of intensified negotiation and conflict in the synchronic temporality of performance, the civic body has a history that stretches back through time to a succession of different relations to Islamic womanhood. With a stronger reliance on production, advertising, and consumption based on identity politics, transnational concepts of Islamic womanhood have created new consumer subjects within the context of a transnational civil society. The civic body has thus become the location of national and transnational forms of cultural difference and its commodification in late capitalism.[50] The abstract civic body has taken precedence over the material body because discussion of the material body would entail recognition of practices of cultural domination and economic exploitation. In either its particularized or universalized manifestations, the civic body exceeds citizenship, that is to say, citizenship is viewed as excess, or as the presence of the absence.

Postscript

The modern history of colonialism, imperialism, and material exploitation based on the sexual, racial, national, and international division of labor has been shaped by different regimes of representation. The representational practices at play, from racism and Orientalism to nationalism and fundamentalism, have become dancing partners with consumer capitalism. Gender identities and subjectivities are at the center of this dance, involving feminists, womanists, nationalists, fundamentalists, and others. Heroic notions of individualism converge with romantic notions of community to create yearning and desire for escape from the boredom of consumption.

Zahra Rahnavard, whose work I have referred to throughout this project, once charged the West with being a system where women are made into "decorative objects." She calls upon her Muslim sisters to question what the "sham civilizations" have made of women, not to act like dolls, and not to display a debilitated will. She asks women to refuse to be part of the harems of the rulers and the communal harems of the streets. Her allusion to the collective appropriation of women in the streets and her rejection of unveiling have made it possible for her to think of the contractual structure of the Muslim family and veiling as sites of women's agency. For Rahnavard, it is through unveiling and Westernization that Muslim women have been turned into objects to be possessed by all men in the public sphere. To resist capitalist rulers and challenge sexual objectification, she asks women to return to veiling and the Muslim family, where women are considered subjects rather than objects of the marriage contract. Is it accidental that Zahra Rahnavard uses the signifier *harem* to talk about the Muslim family? Did she know, when she picked the veil as a signifier of resistance to consumerism and imperialism, that she would become complicit with the Islamic fashion industry? When she wrote about the economics of unveiling, did she know that she was trapped in the gaze of modernity and its ways of seeing? Or, was it the lure of a self-regulating liberal subject that made her to choose the "freedom to veil"?

In the May 2002 issue of *Vogue* magazine, an article entitled "Beneath the Burqua"[1] begins this way: "Near Chicken Street, a thoroughfare lined with shops in downtown Kabul, three burquas paused in front of me and peered out from the netting that covered their eyes. From behind the muffled blue nylon cloth, one spoke in halting English. What is your name? she said, what are you doing here? Her friend began to laugh. It sounded strange to hear something joyful coming from behind the burqua." After this surprising opener, which displays an obsession with the veil, the reporter relates how she finally got to talk to one of the three: "But the third, the bravest, the leader of the gang, rolled back the nylon to reveal a young girl in her twenties named Sahaila. Her hair was dyed blonde; she wore pink lipstick and blue eyeliner. She stared at me defiantly, a smile twitching at the corner of her lips, Ah, you see, she said, I am a person after all." The woman under the burqua only becomes a real person and achieves the status of subject for the reporter when the reporter sees that the young woman has bought into the signifiers of Western, white femininity—blonde dyed hair, blue eyeliner, and pink lipstick.

For the reporter from *Vogue* magazine, the conditions that open women up to objectification according to fundamentalists are the very conditions that lead to the possibility of subjecthood for Afghani women. These representational practices call upon Afghani women to take on the marks of white, Western femininity to become subjects, while for fundamentalists it is the negation of and the break from this subject position that constitute the subject.[2] If the moment of recognition of the subjecthood of the other is defined by the presence of representational signifiers of a white, Western subject position, then what conclusions can we draw about the significance of subjects constituted through engagement with such representational practices? Paradoxically, what if both compliance with and rebellion against this particular subject position are themselves constitutive of a desire based on self-fashioning, whereby the creation of taste, style, and emotional attachment to

particular notions of embodiment become a crucial part of social regulation and control? What would it mean for the order of domination and
resistance to determine the subject's relationship to the body? What if
the subject is produced by a certain conceptual necessity or a notion of
the past that closes the history? Or, is it possible to abandon the notion
of the subject altogether through transnational feminist pedagogies and
practices that incessantly expose the discrepancy between the subject as
produced by particular historical narratives and the relentless resistance
to such a regime of signification?

Glossary of Important
Names and Terms

Author's Note: A full study of the terms included in this glossary would require careful examination of religious texts, historical conditions, and cultural debates. The definitions I offer here are limited to the usage and circulation of these terms in the context of modern Iran and the Iranian revolution of 1979.

Ali Shari'ati (1933–1977)	Dr. Shari'ati was a modernist Iranian thinker and sociologist who opposed the shah's Westernization plans. His existentialist interpretation of Islam was popular among many revolutionary students. He was murdered by SAVAK (the shah's intelligence agency) in London in 1977. Sometimes referred to as the Fanon of Iran, Shari'ati's writings bring together Islam, modernity, and Third World revolutionary ideas. His writings include *Fatima Is Fatima, After Shahadat, What Is to Be Done?* and *Hajj.*
Allah-o Akbar	"God is great." *Allah-o Akbar* is repeated during the Muslim prayer at each change of position. This phrase was used during the Iranian revolution as the spiritual weapon of the masses in attacking enemies of Islam. During the Iran-Iraq war, it was used to build up courage in life-threatening situations.
Andarouni	Traditionally, middle- and upper-class houses assigned the outer part of the house, called the *biruni,* to men, and the inner part, called the *andarouni,* to women. Each space had its own doorway, and the two spaces were connected through a corridor, so that the kitchen could be accessed from both sides of the house.

Ashura
The tenth day of Muharam, when Imam Hussein was martyred. Iranian Shia Muslims commemorate this day by organizing parades in which men beat themselves bloody to recall the suffering of Imam Hussein and his family, singing tragic songs about his martyrdom. Women are spectators, watching the parade without taking an active role, but they express grief when they are moved by the scene.

Ayatollah Khomeini (1902–1989)
Ruhollah Musavi Khomeini was the leader of the Iranian revolution of 1979. A student of the Faiziyah Madreseh in Qum, he was arrested by the shah's regime in the 1963 Faiziyah raids, leading to riots in several cities. He was exiled to Iraq in 1964 as a result of his sermons, in which he opposed the shah's regime. He continued his political activities in exile and taught theology in Iraq until 1978. During the revolutionary insurgency, he left for Paris, later returning to Iran to lead the revolution. Khomeini returned to Iran on February 1, 1979, and was given the title Leader of the Revolution and Nayib-e Imam (*imam*'s representative).

Basiji
Mobilized to work for the Islamic revolution.

Bonyad-e Shahid
The Martyrs' Foundation, a state institution in charge of the welfare of martyrs' families.

Chador siah
The black chador, a long black veil covering the whole body except face, hands, and feet. Before the Iranian revolution, women used to wear floral, colorful, and sometimes very transparent chadors made from delicate tissues, including silk and lace. During and after the revolution, a thick black chador replaced all other versions and became the national dress for women.

Estekbar-e jahani
The powerful of the world.

Faghih
Scholar of Islamic jurisprudence.

Fatima
Fatima-ye Zahra (Fatima the Resplendent) was one of the three daughters of the prophet Muhammad, and was regarded by him as one of the four exemplary women in Islam. She married Muhammad's cousin, Ali-ibn Abi Talib, and is revered by both Shiites and Sunnis.

Ghafeleh-e tamadon
"Caravan of civilization." An evolutionary reference to civilization moving toward progress.

Ghalb-e tarikh	"The heart of history." This expression was used during the Iranian revolution as a cultural reminder that martyrs would always stay in the people's heart. The location of martyrs in the heart rather than the brain indicates Shiites' affective, embodied, and emotional commemorative practices.
Gharbzadeh	"Westoxicated," a cultural disease resulting from exposure to Western culture and values. The prominent Iranian intellectual and writer Jalal-e Al-e Ahmad (1923–1969) was the first to use this term in his influential book *Garbzadegi*. A partial version of the book was circulated in 1962 and the uncensored complete version was published during the Iranian revolution. The book criticized Iranian intellectuals for their loss of identity and their compliant assimilation to the West. To cure this disease, Al-e Ahmad proposed a return to indigenous identity and Islamic traditions. *Garbzadegi* was a popular term during and after the Iranian revolution. The project of Cultural Revolution and the "purification of the educational institutions" in the postrevolutionary era targeted those who were accused of being contaminated by the West and could not be cured. *Zan-e gharbzadeh* designates a Westoxicated woman.
Haram	Prohibited by Islamic law.
Hezbullahi	One who belongs to or believes in Hezbullah (Party of God). Hezbullah emerged in Iran during street demonstrations of 1979 and later formed militias.
Hijab	Literally, the veil that separates man from God. Its common meaning is the adherence to certain standards of Islamic women's dress (not necessarily the veil).
Imam	For Shiite Muslims, *imam* is the title of Ali and his descendants through Fatima, and refers to an intermediary between man and God with spiritual, mythical, and civil authority. In postrevolutionary Iran, *imam* has been used as a title for Ruhollah Khomeini and is an abbreviated form of *nayib-e imam* (*imam*'s representative).
Imam Hussein (624–680 A.D.)	The second son of Imam Ali and Hazrat-e Fatima, he was killed in Karbala on his way to Kufah in Iraq. His martyrdom has made him a tragic figure in Shia history. Every year, masses of Shia Muslims

	commemorate his death by organizing religious performances and parades.
Jahiliyya	The age of ignorance. Historically, this referred to the pre-Islamic era.
Jihad	Holy war, an inevitable war for the defense of what is sacred. Holy war relating to one's needs and desires is called *jihad-e akbar* (major jihad). Holy war directed against enemies of Islam is called *jihad-e asghar* (minor jihad). Holy war on one's passions or self-love is called *jihad-e nafs*.
Karbala-ye Husseini	A city in Iraq where Imam Hussein (the grandson of the Prophet Muhammad) and seventy-two companions were killed in 680 A.D. (the tenth day of Muharam in the sixty-first year of Hijrah). Karbala is the site of the holy tomb of the twelve Imam Shiites. The clay of Karbala is made into small stamps for prayer purposes.
Khaneh	House.
Khar Mazhab	Mindless follower of religion (one who follows religion like a donkey).
Laleh Zar	An old, narrow street in Tehran, where there were many women's clothing merchants, selling in particular women's underwear, which was exhibited publicly. It was also the location of some of the first nightclubs in Tehran.
Mafatieh-el Jenin	Shiite book of prayer.
Mahboob	The beloved.
Mahr	Dowry, a husband's economic obligation to pay the wife a certain amount agreed upon by both parties.
Maktabi	A term that emerged mainly during the revolution in Iran, *maktabi* refers to one who is indoctrinated in Islam. *Maktab* has two meanings: an Islamic primary school or a dogma or doctrine.
Mam-e Vatan	The motherland.
Mardanegi	Masculinity, as opposed to *zananegi* (femininity).
Marja'e taghlid	Literally means the reference point of emulation. In the Usuli school of Shiism, this refers to a religious authority who can arrive at unprecedented decisions in theology and religious law. A *marja'e taghlid* is followed by *muqallids* (followers). Each person chooses his or her own *marja'e taghlid*.

Mazdak (early 6th century A.D.)	A Persian priest and the leader of Zoroastrian Mazdaeism. Mazdak advocated dualism and was put to death, along with many of his followers. Because of his egalitarian views, Mazdak was revisited by socialist movements in Iran as an indigenous figure representing early socialist and communist ideals.
Mostakbar, mostakbaran	The rich and the powerful.
Mostaz'af, mostaz'afan	The poor and the powerless, the dispossessed.
Nafaqa	Economic support provided by the husband to the wife during the waiting period for divorce.
Pahlavi Regime (1924–1979)	A dynasty in Iran established by Reza Khan Pahlavi, a leader of an Army Cossack brigade and a dictator who sought to modernize Iran. Reza Shah was exiled at the beginning of World War II. His son, Mohammad Reza, replaced him, remaining in power until he was overthrown in the 1979 revolution.
Posht-e jebheh	"Behind the battlefield." This term was used during the Iran-Iraq war to recognize the contributions of those (such as women) who could not be at the front but contributed from behind the battlefield.
President Khatami (1943–)	President Khatami was elected the fifth president of the Islamic Republic of Iran in 1997 by a 70 percent majority, including a majority of the women's vote, and was reelected in 2000. His writings include *Az Donyay-e Shahr ta Shahr-e Donya* [From the World of the City to the City of the World] and *Gofteguy-e Tamadonha* [The Dialogue of Civilizations].
Raz va niyaz	Telling one's secrets, needs, and desires to another. It is used to refer to both amorous conversations or conversations with God.
Rohaniyat	A term that refers to the Islamic clergy in Iran. *Rohaniyat* refers to an aspect of divine knowledge that is acquired by the soul *(rouh)* rather than a transient spiritual state.
Rowzeh-e zananeh	A social and religious women's gathering where religious texts are read in a melodious tone and food and refreshments are served by the hostess. One may throw a *rowzeh* to ask the saints to fulfill a wish or to repay a wish that has come true. Women who perform *rowzeh khani* (recitation of the Quran, prayers, or religious songs) for women's gatherings and

	ceremonies are called *mulla* (the learned) and are compensated for their services.
Sadeq Hedayat (1903–1951)	One of Iran's most controversial writers, his stories often have tragic endings and represent nostalgia for an "Indo-European" Iranian past. His writings include *Zendeh Be-Gur* [Buried Alive] (1930), *Seh Qatreh Khun* [Three Drops of Blood] (1932), *Vagh Vahg-i Sahab* [Mr. Bow Wow] (1933), and *Sag-i Velgard* [The Stray Dog] (1942), *ʿAlaviyeh Khanoum* (1933), and *Buf-i Kur* [The Blind Owl] (1937, 1941).
Saqqakhaneh	A small water dispenser placed in a paved area, decorated with a hand, and dedicated to Hussein's half-brother, Abbas, whose hands were cut off before he could reach out to drink water in Karbala, leaving him to die thirsty. A *saqqakhaneh* is frequently placed in alleys of the bazaar, the old part of cities, and in the middle of *tekiyeh* or other religious spaces to commemorate the tragedy of Karbala. It is forbidden for a Muslim to slaughter an animal before giving it water.
Seyavash	A character in *Shahnameh,* Seyavash was the son of Kaikavoos and is considered an Iranian hero. He was killed by the jealous Garsivaz, brother of Afrasiab, the king of Tooran territories.
Shahid, shohada	Martyr(s).
Shahnameh	The Epic of Kings, composed in the tenth century by Ferdowsi and considered to be the crown jewel of Persian literature. The epic has historical legitimacy for many Iranians, who cherish its limited use of Arabic. For many, this book symbolizes a glorious past and is used as a testimony to Iranians' nationhood, independence, and resistance to Arabization.
Shemr	The general who killed Imam Hussein in Karbala; also used to designate a cruel and ruthless person.
Shirbaha	The economic value of a woman's breastfeeding and childrearing.
Taghut	Idolatry. *Taghuti* (followers of *taghut*) became a popular term during the Iranian revolution, when it was applied to counterrevolutionaries, specifically those who defended the shah's regime, and the rich and powerful elite from the Pahlavi regime.
Talabeh	A student of Islam.
Taʿzieh	Shiite passion plays. The primary theme of *taʿzieh* is the tragedy of Karbala and the martyrdom of Imam Hussein and his family.

Tekiyeh	An arena theater for *ta'zieh* and other religious plays and ceremonies, as well as everyday ceremonies from memorials to charity events. The *tekiyeh* is an urban space located in the middle of each neighborhood or locality, and is architecturally designed as a square space with two to four open gates to the neighborhood. It is in the cultural style of the particular locality and is open to people from various social classes. In traditional architecture, the *tekiyeh* is designed to be a neighborhood space that people cross several times a day.
Ulama	Religious savants.
Ummat	The Islamic community.
Vahdat-e kalemeh	"The unity of words." This expression was used by Imam Khomeini to privilege ideological unity over unity of action.
Velayat-e Faghih	The Guardianship of the Islamic Legal Authorities, the political center of the Islamic Republic of Iran, which attributes the highest level of authority to the governance of the *faghih*.
Yar, yaran	A term used mostly in poetic language to refer to someone who could be a lover, a friend, or a comrade.
Za'if, za'ifeh	One who is weak and in need of protection. In more religious or traditional families, it was not proper for men to refer to their wives by their proper names in conversation; instead, men would refer to their wives either as *za'ifeh* or as the mother of their sons (i.e., "Hassan's mother").
Zan	Woman; the opposite of *mard*, or man.
Zan-e hich va pouch	Ali Shari'ati's reference to a woman in her nothingness, a worthless woman, a woman without consciousness of self.
Zeinab	Imam Ali's daughter and Imam Hussein's sister, Zeinab took leadership and became famous for her historic speeches after the Karbala massacre.

Notes

Introduction

1. Some Iranian immigrants prefer to trace their roots to the ancient civilization of Persia rather than the modern nation of Iran. For them, the word *Persian* is not associated with contemporary Iranian politics, which includes the nation-state, the Islamic revolution, and the hostage crisis. Claiming Persia as an ancient civilization and Persianness as a site of cultural belonging strategically dislocates Iranians from a modern history of immigration and displacement, enabling them to deal with anti-Iranian racism and xenophobia. However, this strategy has produced its own nostalgic notions of an imaginary homeland that is located in the timeless golden age of Persia. I will use *Persian* and *Iranian* interchangeably to include both versions of identity.

2. I had traveled to the West before my displacement from Iran, but it was the displacement itself and the submission to the regulatory, cultural, and economic processes of immigration and racialization that made me aware of such history. As Caren Kaplan writes, "The imbuement of space with time leads to spatializing via the production of histories" (1996, 168). I see my text as part of the historical production of identities and subjectivities.

3. Emma Perez refers to what is repeated without any kind of evolutionary or revolutionary transformation as "things said" (1999, 31).

4. I am referring to popular performers of *ta'zieh*.

5. Tani Barlow (1993) refers to colonial or semicolonial modernity in China to talk about the historical mission of a gendered, class-stratified, and male-dominated elite that wrought its national political position through a strategy of appropriating knowledge from colonial powers. I use the

concept in similar fashion, adding a racial component to it in order to include the process of Westernization.

6. For an analysis of the modern constructions of location, see Kaplan (1996).

7. Referring to the great variety of essentialisms applied to races, peoples, and cultures, Guillaumin writes: "Without a doubt, the notion of race, in its basic form and reduced to the term itself, today no longer belongs to the primary unity of the system of racist thought. Such essentialism of genetic-bodily color can make do with many other terms or categories. In the past, use of the term ethnic group, assumed to avoid the pitfalls of racist thought, had quickly reintegrated it. At present, the term culture appears to be following a similar trajectory. The same syncretism is designated by the other perceptive extreme: not the physical, but the mental, not the concrete but the symbolic" (1985, 218–19).

8. Iranian immigrants are not a homogenous group but divided by class, gender, ethnicity, and history of immigration. See Moallem (2000).

9. With the collapse of communism, new regimes of "otherness" have been set in place to allow the political discourses of liberal democracies to function without disruption. I direct the interested reader to Jelica Sumic-Riha's discussion of the discourse of democracy in relation to the constitutive outside through which it achieves its closure (1996).

10. Cold War security metaphors have been retooled to construct an Islamic fundamentalist global threat to the West (Esposito 1993; Pieterse Nederveen 1994). Fundamentalism has served to distinguish between Western allies and enemies in the Middle East, South Asia, and North Africa. The U.S. media's initial attribution of the Oklahoma City bombing to Muslim fundamentalists is an example of the outgrowth of these ideas.

11. Along these lines, some theorists have gone so far as to talk about a worldwide rivalry based on the cultural fault lines separating the West and Islam. Samuel Huntington's *The Clash of Civilizations?* and its outlook on future global conflicts between Islam and the West is an excellent example of this (1993).

12. For a critical review of this sociological literature, see Naderi (1990).

13. I call it a claim because modernity never overcame religion. I believe that we can only talk about a postreligious and post-traditional world by abandoning modern notions of religion and tradition.

14. Ashis Nandy notes that the hegemony of a masculine Christianity and its Eurocentric way of looking at faiths was integrated in the colonial states and subsumed a set of clear polarities, including true faith versus its distortions, civil versus primordial, and great traditions versus local cultures (1998, 323).

15. For example, Radhakrishnan argues that the secular is made to function naturally and namelessly as a Western norm (1996, 160).

16. Chatterjee attributes this to the limits of the conceptual world of liberal political theory and its definition of universal needs, which only

includes material needs, such as health care or education, and not cultural goods, such as religious freedom, free speech, and free association (1998, 366). Bhargava agues that the problem with secularism is related to the lack of a theory that might offer a sketch of how religion and politics must relate after separation (1998, 488).

17. Derrida's terms (2001, 87).

18. As noted by Fischer and Abedi, "Western audiences, out of ignorance, yield too easily to fundamentalist Muslim claims that Islam is prescriptive in simple ways. To argue otherwise requires knowledge of Islamic hermeneutics, dialectics, and dialogics. This knowledge is difficult for those who have lost contact with their own Christian and Jewish traditions of hermeneutics, dialectics, and dialogics, or with those of ancient Greece which too often are nostalgically idealized and hypostasized into paragons of virtue no longer viable" (1990, 147).

19. *Unfreedom* is not a word, but I use it to refer to the negation of the concept of freedom. I am insisting on its use because it conveys something that no other word does.

20. See Kintz (1997), Sahgal and Yuval-Davis (1994), Hawley (1994), and Sarkar and Butalia (1995) for an extensive discussion of women and fundamentalism.

21. See Mazumdar (1992), Honig-Parnass (1994), Sahgal and Yuval-Davis (1994), Afshar (1994), and Diamond (1995) for further discussion.

22. For a discussion of women in various religious nationalist and fundamentalist movements, see Jayawardena and de Alwis (1996), Brasher (1998), Griffith (1997), and Bacchetta (1996).

23. I am not arguing that security concerns are either new or limited to the emergence of the Islamic movements in the region, since area studies in general and Middle Eastern studies in particular have always had complex historical connections with the security concerns of the Cold War. I am concerned with the reconfiguration of these security purposes in the context of new forms of globalization.

24. Gurnah (2000) traces the historical moment back to instructions for an enquiry in the sixteenth century by the government of Elizabeth I of England on the numbers, activities, and employment of what were then called "strangers among us," a term that continues to be applied to those "strangers" from postcolonial territories in the contemporary context.

25. I agree with Stuart Hall that tradition has no fixed or inscribed position or value for its own sake and cannot be treated in an ahistorical manner (1991b, 236–37).

26. These discourses define women's lives through violence, as in the focus on female circumcision rather than poverty, and in so doing authorize those who claim the power to decide what counts as violence. In opposing violence against women, many Western global feminists rely on an abstract notion of gender violence and attempt to protect women victims from their non-Western patriarchal societies. These attempts converge in cultural-

nationalist projects of silencing women by producing and reproducing semantic fields that are organized around notions of violence and nonviolence. For an excellent critique of the discourse of gender violence and global feminism, see Grewal and Kaplan (1994), Abusharaf (1998), and Mani (1989).

27. Iran is a multiethnic, multireligious country. Kurds, Azerbaijanis, Baluchis, Lurs, Arabs, and Bakhtiari constitute the major ethnic groups. Farsi is the dominant language in Iran. The majority of Iranians are Shiite Muslims, but there are also Sunni Muslims, Baha'is, Zoroastrians, Jews, Armenians, and Assyrians. In addition, between one and two million Afghan refugees and more than half a million Iraqi refugees live in Iran.

28. I do not refer to research documents in this book to advocate any version of empiricism. My methodology is inspired by poststructuralism, feminist epistemologies, and cultural studies in its critique of empiricism.

29. The screening of Iranian movies in the space of international film festivals is characterized by the presence of Iranian diasporic communities and discussion about the stories afterward. Some of the film screenings have become a place where the diaspora raises the issue of gender. In Iran, urbanized and educated women respond and engage with these film productions in a dynamic way. For example, in the spring of 2000, the screening of a movie called *Shokaran* created an intense controversy among and contestation by women nurses. The film used similar images to the Hollywood depiction of the femme fatale and portrayed an affair between a female nurse and a married man. Women nurses objected to the depiction of nurses in the film. Nurses argued that the film complemented popular prejudices against them as loose and immoral women with questionable motives for working night shifts. A mediation meeting between the director and female representatives of nursing associations was scheduled by a film magazine so that the director could explain the reasons for such a depiction of nurses and the representatives could explain their reactions to it. These discussions are examples of the importance of film commentary in challenging or perpetuating patriarchal cultural norms and sexist scapegoating of women, as well as of women's contestation and resistance to such representational practices.

30. I refer to Persianness to talk about contemporary essentialist notions of a distinct cultural identity located within the borders of a specific territory and separated from other cultures or nations.

31. Both are significant tragic male heroes. Seyavash is a pre-Islamic mythological figure in Persian epic poetry who was killed in the land of Turan (Iran's rival), and Imam Hussein (Shia's third imam) was martyred in Karbala. Both heroes represent irreconciliation between good and evil, as well as the destruction of the forces of good by the forces of evil.

32. This is the Shia holy month when the slaughter of Hussein's family took place.

33. Karbala is the name of the city where the tragedy of Imam Hussein's family happened. People refer to Karbala-e Husseini to talk about the event or the tragedy of Hussein.

Chapter 1. Fields of Visibility

1. Examples include the West, Islam, veiled women, Western women, etc.

2. According to Ali Shari'ati, one of the most influential Muslim intellectuals of modern Iran, ummat is an Islamic concept, referring to a group of people who live together (1979, 35–37). Shari'ati notes that ummat is similar to concepts such as nation, people, race, and mass. He makes a case for a modern interpretation of ummat by linking it to *imamat* (Shia leadership). He prefers ummat to other modern notions, such as nation, ethnic group, or tribe, because their meanings are static. Ummat is dynamic and reflects movement toward human progress (1980, 38–39). Shari'ati argues that it refers to a dynamic group of humans who are united in a common goal, move toward that goal, and believe in collective leadership (1980, 39–40).

3. In the *Prison Notebooks*, Gramsci refers to hegemony as cultural domination that works through consent and moral and intellectual persuasion (1971, 57).

4. While there is an increasingly large body of literature of postcolonial and transnational feminist scholarship dealing with areas such as East Asia, South Asia, and Latin America, there is still no significant intellectual and scholarly exchange between these areas and the Middle East.

5. Said refers to traveling theory to talk about this phenomenon, and Clifford investigates the relationship between cultural production and reception. For an extensive discussion of both Said and Clifford, see Kaplan (1996, 101–42).

6. This study does not address what Tavakoli-Taraghi calls "Persianate modernity"—a term for the period "predating the consolidation of modern nation-states and the co-optation of modernity as a state-legitimating ideology" (1998, 5–6).

7. The nonfiction texts do not concentrate exclusively on Persia. Some of them set only a chapter or two in Persia, and typically they take place in other parts of Asia and the Middle East.

8. See Stoler (1995); Parama Roy (1998); Grewal (1996); McClintock (1995).

9. As McClintock notes, despite anticolonial nationalisms' investment in the rhetoric of popular unity, most have served to institutionalize gender power through marital laws where women's political relation to the nation is subsidiary to men's through marriage (1992, 92).

10. Neither Englishness nor Frenchness was a homogeneous category. Even in the British Isles, Englishness masked and covered over the antagonism and conflicts between the Irish and Scottish. As has been well documented by Martin Bernal in *Black Athena,* the central mythos of Western civilization, i.e., classical Greece, is deeply embedded in the self-understanding of the ruling classes of imperial Europe. Bernal claims that European identity is anchored through ancient Greece and then stipulates that there is, of course, no homogeneity within individual European national identities, much less within a pan-European identity. As a result, Bernal argues that the deep roots of classical civilization in Egypt and in the Middle East have been suppressed for racist reasons. For a review of *Black Athena,* see Boal (1990).

11. See Mitchell for an in-depth analysis of such a representation of the world in colonial and postcolonial orders (1991). Guillaumin's research on the juxtaposition of race, gender, and sexuality in colonial discourse also provides an important frame for the understanding of the discourses of power as they produce a complex system of domination (1972).

12. For an extensive discussion of the construction of home and harem, see Alloula (1986); Grewal (1996); Kaplan (1992; 1996); Shohat and Stam (1994).

13. She cites both British and U.S. government documents (in particular the Truman papers), as well as *Time* magazine's issue of January 7, 1952.

14. I agree with Guillaumin that the institutionalization of the idea of a natural group or a naturalized given of social relationships as a category sanctioned at the level of the state was accomplished not by the scientific community, regardless of their efforts in that direction, but by the legal system (1995, 147).

15. By focusing on colonialism, gender, and religion, Donaldson and Kwok offer a recent complex picture of Christianity's crucial role in promoting the Anglo-European imperialist project (2002).

16. Sayyid Jamal ad-Din al-Asadabadi/Afghani (1838–1897) is one of the most dramatic anticolonial figures of nineteenth-century Middle Eastern history. His Islamic revival and his reinterpretation of the Islamic past in modern and nationalist terms achieved great popularity in the Middle East. For an excellent biography and translation of some of his ideas, see Nikki R. Keddie (1983). Also see Algar (1973) for a discussion of an appeal to religion for political purposes by reformists such as Sayyid Jamal ad-Din al-Asadabadi and Mirza Malkum Khan.

17. This slogan was also used to mobilize the Iranian masses during the revolution of 1979.

18. Afghani also founded an influential periodical and established, with Syrians Muhammad Rashid Rida and Muhammad Abduh, an Islamic reform movement called *Salafiyya,* "return to *Salaf* or the ancestor." This movement advocated going back to the notion of a true Islam and cleansing it of the formalism of outdated scholastic theology in order to bring it

into harmony with modern scientific thought. The Salafiyya movement of this time is a proactive rather than defensive reform movement. It was brought to its activist form by the Muslim Brothers in Egypt.

19. See, among others, Alloula (1986).

20. As stated by Goldberg, "Corporeal properties furnish also the metaphorical medium for distinguishing the pure from the impure, the diseased from the clean and acceptable, the included from the excluded" (1990, 306).

21. For example, Bandar Abbass was a port of entry and exit for about a half a million pounds' worth of British-Indian trade, according to H. J. Whigham (1903, 66).

22. A number of critics refer to consumer capitalism to conceptualize the development of consumer society as it relates to systems of production. For some writers, consumption is gradually replacing production by organizing society around consumerism and the display of commodities (Baudrillard 1970; Slater 1997; Veblen 1979).

23. Zerinski gives the example of a number of American Presbyterian missionary women, who visited women in the *andarouni* (the inside of the houses, where missionary men could not penetrate) and were mainly responsible for working with Iranian women to save them from their oppressive situation and convert them, not necessarily to Christianity as a religion, but to Westernization and to Christian values and mores (1993).

24. I refer to what Zakia Pathak and Rajeswari Rajan describe as the creation of "an alliance between protector and protected against a common opponent from whom danger is perceived and protection offered or sought, and where this alliance tends to efface the will to power exercised by the protector" (1989, 566). These discourses constitute gendered and racialized subject positions in the very act of making the violence visible.

25. The foundation of various presses inside and outside Iran (e.g., in Turkey, Geneva, and London), especially in the second half of the nineteenth century, permitted the early emergence of the discourse of Westernization and modernization among the local elite.

26. For more information on *Qanun,* see Hamid Algar (1973). The movement for the codification of Islamic law in Iran cannot be separated from the European colonial need for hegemonism and for control of sharia courts in parts of North Africa and the Middle East. Marnia Lazreg argues that, in Algeria, "the shift of emphasis from accommodating Islamic law to reforming it was motivated as much by a desire to rally women to the colonial aim of keeping Algeria French, as by the bureaucratic imperative of rationalizing the legal system by doing away with considerations of ethnic difference" (1994, 90). It is ironic that Mirza Malkum Khan sometimes refers to his pseudo-Masonic foundation, the League of Humanity, as "the Party of God," or *Hezbullah,* to invoke its compatibility with Islam (Algar 1973, 231).

Chapter 2. The Civic Body and the Order of the Visible

1. Zahra Rahnavard, a contemporary Muslim political activist, writes, "My Hijab pounds you. My Hijab is the embodiment of Islam; it is the sworn enemy of you, the ruling powers, materialistic systems, whether Marxist or bourgeois. With my Hijab, I portray the Islamic ideology, embody Islam" (1990, 25).

2. California's Propositions 187 (the 1994 initiative that denied social services to illegal immigrants) and 209 (the 1996 initiative that ended affirmative action) provide an interesting case of such regulation and intervention. The more the Californian globalized economy becomes dependent on the labor of sweatshops, the more immigrant bodies are despised.

3. I am referring to the Eurocentric and Orientalist construction of the "West" and the "Rest," which specifically posits "Europeanness" in opposition to Muslim "otherness" (Said 1979).

4. Cf. Grewal's *Home and Harem* (1996); and the contributions of Lazreg (1994); and Layoun (1992).

5. Only recently has feminist scholarship on women in right-wing and fundamentalist movements begun to contribute to the study of these important metaphors and political tropes.

6. The importance of religious nationalism and the role of the national church in the process of nation-state building in Europe cannot be underestimated, as seen in the examples of the Puritan Revolution in England and the French Revolution in France, with its tension between republican and Catholic values. Foucault's work on the genealogy of modern regimes of governmentality and the impact of Christianity on the formation of the self within a wider Christian tradition in the West provides us with a number of examples of the network of power relations influenced by religious discourses (see Carrette 1999 and 2000 for a careful discussion of Foucault's contribution). Indeed, modern nations always define themselves with or against a dominant religion. As Liobera has demonstrated (1994), in modern nationalism it is essential to subscribe to a particular religious dogma.

7. As Wendy Brown observes, "The constitutive terms of liberal political discourse depend upon their implicit opposition to a subject and set of activities marked 'feminine,' and at the same time obscure both this dependence and this opposition" (1995, 152).

8. Cf. Anne McClintock's formulation, "The global progress of history represented as the commodity progress of the Family of Man" (1995, 57).

9. According to Judith Butler, "As the condition of becoming a subject, subordination implies being in a mandatory submission" (1997b, 7).

10. Although Benedict Anderson's notion of imagined community is fruitful, it lacks precision in relation to the sexual and racial orders of nationalism. For an interesting critique of Anderson, see Probyn (1999).

11. For example, in present-day Europe (especially in England and France) and in the context of the neoracism experienced by Muslim

communities (Balibar 1991), women have a different investment in negotiating issues of work, education, and domestic violence. See Brah (1996); Ali
(1992); and Khanum (1992) for more information.

12. I call it pseudo-nationalism because of its deep dependence on colonial and external powers. The construction of nationalism in Iran goes beyond Reza Shah. Indeed the nationalist movement is for the most part an
adversary and an opposing force to Pahlavi's regime.

13. In his "Essai sur l'inégalité des races humaines," Gobineau wrote that
the Aryans of Persia had declined because they had mixed with the Semites
(1967).

14. Vaziri has noted that "eminent Orientists have tried to knit together
historical documents to identify the Farsi language with the land of Iran and
to create a textual argument that the various dynasties in the post-Islamic
period were connected and each sought to revive the old Iranian culture"
(1993, 93).

15. For an extensive study of these transformations, see Vaziri (1993).

16. *Haji* is an honorable title for someone who has made the pilgrimage
to Mecca. Pilgrimage to Mecca is often identified with wealth, since it is required only when someone can afford it financially, after payment of Islamic
dues and taxes and after the spiritual decision to live a pious life.

17. According to Katouzian, women were not even allowed to wear a
scarf, and in the summer of 1935 Reza Shah ordered all men to wear the
European bowler hat (2000, 335–36).

18. The body of a tribal woman became a signifier for Iranian backwardness. The first Farsi language film, called *The Lore Girl,* opened in Tehran
in 1935. Akrami describes it as "a love story about a government inspector
and a beautiful girl from the Lore tribe who flee to India after the girl's parents are killed by fellow tribesmen. They get married in Bombay and several years later, upon learning that the rule of law and order has been restored by Reza Shah's regime, return to Iran. The first Iranian talkie was a
propaganda piece. No wonder a few years later, the exhibitors called the
title of the film *Yesterday and Today* upon re-release" (1987, 134).

19. Yet the relation between the two was ambivalent, since it was based
at times on an alliance with some of the *ulama* and at other times on an
antagonism.

20. For more information on Reza Shah's modernization project, see
Asiqipur (1968).

21. See Najmabadi (1998b) for a discussion of the modernization and scientific concepts of motherhood and wifehood.

22. Flavia Agnes argues that, in colonial India, Muslim women's rights
upon marriage were superior to those of Englishwomen. She adds that,
even though the provisions of sharia reflect male bias, Islamic principles in
marriage laws could be used in favor of women (1996, 2835–37). Hoodfar
gives the example of the Islamist Iranian women who campaigned for the
ojrat ol-mesal (wages for housework) law, which passed in December 1991,

using the argument that Islam is against exploitation, that women have no obligation to work in their husband's house, and that if they do, they are entitled to a wage (1999, 35). Both Shahla Haeri (1989) and Homa Hoodfar (1999) have argued that Muslim marriage is defined as a relationship based on a contract into which both men and women can insert conditions, although patriarchal cultural beliefs and pressures largely prevent women from doing so.

23. For a summary of the Personal Status Laws in pre- and postrevolutionary Iran, see Kar and Hoodfar (1996).

24. An adequate explanation of Pahlavi's regime and the socio-political and socio-economic causes of the Iranian revolution is far beyond the scope of this chapter, but a substantive amount of research has been published on this topic in the last two decades. See Keddie (1981) and Skocpol (1982).

25. I am not arguing that all Iranian women were passive victims of forced unveiling by Reza Shah's regime; indeed, some women refused to collaborate, while others supported forced unveiling. What I am arguing is that the repressive state did not represent either the collective will of women or even the will of a particular group of women; rather, the state used forced unveiling as an important part of its project of modernization and Westernization.

26. A famous revolutionary slogan chanted by the Guardians of the Revolution was "We are your army, Khomeini, ready to take your orders."

27. See, for example, the poetry of Iraj Mirza and Mirzadeh Eshghi.

28. For example, as noted by San'ati, Sadigeh Dawlatabadi, the editor of the first women's magazine, *Zaban-e Zanan* (Women's Words), started to participate in cultural and social activities without a veil after her return from an international women's conference in Paris in 1927 (San'ati 1993, 69).

29. Along with such transformations, homophobic language started to become an important site of the everyday construction of sexual identities and practices in modern Iran. In everyday language and jokes, the geographical and cultural diversity of Iranian society was used to discipline bodies by associating male homosexuality and women's perversity with certain localities in Iran and opposing them to the hegemonic model of masculinity. For example, men from the northern part of Iran were thought to lack virility *(bi-ghyrat)*, Khasvini men were depicted as natural homosexuals, and men from the Azerbyjan were constructed as hyper-virile. Such language was politicized during the Iranian revolution of 1979 and was a site of class revenge against the Islamic elite. One of the important leaders of the Islamic Republic, Ayatollah Rafsanjani, was mocked by the public because of his resemblance to a *khajeh* (transgendered man) because of his beardlessness, which was perceived as a lack of proper masculinity.

30. The category *khajeh* refers to transgendered men, who had an ambiguous relationship with influential men and women in the dynasty. With the expansion of visual media, *khajeh* was used to consolidate

normative, heterosexist masculinity, distinguishing it from other forms of masculinity.

31. I agree with Najmabadi (1991) that this abstraction was not strictly related to the labor market's intensive need for women's participation, but was also part of the larger project of state-building, which brought women into educational institutions, the labor force, and an expanding bureaucracy.

32. Masses of "obsolete" citizens, in Nandy's terms, form the underground of the modern city (1998, xi).

33. As Inderpal Grewal states, "The domestic space . . . is also a political entity invested with history and tradition represented through female bodies located within it" (1996, 230).

34. As Doreen Massey argues, in the broader Western mode of dualistic thinking, "it is time which is aligned with history, progress, civilization, politics and transcendence and coded masculine. And it is the opposites of these things which have, in the traditions of Western thought, been coded feminine. The exercise of rescuing space from its position, in this formulation, of stasis, passivity and depoliticization, therefore, connects directly with a wider philosophical debate in which gendering and the construction of gender relations are central" (1994, 6).

35. Document number 112, *Vaghe-eye Kashf-e Hijab: Asnad-e montasher nashodeh-e kashf-e hijab dar asr-e reza khan* [The Event of Unveiling: Unpublished Documents from the Event of Unveiling in the Reza Khan Era], collected by Morteza Jafari, *Sazeman-e Madarek e Farhangi Enghelab-e Eslami* [The Organization for the Cultural Documents of the Islamic Revolution] (Tehran: Moaseseh-e Pajouhesh va Motalcat-e Farhangi [The Institute for Research and Study of Culture], 1992 [1371]), 241.

36. *Gharbzadeh* is a portmanteau word that might be translated as "West-struck." The concept of *gharbzadegi* (abduction by the West) was introduced in a 1962 book of the same name by Jalal-e Al-e Ahmad, an Iranian writer and cultural critic. It was popularized and very widely used by secular and religious oppositional movements to describe the colonizing effects of Westernization.

37. George Simmel (1971) argues that fashion can be employed as a measure of the civilizing process. A number of scholars identify clothing and fashion as a manifestation of class structure and social privilege. According to Roland Barthes, fashion is a system of meaning constructed from visual and linguistic details (1985, 18).

38. The shah's propaganda machine used notions of respectability to attack women who joined the guerrilla movement. The accusation that communists were against religion and moral values because they were against marriage, which made them for the deliberate exchange of women, was an important propaganda tool. The regime characterized Muslim guerrilla women as Islamic Marxists and used the same propaganda tools, claiming their Islam was contaminated by Marxism. As far as women were concerned, the shah's regime became a defender of religion and moral values.

39. Ashraf-e Dehqani was born in 1949 into a poor working family in Azerbaijan. Ashraf joined the Organization of the Iranian People's Fedai Guerrillas at the beginning of the guerrilla armed struggle in the late 1960s or early 1970s. After the Battle of Siahkal in February 1971, numerous members of the organization were arrested, including Ashraf and her brother Behrooz Dehqani, who was tortured and killed in prison.

40. In the literature on colonialism and Orientalism, such oppositional logic and its dependence on the categories it has excluded have been extensively discussed (Said 1979; Behdad 1994). Only in recent feminist writing have systematic connections been forged among colonial and postcolonial politics, gender-sex relations, and issues of citizenship (Spivak 1988a; Grewal 1996; Grewal and Kaplan 1994; Alexander and Mohanty 1997).

41. In Malaya, another postcolonial society discussed by Aihwa Ong, the postcolonial state used modern concepts and practices to manage women's hygiene, sexuality, and health while also providing employment, which challenged the moral authority of men over women (1995, 170–71).

42. A comparative study of this process in different geopolitical locations should be undertaken to situate the interlocking forms of particularism and universalism in the construction of women as a category of identity.

43. In her discussion of Hawthorne's comprehension of America, Lauren Berlant explains how he adjudicates the "overlapping but differentially articulated positions: the official and the popular; the national and the local; the rule of law and the rule of men; the collective and the individual; the citizen as abstraction and the citizen as embodied, gendered; utopia and history; memory and amnesia" (1991, 5–6). Also, Doris Sommer discusses the relations between various Latin American romantic novels and patriotic historiography, directly linking this genre of writing to the history of nation-building (1991).

44. With the erosion of nation-states and the expansion of new technologies, international forms of governmentality, and worldwide feminist movements, the discourse of protection is now in crisis. Unable to regulate borders in the old ways in the contemporary postmodern era, these discourses have been disrupted and reinvented through new mechanisms.

45. Mary Douglas (1980) argues that all borderlands are potential sites of pollution and contamination.

Chapter 3. The Tragic Paradox of Revolution

1. Many authors, poets, songwriters, and filmmakers used such subversive means of communication to reach various audiences. One of the classic examples of this tradition of cultural resistance was the famous children's book *The Little Black Fish*, written by the Azerbaijani writer and teacher

Samad-e Behrangi, which became a classic revolutionary text for both adults and children.

2. See Chelkowski and Dabashi for an illustration of visual representations of the Iranian revolution of 1979 (1999).

3. Mazdak advocated social justice, the distribution of wealth, and the equality of men and women. According to modern leftist revolutionary readers, Mazdak articulated an early form of communism in the context of the Persian empire. Mazdak and many of his followers were persecuted and killed by Crown Prince Kosrow Anushirvan.

4. The myth of Seyavash is a section of *Shahnameh*, the epic of kings written by the Persian poet Ferdowsi (940–1020 B.C.). Seyavash was the son of an incompetent Persian king called Kavus. Seyavash refused his father's orders to return hostages to the Persian court, where they would be killed. He resisted the sexual advances of his stepmother, Queen Sudabeh, and exiled himself in the land of Turan, Iran's enemy. Afraseyab, the ruler of Turan, received him and married him to his daughter, but soon Seyavash was accused by Afraseyab's brother of military treason and organizing a military coup against Afraseyab. Seyavash was killed in exile and his son, who was brought up in secret, escaped to Iran, hoping to return to Turan to avenge his father's killing. For an English translation of the Seyavash's story, see Ferdowsi 1992.

5. For an illuminating analysis of the impact of the media in the Iranian revolution of 1979, see Fischer and Abedi (1990).

6. Foucault's writing on ancient subjectivity is suggestive. He suggested the need for more research on the many radically different styles of existence.

7. Cited by D'Isanto (1999, 6). Vattimo argues, "Being coincides with the historical transmission of messages that unfold in time, and of which we can never have an exhaustive understanding" (cited by D'Isanto 1999, 7).

8. Shari'ati justifies such a return by referring not only to the Shia past but also to twentieth-century revolutionaries such as Régis Debray and his statement on crying as an expression of emotionality and humanity (1971, 14).

9. A traditional form of entertainment in which a *pardeh* (screen)—usually a painting of the event on a canvas—is used to depict the story of Karbala. Pardeh-dari was used to tell the epic stories of *Shahnameh*, a national epic and the longest poem written by the Persian poet Ferdowsi. This form of entertainment brings together Shiite mythology and pre-Islamic popular culture.

10. *Saqqakhaneh* refers to "a small water dispenser located in the alley of the bazaar and in the streets in the older quarter of Iranian towns. It is dedicated to Hussein's half-brother and standard-bearer, Abbas, and usually placed in a tiled niche decorated with pictures relating to Karbala" (Chelkowsi and Dabashi 1999, 61). This school was formed by painters in

Iran and the West and helped keep the theme of Karbala and the imagery of the coffeehouse tradition alive.

11. The martyrdom of Imam Hussein is currently back in Iranian theater. *Pol* (The Bridge), which was one of the popular plays in April–May 2003 in Tehran, was a reconstruction of the Ashura uprising and the tragedy of Karbala. The playwright, Mohammad Rahmanian, offered a new historical view of the Imam Hussein tragedy by transforming it into a play where forces of good and evil are not simply posited but investigated throughout the story. The participation of the epic poet, the masked actor, and the narrator in this process reveals the tension between history and memory in the literary reconstruction of the tragedy of Karbala.

12. The growing transnational movements of capital and labor, migration, and the compression of time and space in the cultural flows of globalization are issues that demand careful examination—and are, unfortunately, beyond the scope of this chapter—with respect to both nationalization and transnationalization. See Kaplan, Alarcón, and Moallem (1999), Appadurai (2001b), Dirlik and Zhany (2000).

13. As Cole and Keddie emphasize (1986, 2), Shiism is not now and never has been a monolithic movement. Furthermore, neither the *Ulama* (religious scholars) nor the followers of this branch of Islam have always been activists or even united in their views. For a multidimensional reading of the Karbala paradigm in its Shiite inflections in Iran, see Fischer and Abedi (1990).

14. In *The Phenomenology of Spirit*, in the section on "Lordship and Bondage," Hegel elaborates on the unhappy consciousness based on the bondsman's recognition of enslavement.

15. Ghafari extensively discusses the inner/outer dynamism of such a dichotomy (1979, 19–30).

16. The concept of *Velayat-e faghih* was challenged after the death of Imam Khomeini, since it raised the question of who has the legitimacy to be the supreme leader. Currently the struggle over the concept of *Velayat-e faghih* distinguishes religious fundamentalists, who advocate the official reading of religion by a particular leader, from religious intellectuals, who advocate religious pluralism.

17. I am referring to Gramsci (1971), Foucault (1980), and the circulation of power in the context of representation, and in particular to the ability, through coercion and seduction, to gain consent in establishing leadership and authority.

18. As John Beverley argues, the function of the nation is to articulate to itself not only elements of other classes or group projects as its own embodiment, but the nation is a necessary signifier for the functioning of hegemonic articulation (1999, 141–42).

19. There is not much engagement between postcolonial or subaltern studies and Middle Eastern studies with regard to the formation of subaltern consciousness and subjectivity in Middle Eastern societies.

Mostaz'af can be seen as the subject position of the subaltern as a social category.

20. In the war of position, in the Gramscian sense, the Islamic movement achieved hegemony over other oppositional movements by establishing a revolutionary agency that was not uniquely defined by class relations. It also distinguished itself from the secular nationalist movements and their primordial notions of the nation by calling for a transnational nation of disempowered Muslims in an alliance with what Fanon would call the wretched of the earth.

21. In this chapter, I have not been able to elaborate on the representation of ethnicity in Iranian cinema. It should, however, be noted that postrevolutionary Iranian cinema has included the representation of various ethno-linguistic groups. For the first time, Turkish, Kurdish, and other languages were finally incorporated into Iranian cinema and recognized as minority languages. For example, *Bashu, the Little Stranger* by filmmaker Bahram Baizai depicts ethnic and regional differences in Iran. The representation of religious minorities, however, is still missing from Iranian film production.

22. For more information on women's participation in the Iranian Revolution of 1979, see Azari (1983) and Paidar (1995).

23. With the postrevolutionary authoritarian imposition of *hijab* on all women, more punitive slogans such as "Ya ru sari ya tu sari" (Veil or tap on the head) emerged to discipline women into conformity. As a result, many women were punished, discriminated against, and excluded from political, social, and economic spheres because of noncompliance with such rules and regulations. For further details, see Tabari and Yeganeh (1982), Afshar (1987), and Adelkhah (1991).

24. Sometimes similar signifiers, such as *hijab* (modesty in general and the Muslim women's dress code in particular) or *chador siah* (a long black veil), are used to refer to veiling.

25. While an Orientalist and Eurocentric view constructs veiling as the ultimate form of Muslim women's victimization and oppression by a backward and barbaric patriarchal order, there are other perspectives on veiling, e.g., what Fanon calls the historic dynamism of the veil (1967). While meanings assigned to dress are fully implicated in power relations, veiling in particular has been defined and manipulated within a range of historically, culturally, and socially variable discourses and practices. In the modern epoch—spanning the period from colonialism and post-/neocolonialism to the emergence of nationalism, fundamentalism, and feminism—veiling, unveiling, and reveiling have become an important site of hegemonic politics and subject formation. A number of prominent Middle Eastern feminist scholars have engaged in an effort to demystify and decenter the dominant, monolithic, Eurocentric, and Orientalist notion of veiling (Abu-Lughod 1986; Ahmed 1992; Hoodfar 1991; Lazreg 1994; and Mernissi 1992). In tracing the cultural basis and effects of imperialism, Grewal

contextualizes the use of veiling within colonial discourses of female incarceration, as it shapes relational nationalist constructs of home and harem (1996).

26. In promoting Islamic *hijab*, Rahnavard writes, "And what of the unrestrained style of the colonialist, capitalist or imperialist systems, which expose you to lustful gazes, abuse you for the stupefaction of minds and the rejection of superior values?" (1990, 9).

27. I use *re*masculation to refer to the social phenomenon that includes the construction of masculinity and the process of emasculation. As I have argued, one of the core components of the colonial civilizing mission in Middle Eastern countries has been the construction of gender identities related to the global construction of race relations. Historically, both Eurocentrism and Orientalism, in their construction of Muslim and Arab otherness, have used masculinity and femininity to legitimize power for Eurocentric subject positions (see Shohat and Stam 1994). This process has led to the emasculation of Muslim men and their subordination to Eurocentric, hegemonic models of masculinity. It has also invented competing models of femininity for women. This process is still at work in the construction of the Muslim other in new Euro-American racist discourses.

28. According to Chelkowski and Dabashi, "Between the years 1979 and 1987, 302 avenues, forty-one squares, thirteen freeways, and seventeen parks had their names changed. The streets in Tehran that bear the names of Shuhada or martyrs of the Islamic revolution and the war against Iraq number more than 1400. Often, before their deaths, the 'martyrs' used to live on the streets or in the quarters of the city named after them" (1999, 121).

29. The underworld of women's responses to the demands of the Islamic *ummat* still needs to be excavated.

30. The bureaucratization of the revolution and the Iran-Iraq war led to the institutionalization of martyrdom in the Islamic Republic.

31. An analysis of Muslim fundamentalist discourse must go beyond the notion of "reality testing," as Gordon maintains (1997). She refutes the Freudian restriction of the haunted field, arguing, "It is precisely the experience of being haunted in 'the world of common reality,' and the unexpected arrival of ghosts, wolves or eerie photographs, that troubles or even ruins our ability to distinguish reality and fiction, magic and science, savage and civilized, self and other, and in those ways gives reality a different coloring" (53).

32. Barthes's (1972) notion of myth as a mode of signification is very useful for an understanding of death and martyrdom in fundamentalism.

33. In these local performances, women's roles are played exclusively by men who dress up in women's clothing.

34. Death has been an important site of philosophical reflection. There are a number of genealogical and sociological studies of death, e.g., Foucault (1978), Derrida (1995), Bronfen (1992), and Kristeva (1982).

35. Murray and Roscoe (1997), in their critique of Eurocentrism in lesbian-gay history, elaborate on male homosexual patterns in various Islamic societies.

36. I am referring to allegory to talk about what Clifford calls the poetic, traditional, cosmological nature of cultural representations (1986, 100).

Chapter 4. The Sacralization of Politics and the Desacralization of Religion

1. The notion of Islamic intellectualism was first discussed in Shari'ati's writings in the 1970s.

2. Ganji, a prominent Islamist journalist who is in prison for his public criticism of religious conservatives and fundamentalists, deploys a reading or interpretation of religion as a form of fascism. He speaks of a fascistic religious movement in Iranian society characterized by a totalistic ideology, attachment to a party led by a single leader, the use of terror, and the movement's exclusive control of the economy, the media, and the military (1999, 11).

I do not mean to be tendentious when deploying labels such as fundamentalist, reformist, and religious. My intention is to characterize the range of religious and political tendencies in a way that accurately reflects ongoing debates and discussions among various individuals and groups in Iran. These exchanges have cost some clergymen, scholars, journalists, and political leaders their freedom. For a sampling of positions with regard to women's issues, see Mir-Hosseini (1999), Haeri (1989), *Zanan* (nos. 59–79, 1999–2001), and Afshar (1998).

3. This includes Shari'ati and Motahari.

4. Both President Khatami's invitation to a dialogue between civilizations and the debate in the West on "the clash of civilizations" reveal the particularism of Western universalisms and cast doubt on this aspect of Western hegemony.

5. The unleashing of religious language and imagery reflects a convergence of American nationalism and religion in post-9/11 cultural representations. Religious phraseology and symbols, talk of "a crusade," and Manichean references to forces of good and evil evoke the image of a militant Christianity conducting a holy war against the Muslim invader.

6. Naficy proposes the notion of "accented cinema's mode of production" to talk about the dominant mode of cultural production that exists side by side with alternative and emergent modes (2001, 43).

7. The political economy of Imam Reza's shrine, one of the richest religious sites in Iran, is a fascinating subject that merits a separate study analyzing its revenue, along with the regulation and distribution of its wealth.

8. Commodification of religion has become an important part of urban life in Iran. For example, next to the Imam Khomeini's shrine in Tehran, there is a souvenir shop where various objects, from posters of the imams to Islamic dress, are displayed for consumers.

9. Ziba Mir-Hosseini has examined the response of the *Houzeh* (the Qom seminaries) to legal problems *(masa'el)* that have arisen in the social arena, including the high-ranking Ayatollah Madani's rulings on matters for which there was no juristic precedent. She notes that out of 450 new problems, 162 concern women and gender issues, such as artificial insemination, abortion, sex-change operations, and contraception (1999, 31–32).

10. Throwing acid is a common form of violence against women in Iran.

11. The *basiji* and revolutionary guards were volunteer forces, composed mainly of young men who took part in nation-building in the postrevolutionary era. Among their tasks was forcing women to conform to Islamic rules and regulations.

12. Completed in 1996, the film was banned immediately after its formal screening and was only released in 1999.

13. Interestingly, in the post–9/11 era, with its concurrent rise of American jingoism and masculinist nationalism, Western anxiety about the impenetrability of the *chador* surfaces through a rumor of Bin Laden's escape from Afghanistan dressed as a woman. In this scenario, we construct Muslim men as possibly wearing the *burqua* or *chador* so as to pass for women.

14. While there should be a distinction between films made in Iran and those made in the diaspora, since they reflect different modes of production and circulation, the compression of time and space (created by the movement of filmmakers and film productions and by the demarcation of these films as Iranian) marks the hegemonic power of nationalism in our highly globalized world.

15. According to Banafsheh-e Sam Giss, a social worker who has worked with *dokhtaran-e farari* (runaway girls), this phenomenon is not limited to the capital. She notes that the most common means of survival for these young girls are prostitution, petty crime, and drug dealing (*Nou-rouz*, 5 Tir 1380 [2001]).

16. A recent phenomenon in Iran involves young girls (with 70% between the age of ten and fourteen) who ran away from their families for various reasons, including family violence, poverty, and forced marriages (Karimi Majd 2000, 3).

17. The debate on the possibilities and limits of pluralism and the toleration of difference within both secularist and religious modern nation-state institutions deserves careful consideration. In the last decade, a rich literature has emerged to shed light on the complex histories of both secularism and religion in modernity and postmodernity, especially in the West and South Asia. For further discussion, see Das 1990; Chatterjee 1998; Castelli 2001; Connolly 1999.

18. Pejman Azarmina, in an article entitled "In Iran, gender segregation becoming a fact of medical life," writes: "Ten years ago only 12.5% of Iranian medical students were women, and the government responded by setting a goal that half of new students will be female. Today, one third of the 22,326 students in Iran's 38 medical schools are women." *Canadian Medical Association Journal* 166, no. 5(2002): 645.

19. Columns such as "What are they (women) complaining about?" in *Payam-e Hajar* are examples of the airing of women's issues across a wide spectrum.

20. Iranian women have participated as delegates at a number of international forums and conferences. They are also involved in transnational circles of Islamic women and have initiated conferences and exhibitions on the issues related to Islam and women. At the same time, the Islamic Republic has replaced the discourse of the shah's regime on women's issues with an Islamic agenda through the Society of Women of the Islamic Revolution (which replaced the state-regulated Iranian Women's Organization) and the Islamic Institute for Women, led by Azam Taleghani, the daughter of Ayatollah Taleghana (a prominent religious figure in the Iranian revolution) and editor-in-chief of the women's journal *Payam-e Hajar*, among other organizations. Islamic identity in relation to women has been continuously refined and rearticulated vis-à-vis global and regional frameworks (e.g., women's rights as human rights discourse, the discourse of development, and approaches taken by nongovernmental organizations and other Islamic countries). For examples of this literature, see Kadivar (1996) and the collection of articles *Zan, Elm, San'at va Tawsi'ah* (1995–96).

21. As Bacchetta argues in the case of the Sangh Hindu nationalism movement, the discourse of Hindu nationalist women ideologues cannot simply be reduced to the discourse of their male counterparts since, even though women and men are both struggling for what they collectively call a "Hindu nation," they do not necessarily have the same goals (1996, 127).

Chapter 5. Transnationalism, Feminism, and Fundamentalism

1. The question "Who are we?" is an important one in ethnic and national movements, which all question technical, scientific, and administrative forms of power.

2. For Foucault, modern societies are less about state control *(étatisation)* than about the governmentalization of the state (2000, 220).

3. Mark Poster, cited by Kaplan (1997).

4. As Pettman argues (1996), an investigation of the international political economy of sexed bodies and the complex human traffic within and

across state borders calls for recognition of the different local, national, state, and even wider political identities that are increasingly located within global structures of power.

5. Feminist interpretation of sacred texts in different religious traditions and their distribution as printed material represent an interesting example of recent changes in power and knowledge relations. This process has facilitated desacralization and has met with resistance from the fundamentalist resacralization movement.

6. A number of scholars have elaborated on the crisis of rationality. For example, Gellner refers to the flourishing of postmodernism and the importance of the idea that everything is a text open to be coded, decoded, and deconstructed in challenging the cognitive elitism of Western philosophy, which claims that, despite the equality of all men and minds (not women), not all cultures and systems of meaning are equal (1992, 20-37).

7. The mobilization of feminism in the United States to serve militaristic and nationalistic goals, especially post-9/11, or what Jennifer Terry calls "state-sponsored feminism," is a good example of the ramifications of such dichotomous views of feminism and fundamentalism (panel discussion for Women's History Month, San Francisco State University, 2002). For a discussion of feminist responses to 9/11 see Bacchetta et al. (2002).

8. The event that is now called 9/11 in popular language was the result of a momentum that brought to the surface the crisis of nation-states, modern regimes of governmentality, and citizenship. It displayed convergences between elements that have been considered antagonistic dichotomies and discursive outlaws, including nationalism and transnationalism, feminism and fundamentalism, religion and secularism, humanism and barbarism, and liberation and oppression. The convergence has continued to haunt our everyday political discourse, shaking the foundational categories of modernity and the radical separation of realms. These convergences are, of course, signifiers of a postmodern world of de/differentiation, where each concept or realm becomes a mirror of its opposite, taking its opposite to its conceptual limits. Throwing food and bombs on the population in Afghanistan, bombing Iraq for the sake of its reconstruction, and going to war for the promotion of peace are examples of these convergences. Such mixing of categories shows a significant turning point in the semiotics of global politics and its regimes of representation. It also indicates an important discursive shift in a number of modern discourses, including nationalism, fundamentalism, humanism, feminism, and secularism.

9. For an excellent overview of transnational feminist theories, see Grewal and Kaplan's introduction to *Scattered Hegemonies* (1994, 1-33).

10. As we see in the example of Iraq and Afghanistan.

11. I agree with Enloe that "to make sense of any militarized social system, you always have to ask about women" (2003, 1199).

12. In spite of emerging scholarship on the body in, for example, feminist and queer studies, there has been very little written on the national and

transnational imagining of the body and how this imagining is invested in notions of motherhood, sisterhood, and wifehood as sites of empowerment, political mobilization, and participation. Recent scholarship on women in the right wing and fundamentalist movements has contributed to the study of these important metaphors and political tropes.

13. Examples include feminist fundamentalists, fundamentalist feminists, and secular fundamentalists.

14. For a definition of U.S. multicultural nationalism, see Moallem and Boal (1999).

15. However, in the case of the recent war in Iraq, the absence of women from the realm of representational practices displaced the body of women to the land of Iraq. The abjectification of women ("their women") left the field of representation wide open to display the bravery and macho masculinity of American and British troops, thus opposed to the emasculated Iraqi men. The land of Iraq and its liberation stood for "the body of Afghani women" and their liberation. The absence of feminist sisterhood with Iraqi women, represented as "militant fundamentalists" or "suicide bombers," turned the feminist gaze inward. In this war we were concerned about our sisters in the military and their safety. For example, in the National Organization for Women's statements urging peace, we can clearly see the lines drawn between us and them in the phrase "the war that carries the danger that their nation will degenerate into an even more militarized or extremist Iraq that dramatically could restrict women's rights." Another example comes from the Feminist Majority, which incessantly claimed sisterhood with Afghani women. Yet, the absence of any declaration of sisterhood with Iraqi women again leads us to suspect a nationalist impulse in feminism. We are only sisters to those who need our protection and are willing to renounce their brothers by joining us. In this case, the nationalism of the civilized should be restored.

16. The best two recent examples of such a spectacle are from the war in Afghanistan and the war in Iraq. In both cases, the representation of Muslim women either as passive victims, in the case of Afghanistan, or suicide bombers, in the case of Iraq, was used as part of the justification for war and military intervention in these two countries. By either taking an outspoken position in defense of the liberation of Afghani women, or a silent one, in the case of Iraqi women, numerous feminist groups in the United States either legitimized or simply became complicit with the military occupation of these two countries by U.S. and British forces.

17. The exclusively male subject of various religious and secular discourses has been challenged by feminist claims for equality. Feminist challenges include both a reconstruction of subjects from within different religious traditions and a secularist rejection of patriarchal religious practices. Both of these forms of feminist challenge are lively and present within the framework of Islam. See, among others, Ahmed (1986), Mernissi (1992), and El Saadawi (1988).

18. Minh-ha has criticized this quest for a lost, pure, authentic identity of the real self, the real Black, and the real Indian or Asian, as located within the locus of all that is considered other (1990, 371).

19. In the case of feminism, Eurocentric notions of Western feminists who conceive of the women's liberation movement as a purely West European and North American phenomenon have been seriously challenged by postcolonial and poststructuralist feminists, critical feminists of color, and Third World feminists. See Hooks (1984), Grewal and Kaplan (1994), Minh-ha (1989), Mohanty (1991b), and Spivak (1988b). In the case of fundamentalism, recent comparative studies of religious fundamentalism have challenged monolithic notions of fundamentalism as uniquely related to Islam. See Moghadam (1994), Yuval-Davis (1992), and Hawley (1994).

20. Grewal and Kaplan's (1994) suggestion of a transnational mode of analysis that insists on the importance of geopolitical forces is very useful.

21. Since 1980, the celebration of the March 8 (Women's Day) in Iran has been replaced by the celebration of the birthday of Fatima Zahra, the prophet's daughter (Adelkhah 1991). Debates in fundamentalist women's journals such as *Puyandegan-e rah-e Zeinab, Payam-e Hajar,* and *Mahjoobeh* also represent such a convergence. Klatch reports that laissez-faire conservative women share a measure of the feminist vision vis-à-vis the construction of gender and the existence of sexual inequality (1987, 152). In her book on newly orthodox Jewish women, Kaufman argues that despite a distrust of feminism on the part of "born again" women, the focus on raising women's status, promoting female interests, and altering gender roles resonates with issues that have long concerned feminists (1991).

22. Sandoval's (1990) critique sheds light on the solidification of gender categories that has resulted from the tendency of white feminism to lean toward reductive, binary understandings of power based on domestic U.S. politics.

23. In her discussion of feminist fundamentalism, Wilson argues that feminists have deployed secular fundamentalist methods in their antipornography campaigns in the United States (1992, 27). Also, the desire to create a safe niche, especially within the institutionalization of feminism, has been identified in the theoretical work of "women of color." See Anzaldua (1990).

24. A number of feminist critiques have exposed the rationalist ideal of masculinity as a neurotic denial of the chaos, decomposition, and death associated with femininity and otherness. This ideal leaves masculinity as an imagined zone of safety encircled by the feminine "other." Hélène Cixous has suggested that in the binary gender pairing, women have been associated with death (1981). Sarah Webster Goodwin and Elizabeth Bronfen argue that the historicization of death requires an examination of its intersection with the history of gender and the simplistic opposition of man/life

and woman/death (1993, 5).

25. Feminist literature raises significant questions vis-à-vis the sexual division of labor in general and domestic work in particular. An important part of this literature explores domestic work as a site of social and economic activity, in which a political economy based on the sex/gender division of labor makes it possible for patriarchy and capitalism to profit from women's unpaid and unrecognized work. The following important sites of women's activities in the family have been identified as pertinent to an understanding of women's position in society: (1) childbearing and childrearing; (2) domestic services; (3) sexual services; and (4) emotional labor and care-taking services. See Delphy (1983), Hochschild (1989), Guillaumin (1995), Juteau and Laurin (1989), Hartmann (1979), Pam Smith (1992), and Walby (1986), among others.

26. For an extensive review of Marxist feminist positions, see Sokoloff (1980). Marxist, socialist, and materialist feminists have played a crucial role in bringing capitalism and patriarchy into dialogue with each other (Hartmann 1979; Delphy 1983; Mies 1986; Walby 1986).

27. As Kamalkhani argues, the convergence of political and religious rituals has created space for the articulation of the "true" and "false" identity of Muslim women (1998, 185).

28. As Anouar Majid argues, creating dialogues and critically redefining old, male-centered canonical documents to expand the spaces of freedom in the Islamic world require a questioning of clerical Islam as well as of unexamined Western social science theories and their bias against Islam (2000, 100–101).

29. For a critique of Western feminist and womanist discourses, see Spivak (1988a, 1988b), Grewal and Kaplan (1996), Lazreg (1994), Mohanty (1991b), and Mani (1989).

30. In the case of Christianity, Castelli suggests that "from the earliest Christian texts and practices, the human body functioned as both a site of religious activities and a source of religious meanings" (1991, 29). In the case of Islam, according to Aït Sabbah, the female body is a field of sacred writing (1984).

31. As Renate Salecl puts it in the case of "the socialist moral majority" in Slovenia and Croatia, "a fetus is also a Croat" (1992, 59).

32. Several essays in Moghadam's (1994) anthology elaborate upon this issue in Jewish, Christian, Hindu, and Muslim fundamentalisms. Controlling women's reproductive powers may be linked to certain claims of the U.S. religious right. However, it is very important to distinguish the particular socio-historical and geopolitical contexts of such discourses in the United States, the Middle East, and elsewhere.

33. In Iran since the Islamic regime, certain civil codes, especially those affecting women, have been replaced by the Islamic Rule of Ethics (the

sharia) interpreted by Iranian Shia clergy. See Tohidi (1991). The convergence of civil codes with sharia has enabled women to legally negotiate their rights and to challenge gender-biased rules and regulations.

34. A great deal of feminist writing has been concerned with the question of feminist consciousness and morality. Liberal feminists have addressed questions from "feminine" virtues to abortion. Radical feminists have taken on the role of reproductive technologies. Socialist feminist theory has analyzed the alienation of women. Poststructuralist feminism has focused on the gaze, double consciousness, and the divided self.

35. A number of feminist scholars draw a direct connection between women's maternalism and the emergence of welfare states (Koven and Michel 1993).

36. In his description of the master/slave relation, Hegel refers to happy consciousness as a slave's (false) self-consciousness prior to the realization of his slavery. For Hegel this form of consciousness is unequal and unilateral, since it reflects the master's perception and does not recognize the reality of the slave's humanity and dignity. As the slave becomes aware of the appropriation of his labor, his consciousness alternates into an unhappy consciousness or a joyous consciousness. The joyous consciousness is formed by the tragic recognition of the truth, which consists of the dominated self's unhappiness, and the joy of the possibility of human freedom. For an excellent reading of Hegel's master/slave relations, see Kojève (1947).

37. Marx and Hegel are not the only philosophers to address the issues of alienation and consciousness of the dominated self. Many other philosophers have written about mystification and perplexity as prominent features of modern social life (Heidegger, Marcuse, and Sartre among them). Feminists have relied extensively on these ideas to talk about women's sexual objectification and feminist consciousness.

38. Grewal's (1996) study of how discursive colonial encounters shaped and linked the distinct constructs of gender and nation provides an excellent theoretical framework for the examination of the conditions that make feminist subject-positions possible in different historical contexts.

39. Elspeth Probyn's (1993) effort to break through such a dichotomy is a contribution to feminism and fertile ground for further reflection.

40. Using the Body Shop trademark as a case study, Caren Kaplan (1995) explores the complicities with and resistances to transnational capital in Euro-American feminist discourses and practices. The signifiers of fundamentalist discourse have been adopted and used in advertising and marketing. Within the framework of the Islamic dress code, Islamic dress has been reinvented in a variety of ways in the Iranian fashion industry. Iran's new "Sarah" doll shadows the Barbie trademark concept (but not its clothing).

41. For example, as Chatterjee discusses (1998), the meaning of secularism in India cannot be reduced to its European conceptions. For some scholars the inadequacy of secularism to address the complex relationship

between majority rule and minority rights in postcolonial non-Western societies requires the abandonment of the concept altogether (Nandy 1998b). For others, the limits of liberal thought and political practice both in the West and in India require "the development of new institutional sites cutting across the divide between state sovereignty on the one hand and people's rights on the other" (Chatterjee 1998, 366).

42. A number of Iranian feminist groups have been able to bring together feminist and gender activists in Iran and in various disaporic locations. For example, the feminist journal *Nimeye Digar,* which is published in the United States, initiated the practice of including writings by women and activists located both in Iran and in the diaspora. In addition, the Iranian Women's Studies Foundation, which organizes an international conference of Iranian women's studies in various parts of the United States, Canada, and Europe, has been instrumental in inviting speakers and panelists from Iran, including women and men who have been active in promoting gender issues and women's rights. While these efforts have been crucial in creating a dialogue between feminist and women activists inside and outside Iran, there has been constant conflict and tension between those Iranian feminists who take a secular fundamentalist position and those who are open to such possibilities. For more information, see the editorials of the International Conference of Iranian Women's Studies' proceedings (in Farsi) published by the Iranian Women's Studies Foundation (http://www.iwsf.org).

43. The Council of Guardians is composed of twelve members, six religious leaders and six legal scholars, who monitor elections and the Parliament.

44. This is a magazine authored by young male clerics from Houzeh-ye Elimiyeh (Theological College). It addresses women's issues in Islam and defends women's rights.

45. For more information about Hojjat-ol-Eslam Sa'idzadeh's views, see Mir-Hosseini (1999, 247–72); *Zanan* 6, no. 37 (Shahrivar–Mehr 1376 [1997]): 50–57.

46. The reform movement in Iran emerged during the election of Mohammad Khatami to Iran's presidency on May 23, 1997. This movement is composed of mostly urban and middle-class individuals, including women, journalists, students, and members of nongovernmental organizations. The reform movement has been pressuring the state to institutionalize a pluralistic vision of Islamic government and the civil society to allow freedom of cultural expression that does not conform to the rules and regulations of the Islamic state. The movement flourished after the election of Khatami with an explosion of publications. In addition, the loosening of restrictions imposed on relations with the West led to the expansion of transnational networks, computer websites, feminist NGOs, professional associations, and scholarly and media networks in the West, especially those involved in the Iranian diaspora in the United States and in various European countries.

This encouraged more exchange between Iranian intellectuals and cultural workers in Iran and in diaspora. A number of Iranian filmmakers, writers, scholars, journalists, and clergymen traveled to various European countries and the United States to participate in seminars and conferences. The movement, which was concentrated in the press and involved the participation of numerous journalists either in criticizing fundamentalist tendencies or in defining a reformist vision of Islam, provoked a series of attacks and killings, along with the imprisonment of some journalists, lawyers, and filmmakers by government or government-related agencies. These events displayed the fragmentation of the Islamic state and the crisis of authority of the state, which was unable to function as a unified or unifying force. Since the Iranian revolution, the Iranian state has had difficulty bringing the ideas of the state and the nation together because of the contradictions between a cultural nationalist notion of Islam and a transnational notion of Islam—meaning a reference to ummat as defined by territorial and national boundaries of Iran and a reference to ummat as it expands beyond the boundaries of the nation-state to include all Muslims. Both problems are related to the new forms of globalization and the decline of the nation-state, as well as to the modernization of Islam in the context of the modern nation-state, which is deeply deficient in dealing with issues of cultural and religious difference.

In the election of 1997, support for the reform movement and the massive participation of various groups in electoral politics created a new investment in the concept of nation, not as an Islamic ummat, but as a voting block or majority able to take part in the political life of the citizens and to change state laws and regulations. However, with the failure of the reform movement and the persecution of reformists by segments of the government, the reform movement has lost its popularity among the masses of Iranians who desire to see social and institutional change. Once focused on electoral politics and the possibility of a state free from a particularistic notion of Islam, the movement has lost its legitimacy and optimism, instead giving way to a sense of despair and a passive reaction to the diasporic movements, including the old monarchists, the constitutionalists, and others who are trying to mobilize to take over the government either through public pressure for a referendum or with the assistance of U.S. forces. For a recent account of the reform movement in Iran, see Yaghmaian (2002).

47. Here I refer not only to the excess of citizen-subjects, the peasantry, the working class, etc., but to the diasporic bodies marked by the relations of race, class, gender, and sexuality. Transnational cultural nationalism contains the multiplicity of bodies and experiences of diasporic women and locates them inside or outside the oppositional consciousness of an anti-West Islamic femininity, denying hybridity and the intermingling of the diasporic subject.

48. See Derrida (1995).

49. It is ironic how inconsequential modernity is with regard to secularization. Secularization is part of the modernization project to construct new identities and sensibilities based on the dichotomous categories of the religious and the secular. However, the definition of the secular and the religious and their meanings in different contexts are problematic.

50. This process is necessary for the diasporic subject. See Probyn (1996) on the question of the "inside and outside" of belonging.

Postscript

1. *Vogue,* May 2002. This article is one of many that reveal an obsession with what is under the *burqua.* There have also been a number of films, works of fiction, and reports focused on what is found behind, beneath, and under the veil.

2. These representational practices are not limited to women's magazines such as *Vogue,* but are widely used by various media. Such notions of Western freedom versus Eastern unfreedom even mobilized many mainstream feminist organizations in their attempt to save Afghani women.

Bibliography

Abrahamian, Ervand. 1991. "Khomeini's Populism." *New Left Review* 186: 102–19.

Abu-Lughod, Lila. 1986. *Veiled Sentiments: Honor and Poetry in a Bedouin Society.* Berkeley: University of California Press.

———. 1998. *Remaking Women: Feminism and Modernity in the Middle East.* Princeton, N.J.: Princeton University Press.

Abusharaf, Rogaia. 1998. "Unmasking Tradition." *The Sciences* (March/April): 23–27.

Adelkhah, Fariba. 1991. *La revolution sous le voile: Femmes islamiques d'Iran.* Paris: Karthala.

Afary, Janet. 1996. *The Iranian Constitutional Revolution, 1906–1911: Grassroots Democracy, Social Democracy, and the Origins of Feminism.* New York: Columbia University Press.

Afshar, Haleh. 1987. "Women, Marriage and the State in Iran." In *Women, State, and Ideology: Studies from Africa and Asia,* edited by Haleh Afshar, 70–86. Albany: State University of New York Press.

———. 1994. "Women and the Politics of Fundamentalism in Iran." *Women Against Fundamentalism Journal* 5, no. 1: 15–20.

———. 1998. *Islam and Feminisms: An Iranian Case Study.* New York: St. Martin's Press.

Agnes, Flavia. 1996. "Economic Rights of Women in Islamic Law." *Economic and Political Weekly,* Oct. 12–19, 2832–38.

Ahmed, Akbar S., and Donnan Hastings, eds. 1994. *Islam, Globalization and Postmodernity.* London: Routledge.

Ahmed, Leila. 1986. "Women and the Advent of Islam." *Signs* 11, no. 4: 665–91.

———. 1992. *Women and Gender in Islam: Historical Roots of a Modern Debate.* New Haven, Conn.: Yale University Press.

Aït Sabbah, Fatna A. 1984. *Women in the Muslim Unconscious.* New York: Pergamon Press.

Akinson, James, trans. 1832. *Kulsum Nane: Customs and Manners of the Women of Persia and their Domestic Superstitions.* London: J. L. Cox and Son.

Akrami, Jamshid. 1987. "The Blighted Spring: Iranian Political Cinema in the 1970s." In *Film and Politics in the Third World,* edited by J. D. Downing. New York: Praeger.

Alarcón, Norma. 1990. "The Theoretical Subject(s) of *This Bridge Called My Back* and Anglo-American Feminism." In *Making Face, Making Soul/Haciendo Caras: Creative and Critical Perspectives by Women of Color,* edited by Gloria Anzaldua, 356–69. San Francisco: Aunt Lute Books.

———. 1996. "Conjugating Subjects in the Age of Multiculturalism." In *Mapping Multiculturalism,* edited by Avery F. Gordon and Christopher Newfield, 127–48. Minneapolis: University of Minnesota Press.

———. 1998. "Chicana Feminism: In the Tracks of the 'Native Woman.'" In *Living Chicana Theory,* edited by Carla Trujillo, 371–82. Berkeley, Calif.: Third Woman Press.

Alavi Tabar, Ali Reza. 2000 (1379). "Mas'leh-e Zanan Dar Iran." *Zanan,* no. 65 (Tir): 44–45.

———. 2001 (1380). "Houqouq-e Zan va Mard Mosavi Ast Na moshabeh: Zanan az Negah-e Allameh Motahari." *Zanan,* no. 75 (Ordibehesht): 38–41.

Al-e Ahmad, Jalal-e. 1962. *Gharbzadegi.* Tehran: Ketab.

Alexander, Jacqui, and Chandra Talpade Mohanty, eds. 1997. *Feminist Genealogies, Colonial Legacies, Democratic Futures.* New York: Routledge.

Alexander, Meena. 1996. *The Shock of Arrival: Reflections on Postcolonial Experience.* Boston: South End Press.

Algar, Hamid. 1973. *Mirza Malkum Khan: A Study in the History of Iranian Modernism.* Berkeley: University of California Press.

———, ed. and trans. 1981. *Islam and Revolution: Writings and Declarations of Imam Khomeini.* Berkeley: Mizan Press.

Ali, Yasmin. 1992. "Muslim Women and the Politics of Ethnicity and Culture in Northern England." In *Refusing Holy Orders,* edited by Gita Sahgal and Nira Yuval-Davis, 101–23. London: Virago Press.

Alice: The Adventures of an English Girl in Persia. 1890. London.

Allen, Theodore. 1994. *The Invention of the White Race.* London: Verso.

Alloula, Malek. 1986. *The Colonial Harem.* Translated by Myrna and Wlad Godzich. Minneapolis: University of Minnesota Press.

Anderson, Benedict. 1991. *Imagined Communities: Reflections on the Origin and Spread of Nationalism.* London: Verso.

Anzaldua, Gloria, ed. 1990. *Making Face, Making Soul/Haciendo Caras: Creative and Critical Perspectives by Women of Color.* San Francisco: Aunt Lute Books.

Appadurai, Arjun. 1996. *Modernity at Large: Cultural Dimensions of Globalization.* Minneapolis: University of Minnesota Press.

————. 2001a. "Grassroots Globalization and the Research Imagination." In *Globalization,* edited by Arjun Appadurai, 1–21. Durham, N.C.: Duke University Press.

————, ed. 2001b. *Globalization.* Durham, N.C.: Duke University Press.

Appelbaum, Richard P. 1996. "Multiculturalism and Flexibility: Some New Directions in Global Capitalism." In *Mapping Multiculturalism,* ed. Avery F. Gordon and Christopher Newfield. Minneapolis: University of Minnesota Press.

Ardalan, Parvin. 2001 (1379). "Zanan Nashriat-e Zanan ra Mo'arefi Mikonad." *Zanan,* no. 71 (Day): 10–13.

Asad, Talal. 1993. *Genealogies of Religion.* Baltimore, Md.: Johns Hopkins University Press.

————. 2003. *Formations of the Secular.* Stanford, Calif.: Stanford University Press.

Asiqipur, Abda al-riza. 1968. *Yadegar-i Guzashtah: Majmu'ah-i Sukhanranihayi Ala-hazrat Faqid Riza Sahh Kabir, Reza Shah, Shah of Iran, 1878–1944.* Tehran: Javidan Publishing.

Assrar, Mostafa. 1997 (1376). *Hemaseh saazan-e ashura.* Tehran: Mohayya Publications.

Aveni, Anthony. 1998. "Time." In *Critical Terms for Religious Studies,* edited by Mark C. Taylor, 314–33. Chicago: University of Chicago Press.

Azari, Farah, ed. 1983. *Women of Iran: The Conflict with Fundamentalist Islam.* London: Ithaca Press.

Azarmina, Pejman. 2002. "In Iran, Gender Segregation Is Becoming a Fact of Medical Life." *Canadian Medical Association Journal* 166, no. 5: 645.

Bacchetta, Paola. 1996. "Hindu Nationalist Women as Ideologues: The Sangh, the Samiti and Differential Concepts of the Hindu Nation." In *Embodied Violence: Communalizing Women's Sexuality in South Asia,* edited by Kumari Jayawardena and Malathi de Alwis, 126–67. New Delhi: Kali for Women.

Bacchetta, Paola, Tina Campt, Inderpal Grewal, Caren Kaplan, Jennifer Terry, and Minoo Moallem. 2002. "Transnational Feminist Practices in Alliance Against War." Statement in *UK Women's Studies Newsletter, Daily Star* (Dhaka), *Manifesto* (Italy), *Revista Estudos Feministas* (Brazil), *Meridians* (vol. 2, no. 2, US), and *Cyberzone* (Italy).

Bachelard, Gaston. 1969. *The Poetics of Space: The Classic Look at How We Experience Intimate Places.* Boston: Beacon Press.

Balibar, Etienne. 1991a. "*Es Gibt Keimen Staat in Europa:* Racism and Politics in Europe Today." *New Left Review* 186: 5–19.

————. 1991b. "Is There a 'Neo Racism'?" In *Race, Nation, Class: Ambiguous Identities,* edited by Etienne Balibar and Immanuel Wallerstein, 17–28. London: Verso.

————. 1991c. "Racism and Nationalism." In *Race, Nation, Class: Ambiguous Identities,* edited by Etienne Balibar and Immanuel Wallerstein, 37–67. London: Verso.

————. 1994. *Masses, Classes, Ideas.* Translated by James Swenson. New York: Routledge.

Barlow, Tani. 1994. "Theorizing Women: *Funu, Guojia, Jiating* (Chinese Women, Chinese State, Chinese Family)." In *Scattered Hegemonies,* edited by Inderpal Grewal and Caren Kaplan, 173–96. Minneapolis: University of Minnesota Press.

————. ed. 1993. *Gender Politics in Modern China: Writing and Feminism.* Durham, N.C.: Duke University Press.

Barthes, Roland. 1972 [1957]. *Mythologies.* New York: Noonday Press.

————. 1985 [1967]. *The Fashion System.* New York: Jonathan Cape.

Bartky, Sandra Lee. 1990. *Femininity and Domination: Studies in the Phenomenology of Oppression.* New York: Routledge.

Bassett, James. 1887. *Persia, The Land of the Imams: A Narrative of Travel and Residence, 1871–1885.* London: Blackie & Son.

Bataille, Georges. 1989. *The Tears of Eros.* Translated by Peter Connor. San Francisco: City Lights.

————. 1992. *Theory of Religion.* Translated by Robert Hurley. New York: Zone Books.

Baudrillard, Jean. 1970. *La société de consommation.* Paris: Gallimard.

Behdad, Ali. 1994. *Belated Travelers: Orientalism in the Age of Colonial Dissolution.* Durham, N.C.: Duke University Press.

Bell, Margaret L. Gertrude. 1894. *Safar Nameh, Persian Pictures: A Book of Travel.* London: Richard Bentley and Son.

Benavides, Gustavo. 1998. "Modernity." In *Critical Terms for Religious Studies,* edited by Mark C. Taylor, 186–204. Chicago: University of Chicago Press.

Berlant, Lauren. 1991. *The Anatomy of National Fantasy: Hawthorne, Utopia, and Everyday Life.* Chicago: University of Chicago Press.

Bernal, Victoria. 1992. *Gender, Culture and Capitalism.* Working Paper No. 160. Boston: Boston University African Studies Center.

Beverley, John. 1999. *Subalternity and Representation: Arguments in Cultural Theory.* Durham, N.C.: Duke University Press.

Bhabha, K. Homi. 1994. *The Location of Culture.* London: Routledge.

Bhargava, Rajeev, ed. 1998. *Secularism and Its Critics.* Delhi: Oxford University Press.

Binder, Leonard. 1988. *Islamic Liberalism: A Critique of Development Ideologies.* Chicago: University of Chicago Press.

Bird, Mary Rebecca. 1899. *Persian Women and Their Creed.* London: Church Missionary Society.

Boal, Iain. 1990. "Facing the Past." *Before Columbus Review* (Spring/Summer): 7–31.

Bourdieu, Pierre. 1984. *Distinction: A Social Critique of the Judgment of Taste.* Cambridge, Mass.: Harvard University Press.

Brah, Avtar. 1996. *Cartographies of Diaspora: Contesting Identities.* London: Routledge.

Brasher, E. Brenda. 1998. *Godly Women: Fundamentalism and Female Power.* New Brunswick, N.J.: Rutgers University Press.

Brière, Claire, and Pierre Blanchet. 1979. *Iran: La révolution au nom de dieu.* Paris: Editions du Seuil.

Bronfen, Elizabeth. 1992. *Over Her Dead Body: Death, Femininity and the Aesthetic.* New York: Routledge.

Brown, Wendy. 1995. *States of Injury: Power and Freedom in Late Modernity.* Princeton, N.J.: Princeton University Press.

Butalia, Urvashi. 1995. "Muslims and Hindus. Men and Women. Communal Stereotypes and the Partition of India." In *Women and Right-Wing Movements: Indian Experience,* edited by Tanika Sarkar and Urvashi Butalia, 58–81. London: Zed Books.

Butler, Judith. 1997a. *Excitable Speech: A Politics of the Performative.* New York: Routledge.

———. 1997b. *The Psychic Life of Power.* Stanford, Calif.: Stanford University Press.

Caputo, D. John. 2001. *On Religion.* London: Routledge.

Carrette, R. Jeremy. 1999. *Religion and Culture by Michel Foucault.* Manchester: Manchester University Press, and New York: Routledge.

———. 2000. *Foucault and Religion: Spiritual Corporality and Political Spirituality.* London: Routledge.

Castelli, Elizabeth. 1991. "'I Will Make Mary Male': Pieties of the Body and Gender Transformation of Christian Women in Late Antiquity." In *Body Guards: The Cultural Politics of Gender Ambiguity,* edited by Julia Epstein and Kristina Straub, 29–49. London: Routledge.

———, ed. 2001. *Women, Gender, Religion: A Reader.* New York: Palgrave.

Chakrabarty, Dipesh. 1998. "Revisiting the Tradition/Modernity Binary." In *Mirror of Modernity: Invented Traditions of Modern Japan,* edited by Stephen Vlastos, 285–96. Berkeley: University of California Press.

Chatterjee, Partha. 1998. "Secularism and Tolerance." In *Secularism and Its Critics,* edited by Rajeev Bhargava, 345–79. Delhi: Oxford University Press.

Chelkowski, J. Peter, ed. 1979. *Ta'ziyeh: Ritual and Drama in Iran.* New York: New York University Press.

Chelkowski, J. Peter, and Hamid Dabashi. 1999. *Staging a Revolution: The Art of Persuasion in the Islamic Republic of Iran.* New York: New York University Press.

Christ, Carol. 1995. *Diving Deep and Surfacing: Women Writers on Spiritual Quest.* Boston: Beacon Press.

Christ, Carol, and Judith Plaskow. 1979. *Womanspirit Rising: A Feminist Reader in Religion.* San Francisco: Harper & Row.

Cixous, Hélène. 1981. "Sorties." In *New French Feminisms,* edited by Elaine Marks and Isabelle de Courtivron, 90–98. New York: Schocken.

Clifford, James. 1986. "On Ethnographic Allegory." In *Writing Culture: The Poetics and Politics of Ethnography,* edited by James Clifford and George E. Marcus, 98–121. Berkeley: University of California Press.

―――. 1989. "Notes on Theory and Travel." *Inscriptions* 5: 177–88.

Cole, Juan R. I., and Nikki R. Keddie, eds. 1986. *Shiʿism and Social Protest*. New Haven, Conn.: Yale University Press.

Connell, R. W. 1987. *Gender and Power: Society, the Person and Sexual Politics*. Stanford, Calif.: Stanford University Press.

Connolly, William E. 1999. *Why I Am Not a Secularist*. Minneapolis: University of Minnesota Press.

Costera, Irene, and Paukje Prins. 1998. "How Bodies Come to Matter: An Interview with Judith Butler." *Signs* 2, no. 23: 275–86.

Daly, Mary. 1978. *Gyn/Ecology: The Metaethics of Radical Feminism*. Boston: Beacon Press.

Das, Veena, ed. 1990. *Mirrors of Violence: Communities, Riots and Survivors in South Asia*. New Delhi: Oxford University Press.

Dehqani, Ashraf. 1978. *Torture and Resistance in Iran: Memoirs of the Woman Guerrilla Ashraf*. New Dehli: Swan.

Deleuze, Gilles, and Félix Guattari. 1975. *Capitalisme et schizophrénie*. Paris: Editions de Minuit.

Delphy, Christine. 1983. "Agriculture et travail domestique: La réponse de La Bergère à Engels." *Nouvelles Questions Feministes* 5 (Spring): 3–17.

Derrida, Jacques. 1993. *Aporias*. Translated by Thomas Dutoit. Stanford, Calif.: Stanford University Press.

―――. 1995. *The Gift of Death*. Translated by David Wills. Chicago: University of Chicago Press.

―――. 1997. *Politics of Friendship*. Translated by George Collins. London: Verso.

―――. 1998. "Faith and Knowledge: The Two Sources of 'Religion' at the Limits of Reason Alone." In *Religion,* edited by Jacques Derrida and Gianni Vattimo, translated by David Webb, 1–78. Stanford, Calif.: Stanford University Press.

―――. 2001. "Above All, No Journalists!" In *Religion and Media,* edited by Hent de Vries and Samuel Weber, 56–93. Stanford, Calif.: Stanford University Press.

Derrida, Jacques, and Gianni Vattimo, eds. 1998. *Religion*. Stanford, Calif.: Stanford University Press.

De Vries, Hent. 2001. "In Media Res: Global Religion, Public Spheres, and the Task of Contemporary Comparative Religious Studies." In *Religion and Media,* edited by Hent de Vries and Samuel Weber. Stanford, Calif.: Stanford University Press.

Diamond, Sara. 1995. *Roads to Dominion: Right-Wing Movements and Political Power in the United States*. New York: Guilford Press.

Dieulafoy, Jane. 1989. *Une Amazone en Orient: Du Carcase à Persépolis, 1888–1882*. Paris: Phébus.

―――. 1990. *L'Orient sous le voile: De Chiraz à Baghdad 1881–1882*. Paris: Phébus.

Di Leonardo, Micaela. 1984. *The Variety of Ethnic Experience: Kinship, Class, and Gender among California Italian-Americans.* Ithaca, N.Y.: Cornell University Press.

Dirlik, Arif, and Xudong Zhang, eds. 2000. *Postmodernism and China.* Durham, N.C.: Duke University Press.

D'Isanto, Luca. 1999. "Introduction." In *Belief,* by Gianni Vattimo, translated by Luca D'Isanto and David Webb, 1–17. Stanford, Calif.: Stanford University Press.

Djebar, Assia. 1988. *Fantasia: An Algerian Cavalcade.* Translated by Dorothy Blair. London: Quartet.

Donaldson, E. Laura, and Kwok Pui-lan. 2002. *Postcolonialism, Feminism and Religious Discourse.* New York: Routledge.

Douglas, Mary. 1980. *Purity and Danger: An Analysis of the Concepts of Pollution and Taboo.* London: Routledge and Kegan Paul.

Dworkin, Andrea. 1974. *Woman Hating.* New York: Dutton.

Ebadi, Shirin. 1994 (1373). *Tarikh-chehe Houghough-e Bashar dar Iran* [History and Documentation of Human Rights in Iran]. Tehran: Roshangaran Publishing.

Eliade, Mircea. 1987 [1957]. *The Sacred and the Profane: The Nature of Religion.* Translated by Willard R. Trask. San Diego, Calif.: Harcourt Brace & Company.

Elias, Norbert. 1978. *The Civilizing Process: The Development of Manners.* Translated by Edmund Jephcott. New York: Blackwell.

El Saadawi, Nawal. 1988. *The Fall of the Imam.* London: Minerva.

Enloe, Cynthia. 1990. *Bananas, Beaches and Bases: Making Feminist Sense of International Politics.* Berkeley: University of California Press.

———. 1993. *The Morning After: Sexual Politics at the End of the Cold War.* Berkeley: University of California Press.

———. 2003. "A Conversation with Cynthia Enloe: Feminists Look at Masculinity and the Men Who Wage War." *Signs* 28, no. 4: 1187–1207.

Esposito, L. John. 1993. *The Islamic Threat: Myth or Reality.* New York: Oxford University Press.

Fahimi, Seyyed Mehdi. 1998. *Farhang-e Jebhe* [The Culture of the War Front. Vol 2: Ethics and Manners]. Tehran: Farhang Gostar and Soroush Publications.

———. 2000. *Farhang-e Jebhe* [The Culture of the War Front. Vol. 1: Written Reminiscences]. Tehran: Farhang Gostar and Soroush Publications.

Fanon, Frantz. 1967. *A Dying Colonialism.* New York: Grove Press.

———. 1968 [1961]. *The Wretched of the Earth.* Translated by Constance Farrington. New York: Grove Press.

Ferdowsi, Abulghasem. 1992. *The Legend of Seyavash.* Translated by Dick Davis. London: Penguin Books.

"Figh and Women's Human Rights: Interview with Ayatollah Bojnourdi." 1997. *Farzaneh: Journal of Women's Studies and Research* 3, no. 8 (Winter): 37–42.

Fischer, M. J. Michael. 2001. "Filmic Judgment and Cultural Critique: The Work of Art, Ethics, and Religion in Iranian Cinema." In *Religion and Media*, edited by Hent De Vries and Samuel Weber, 456–86. Stanford, Calif.: Stanford University Press.

Fischer, M. J. Michael, and Mehdi Abedi. 1990. *Debating Muslims: Cultural Dialogues in Postmodernity and Tradition*. Madison: University of Wisconsin Press.

Foran, John. 1997. "The Comparative-Historical Sociology of Third World Social Revolutions." In *Theorizing Revolutions*, edited by John Foran, 227–67. London: Routledge.

Foucault, Michel. 1961. *Histoire de la folie à l'âge classique*. Paris: Plon.

——. 1978. *The History of Sexuality: An Introduction*. Translated by Robert Hurly. Vol. 1. New York: Pantheon.

——. 1979a. *Discipline and Punish: The Birth of the Prison*. Translated by Alan Sheridan. New York: Vintage Books.

——. 1979b. " 'L'esprit d'un monde sans esprit': Entretien avec Michel Foucault." In *Iran: La révolution au nom de dieu*, edited by Claire Brière and Pierre Blanchet, 227–41. Paris: Editions du Seuil.

——. 1980. *Power/Knowledge: Selected Interviews and Other Writings, 1972–1979*. Edited and translated by Collin Gordin. New York: Pantheon.

——. 1989. *Foucault Live (Interviews, 1966–1984)*. Translated by John Johnston, edited by Sylvère Lotringer. New York: Semiotext(e) Foreign Agents Series.

——. 1991. *Remarks on Marx, Conversations with Duccio Trombardori*. Translated by James Goldstein and James Cascaito. New York: Semiotext(e).

——. 1994a. *Dits et écrits: 1954–1988*. Paris: Gallimard.

——. 1994b. "Inutile de soulever?" In *Dits et écrits*, vol.3, 790–94. Paris: Gallimard.

——. 1997. *Il faut défendre la société: Cours au Collège de France (1975–1976)*. Paris: Hautes Etudes, Gallimard and Seuil.

——. 2000. *Power: Essential Works of Foucault 1954–1984*. Edited by James D. Faubion. New York: New Press.

Gafari, Hadi. 1979. *Hamd Mi Amouzad*. Tehran: Bessat.

Ganji, Akbar. 1999 (1378). *Talaghi-ye facisti az Din va Dolat* [Fascistic Interpretation of Religion]. Tehran: Entesharat-e Tarhe nou.

Gellner, Ernest. 1992. *Postmodernism, Reason and Religion*. London: Routledge.

Gobineau, Conte de. 1865. *Les religions et les philosophies dans l'Asie Centrale*. Paris: Librarie Académique.

——. 1967 [1854]. *The Inequality of Human Races*. Translated by Adrian Collins. New York: Howard Fertig.

Goldberg, Theo David, ed. 1990. *Anatomy of Racism*. Minneapolis: University of Minnesota Press.

Göle, Nilufer. 1996. *The Forbidden Modern: Civilization and Veiling*. Ann Arbor: University of Michigan Press.

Goodwin, Sarah Webster, and Elizabeth Bronfen, eds. 1993. *Death and Repre-*

sentation. Baltimore, Md.: Johns Hopkins University Press.

Gordon, Avery. 1997. *Ghostly Matters: Haunting and the Sociological Imagination*. Minneapolis: University of Minnesota Press.

Gorgi, Monir, and Massoumeh Ebtekar. 1994. "A Brief Study on the Influence of Pre-Islamic Cultures: On the Contemporary Status of Muslim Women." *Farzaneh* 1, no. 4 (Summer–Fall): 145–58.

Gosh, Bishnupriya, and Brinda Bose. 1997. *Interventions: Feminist Dialogues on Third World Women's Literature and Film*. New York: Garland Publishing.

Graham-Brown, Sarah. 1988. *Images of Women: The Portrayal of Women in Photography of the Middle East 1860–1950*. New York: Columbia University Press.

Gramsci, Antonio. 1971. *Selections from the Prison Notebooks of Antonio Gramsci*. Edited by Quintin Hoare and Geoffrey Nowell Smith. New York: International Publishers.

Grewal, Inderpal. 1993. "Reading and Writing the South Asian Diaspora: Feminism and Nationalism in North America." In *Our Feet Walk the Sky: Women of the South Asian Diaspora*, edited by the Women of South Asian Descent Collective, 226–36. San Francisco: Aunt Lute Books.

———. 1996. *Home and Harem: Nation, Gender, Empire, and the Cultures of Travel*. Durham, N.C.: Duke University Press.

Grewal, Inderpal, Akhil Gupta, and Aihwa Ong. 1999. "Introduction: Asian Transnationalities." *Positions* 7, no. 3 (Winter): 653–66.

Grewal, Inderpal, and Caren Kaplan. 1996. "Warrior Marks: Global Womanism's Neo-Colonial Discourse in a Multicultural Context." *Camera Obscura* 39 (September): 5–33.

———, eds. 1994. *Scattered Hegemonies: Postmodernity and Transnational Feminist Practices*. Minneapolis: University of Minnesota Press.

———. 2000. "Postcolonial Studies and Transnational Feminist Practices." *Jouvert* 5, no. 1 (Autumn): http://socialchass.ncsu.edu/Jouvert/vsiyGrewal.htm.

Griffith, R. Marie. 1997. *God's Daughters: Evangelical Women and the Powers of Submission*. Berkeley: University of California Press.

Grosz, Elizabeth. 1994. *Volatile Bodies: Toward a Corporeal Feminism*. Bloomington: Indiana University Press.

Guillaumin, Colette. 1972. *L'idéologie raciste: Genèse et langage actuel*. Paris: Mouton.

———. 1985. "Avec ou sans race." *Le genre humain*, no. 11: 215–22. Paris: Editions Complexe.

———. 1995. *Racism, Sexism, Power and Ideology*. London: Routledge.

Gurnah, Abdulrazak. 2000. "Strangers Settled among Us." Paper presented at the Recasting European History: National Consciousness, Migration, Multicultural Lives Conference, Bremen, Germany, May 18–21.

Habermas, Jürgen. 1975. *Legitimation Crisis*. Boston: Beacon Press.

———. 2002. "The Unrest Is Growing: Interview with Christiane Hoffmann." *Frankfurter Allgemeine Zeitung*, June 18, 2002.

Haeri, Shahla. 1989. *Law of Desire: Temporary Marriage in Shiʻi Islam.* Syracuse, N.Y.: Syracuse University Press.

Hale, Sandra. 1999. "Mothers and Militias: Islamic State Construction of the Women Citizens of Northern Sudan." *Citizenship Studies* 3, no. 3: 373–86.

Hall, Stuart. 1991a. "The Local and the Global: Globalization and Ethnicity." In *Culture, Globalization and the World-System,* edited by Anthony D. King, 19–40. Binghamton: Department of Art and Art History, State University of New York Binghamton.

———. 1991b. "Notes on Deconstructing 'The Popular.'" In *People's History and Socialist Theory,* edited by Raphael Samuel, 227–39. London: Routledge and Kegan Paul.

———. 1991c. "Old and New Identities." In *Culture, Globalization and the World-System,* edited by Anthony D. King, 41–68. Binghamton: Department of Art and Art History, SUNY Binghamton.

———. 1996. "The West and the Rest: Discourse and Power." In *Modernity: An Introduction to Modern Societies,* edited by Stuart Hall, David Held, Don Hubert, and Kenneth Thompson, 184–227. Cambridge: Blackwell Publishers.

———, ed. 1997. *Representation: Cultural Representations and Signifying Practices.* London: Open University.

Hamilton, Peter. 1997. "Presenting the Social: France and Frenchness in Post-War Humanist Photography." In *Representation: Cultural Representations and Signifying Practices,* edited by Stuart Hall, 75–150. London: Sage Publications and the Open University.

Hanafi, Hassan. 1990. "De l'orientalisme à l'occidentalisme: L'orientalisme interrogations." *Peuples Méditerranéens* 50 (Jan.–Mar.): 115–19.

Hartmann, Heidi. 1979. "Capitalism, Patriarchy and Job Segregation by Sex." In *Capitalism, Patriarchy and the Case for Socialist Feminism,* edited by Zillah R. Eisenstein, 206–47. New York: Monthly Review Press.

Hashemi, Faezeh. 1997. Interview. *Asahi Shimbun,* Tokyo, Feb. 6, 1997.

Hawley, Stratton John, ed. 1994. *Fundamentalism and Gender.* New York: Oxford University Press.

Hedayat, Sadeq. 2001 [1930–1946] (1324). "Haji Agha," "Albesat-el eslamieh elal elbelade elfaranjieh," and "Toup-e Morvari." In *Afsaneh-e Afarinish.* Paris: Farzad Publications.

Hegel, G. W. F. 1967 [1910]. *The Phenomenology of Spirit.* Translated by George Lichtheim. New York: Harper Torchbooks.

Heiss, Mary Ann. 1997. *Empire and Nationhood: The United States, Great Britain, and Iranian Oil, 1950–1954.* New York: Columbia University Press.

Hentsch, Thierry. 1988. *L'orient imaginaire: La vision politique occidentale de l'Est méditerranéen.* Paris: Editions de Minuit.

Hobsbawm, E.J. 1990. *Nations and Nationalism since 1789.* Cambridge: Cambridge University Press.

Hochschild, Arlie Russell. 1989. *The Second Shift: Working Parents and the Revolution at Home.* New York: Viking-Penguin.

Honig-Parnass, Tivka. 1994. "Jewish Fundamentalism and Oppression of Women as Inherent in the Jewish-Zionist State." *Women Against Fundamentalism Journal* 1, no. 5: 21–24.

Hoodfar, Homa. 1991. "Return to Veil: Personal Strategy and Public Participation in Egypt." In *Working Women: International Perspectives on Labour and Gender Ideology,* edited by Nanneke Redclift and M. Thea Sinclair, 104–24. London: Routledge.

———. 1999. "The Women's Movement in Iran: Women at the Crossroads of Secularization and Islamization." *Women Living under Muslim Law: International Solidarity Network.* Paris: Women's Movement Series, no.1 (Winter 1999): 3–46.

Hooks, Bell. 1984. *Feminist Theory: From Margin to Center.* Boston: South End Press.

———. 1990. *Yearning: Race, Gender, and Cultural Politics.* Boston: South End Press.

Horkheimer, Max, and Theodor W. Adorno. 1987 [1944]. *Dialectic of Enlightenment.* New York: Continuum.

Hosseinjani, Abolgassem. 1998. *Hussein, Ehyagat-e Adam* [Imam Hussein: The Reviver of Man]. Tehran: Soroush.

How to Win Over Moslem Races. 1906. London: Fleming H. Revell Company.

Hume-Griffith, M. E. 1909. *Behind the Veil in Persia and Turkish Arabia: An Account of an Englishwoman's Eight Years' Residence amongst the Women of the East.* 2d ed. London: Seeley.

Huntington, Samuel P. 1993. "The Clash of Civilizations?" *Foreign Affairs* 72, no. 3 (Summer): 22–49.

Jakobsen, Janet J., and Ann Pellegrini. 2000. "World Secularisms at the Millennium." *Social Text* 64, vol. 18, no. 3 (Fall): 1–27.

———. 2001. "Getting Religion." In *Women, Gender, Religion: A Reader,* edited by Elizabeth Castelli, 518–28. New York: Palgrave.

Jame'eh madani va Iran-e emrooz. 1998 (1377). Tehran: Naghsh-va Negar.

Jayawardena, Kumari, and Malathi de Alwis. 1996. *Embodied Violence: Communalizing Women's Sexuality in South Asia.* New Delhi: Kali for Women.

Joseph, Suad. 1996. "Gender and Citizenship in Middle Eastern States." *Middle East Report* 198 (Jan.-Mar.): 4–10.

———. 1999. "Descent of the Nation: Kinship and Citizenship in Lebanon." *Citizenship Studies* 3, no. 3: 295–318.

Juteau, Danielle, and Nicole Laurin. 1989. "From Nuns to Surrogate Mothers: Evolution of the Forms of the Appropriation of Women." *Feminist Issues* 9, no. 1 (Spring): 13–40.

Kadi, Joanna, ed. 1994. *Food for Our Grandmothers: Writings by Arab American and Arab Canadian Feminists.* Boston: South End Press.

Kadivar, Jamileh. 1996 (1375). *Zan.* Tehran: Etella-at Publishers.

Kamalkhani, Zahra. 1998. "Reconstruction of Islamic Knowledge and Knowing: A Case of Islamic Practices among Women in Iran." In *Women and Is-*

lamization: Contemporary Dimensions of Discourse on Gender Relations, edited by Karin Ask and Marit Tjomsland, 177–93. Oxford: Berg.

Kandiyoti, Deniz, ed. 1991. *Women, Islam and the State*. Philadelphia: Temple University Press.

———. 1996. *Gendering the Middle East: Emerging Perspectives*. Syracuse, N.Y.: Syracuse University Press.

Kaplan, Caren. 1992. "Resisting Autobiography: Out-Law Genres and Transnational Feminist Subjects." In *De/colonizing the Subject*, edited by Sidonie Smith and Julia Watson, 115–68. Minneapolis: University of Minnesota Press.

———. 1995. "A World Without Boundaries. The Body Shop's Trans/national Geographics." *Social Text* 43 (Fall): 45–66.

———. 1996. *Questions of Travel: Postmodern Discourses of Displacement*. Durham, N.C.: Duke University Press.

———. 1997. "Precision Targets: Discourses of Location and the Marketing of Global Positioning Systems." Available at http://www.geog.ubc.ca/iiccg/papers/kaplan_C.html.

———. 2002. "Transporting the Subject: Technologies of Mobility and Location in an Era of Globalization." *PMLA* 117, no. 1 (Jan.): 32–42.

Kaplan, Caren, Norma Alarcón, and Minoo Moallem. 1999. *Between Women and Nation: Nationalisms, Transnational Feminisms, and the State*. Durham, N.C.: Duke University Press.

Kaplan, Caren, and Inderpal Grewal. 1994. "Transnational Feminist Cultural Studies: Beyond the Marxism/Poststructuralism/Feminism Divides." *Positions* 2, no. 2.

Kar, Mehrangiz. 1991. *Fereshteh-e Edalat va Pareh-haye Douzakh*. Tehran: Entesharat-e Roshanaran.

———. 1997. *Houghough-e Siasi-e Zanan-e Iran* [Political Rights of Iranian Women]. Tehran: Roshangaran and Women Studies Publishing.

———. 2000a. *A Research about Violence Against Women in Iran*. Tehran: Roshangaran and Women Studies Publishing.

———. 2000b (1379). *Musharakat-e Siyasi-e Zanan: Mavani'va Emkanat*. Tehran: Rowshangaran va Motaleat-e Zanan.

———. 2001a (1380). *Kudam haqq? Kudam taklif?: Darbarah-i vaz'iyat-i huquqi-i zan dar khanvadah*. Tehran: Jamiah-i Iraniyan.

———2001b. "Women's Struggles in Iran from the 1979 Revolution to 1999." In *Globalization, Gender, and Religion*, edited by Jane H. Bayes and Nayereh Tohidi, 177–201. New York: Palgrave.

Kar, Mehrangiz, and Homa Hoodfar. 1996. "Personal Status Law as Defined by the Islamic Republic of Iran: An Appraisal." *Special Dossier: Shifting Boundaries in Marriage and Divorce in Muslim Communities* 1 (Fall): 7–36.

Karimi Majd, Roya. 2000 (1379). "Inja Tanha Khaneh-e Amn-e Dokhtaran-e Farari Ast/ Here Is the Only Safe Place for Girls on the Run." *Zanan*, no. 70 (Azar): 2–8.

Kashi, Mohamad Javad. 2000a (1379). "Zan dar Kalam-e Siasi: Tahlili az Olgouy-e Zan dar Negah-e Doctor Ali Shari'ati." *Zanan*, no. 70 (Azar): 54–59.

———. 2000b (1378). "Zarourat-e Kankashi Tazeh dar Tarif-e Masail-e Zanan." *Zanan*, no. 61 (Esfand): 62–64.

Kasravi, Ahmad. 1975 [1324]. *Khaharan va Doktaran-e Ma* [Our Sisters and Daughters]. Tehran: Payman Publications.

Katouzian, Homa. 2000. *State and Society in Iran: The Eclipse of the Qajars and the Emergence of the Pahlavi*. London: I. B. Tauris Publishers.

Kaufman, Renee Debra. 1991. *Rachel's Daughters: Newly Orthodox Jewish Women*. New Brunswick, N.J.: Rutgers University Press.

Keddie, Nikki R. 1981. *Roots of Revolution: An Interpretive History of Modern Iran*. New Haven, Conn.: Yale University Press.

———. 1983. *An Islamic Response to Imperialism: Political and Religious Writings of Sayyid Jamal ad-Din al-Afghani*. Berkeley: University of California Press.

Kemp, Norman. 1953. *Abadan: A First-Hand Account of the Persian Oil Crisis*. London: Allan Wingate.

Khanum, Saeeda. 1992. "Education and the Muslim Girl." In *Refusing Holy Orders*, edited by Gita Sahgal and Nira Yuval-Davis, 124–40. London: Virago Press.

Khomeini, Sayyid Ruhollah Musavi. 1974. *Speeches: Selections*. Tehran: Anjuman-i Islami-i Danishjuyan dar Amrika va Canada.

———. 1978a. *Hukumat-e Islami: Velayat-eFaqih*. Tehran: Amir Kabir.

———. 1978b. *Khomeini va Junbish: Khutbah-ha va I'lamiyah-ha va Namah-ha va Fatava*. Vol. 1. Tehran: Alfatah Publishers.

———. 1980. *Selected Messages and Speeches of Imam Khomeini*. Tehran: Ministry of National Guidance.

———. 1981a. *Islam and Revolution: Writings and Declarations of Imam Khomeini*. Translated and annotated by Hamid Algar. Berkeley: Mizan Press.

———. 1981b. *Khumeini Speaks Revolution*. Karachi: International Islamic Publishers.

———. 1982. *Majmu'a-i az Maktubat, Sukhanraniha, Payamha va Fatavi-i Imam Khumayni az Nimeh-i Duvvum-i 1341 ta Hijrat bih Paris, 14 Mihr Mah-i 1357*. Tehran: Intisharat-i Chappakhsh.

———. 1984. *Kungrah-I Ibadi-yi siyasi-yi hajj: Majmu'a-i Sukhanan va Payamha-yi Imam Khomeini* [Collection of Lectures]. Tehran: Markaz-i Tahqiqat va Intisharat-i Hajj.

———. 1986. *Simay-e Zan dar Kalam-e Imam Khmeini*. Tehran: Vezarat-e Ershad-e Islami.

———. 1987 (1366). *Faryad-i Baraat: Payam-i Imam khomeini bih Hujjaj-i Bayt Allah al-Haram, Zi Hijjah 1407*. Tehran: Vizarat-e Farhang va Irshad-e Eslami, Sazamn-e chap va Intisharat.

———. 1991. *Quran, Bab-i ma, Rifat-i Allah: Majmu'a-i Bayanat va Nivishtah, ha-yi Hazrat Imam Khomeini dar Barah-i Quran*. Tehran: Markaz-i Pakhsh Payam-i Azadi.

———. 1994. *Khatirah va Hikayat az Zaban-i Hazrat-i Imam-i Khumayni, Hikayatha-yi Talkh va Shirin.* Tehran: Muassasah-i Farhangi-i Qadr-i Vilayat.

Kintz, Linda. 1992. *The Subject's Tragedy: Political Poetics, Feminist Theory, and Drama.* Ann Arbor: University of Michigan Press.

———. 1997. *Between Jesus and the Market: The Emotions that Matter in Right-Wing America.* Durham, N.C.: Duke University Press.

Klatch, Rebecca E. 1987. *Women of the New Right.* Philadelphia: Temple University Press.

Kojève, Alexandre. 1947. *Introduction à la lecture de Hegel.* Paris: Editions Gallimard.

Koven, Seth, and Sonya Michel. 1993. *Mothers of a New World: Maternalist Politics and the Origin of Welfare States.* New York: Routledge.

Kristeva, Julia. 1982. *Pouvoirs de l'horreur.* Paris: Editions du Seuil.

Lawrence, Bruce B. 1989. *Defenders of God: The Fundamentalist Revolt Against the Modern Age.* New York: Harper & Row.

Layoun, Mary. 1992. "Telling Spaces: Palestinian Women and the Engendering of National Narratives." In *Nationalisms and Sexualities,* edited by Andrew Parker, Mary Russo, Doris Sommer, and Patricia Yaeger, 407–23. New York: Routledge.

Lazreg, Marnia. 1994. *The Eloquence of Silence: Algerian Women in Question.* New York: Routledge.

Le Doeuff, Michele. 1977. "Women and Philosophy." *Radical Philosophy* 17 (Summer): 2–11.

Liobera, Joseph R. 1994. *The God of Modernity: The Development of Nationalism in Western Europe.* Oxford: Berg Publishers.

Liu, H. Lydia. 1995. *Translingual Practice: Literature, National Culture, and Translated Modernity, China 1900–1937.* Stanford, Calif.: Stanford University Press.

———. ed. 1999. *Tokens of Exchange: The Problem of Translation in Global Circulations.* Durham, N.C.: Duke University Press.

Lovibond, Sabina. 1996. "Meaning What We Say: Feminist Ethics and the Critique of Humanism." *New Left Review,* no. 220 (Nov./Dec.): 98–116.

Lowe, Lisa. 1996. *Immigrant Acts: On Asian American Cultural Politics.* Durham, N.C.: Duke University Press.

Macciocchi, Maria-Antonietta. 1974. *Pour Gramsci.* Paris: Editions du Seuil.

Mackie, Erin. 1997. *Market à la Mode: Fashion, Commodity, and Gender in the Tatler and the Spectator.* Baltimore, Md.: Johns Hopkins Press.

Mahmoud. 1990 (1369). "You are from which tribe, my sister?" In *Zan dar ayeneh-e defa'e moggadas* [Woman in the Mirror of Sacred Defense], 64–75. Tehran: Publishing Arm of the Islamic Guards.

Majid, Anouar. 2000. *Unveiling Traditions: Postcolonial Islam in a Polycentric World.* Durham, N.C.: Duke University Press.

Majidi, Majid. 1999. *Children of Heaven: Script, Interview, Critique.* Tehran: Farhang Kavesh Publication.

Malcolm, Mrs. Napier. 1911. *Children of Persia*. Edinburgh: Oliphant, Anderson & Ferrier.

Malcolm, Sir John. 1827. *Sketches of Persia: From the Journals of a Traveler in the East*. Vol. 1. London: John Murray.

Malkum Khan, Mirza. 1948 (1327). *Majmuah-i âsar-i Mirza Malkum Khan, 1833–1908* [Collected Works]. Tehran: Intisharat-i Elmi.

———. 1976. *Qanun* [The Law]. Edited by Huma Natiq. Tehran: Amir Kabir.

Mani, Lata. 1989. "Contentious Traditions: The Debate on Sati in Colonial India." In *Recasting Women*, edited by Kum Kum Sangari and Sudesh Vaid, 88–126. New Dehli: Kali for Women.

Marsh, Cunliffe Hippisley. 1877. *A Ride through Islam: A Journey through Persia and Afghanistan to India, via Meshed, Herat and Kandahar*. London: Tinsley Brothers.

Marty, Martin E., and Scott R. Appleby, eds. 1991. *Fundamentalisms Observed*. Chicago: University of Chicago Press.

Masiello, Francine. 1992. *Between Civilization and Barbarism: Women, Nation and Literary Culture in Modern Argentina*. Lincoln: University of Nebraska Press.

Massey, Doreen. 1994. *Space, Place, and Gender*. Minneapolis: University of Minnesota Press.

Mazumdar, Sucheta. 1992. "Women, Culture and Politics: Engendering the Hindu Nation." *South Asia Bulletin* 12, no. 2 (Fall): 1–24.

McClintock, Anne. 1992. "The Angel of Progress: Pitfalls of the Term 'Post-Colonialism.'" *Social Text*, no. 32: 84–98.

———. 1995. *Imperial Leather: Race, Gender and Sexuality in the Colonial Contest*. New York: Routledge.

Mehrabi, Mas'ud. 1984. *Tarikh-i Sinema-yi Iran*. Tehran: Film Publications.

Mernissi, Fatima. 1987. *The Fundamentalist Obsession with Women*. Pakistan: Simorgh.

———. 1991. *The Veil and the Male Elite: A Feminist Interpretation of Women's Rights in Islam*. Boston: Addison-Wesley.

———. 1992. *Islam and Democracy: Fear of the Modern World*. Translated by Mary Jo Lakeland. Boston: Addison-Wesley.

———. 1996. *Women's Rebellion and Islamic Memory*. London: Zed Books.

Methods of Mission Work Among Moslems. 1906. London: Fleming H. Revell Company.

Mies, Maria. 1986. *Patriarchy and Accumulation on a World Scale: Women in the International Division of Labor*. London: Zed Books.

Milani, Tahmineh. 1997. *Dou Zan*. Tehran: Tofigh Afarin.

———. 2001. "Ma ra az Rishe Michinand Valei Az Shakheh Miruryam/They Cut Me from the Root, I Grow from the Stem: A Dialogue between Effat Mahbaz and Tahmineh Milani." *Iran-e Emrooz*. Available at www.iranemrooz.de/goftgu/milani0404.html.

Minh-ha, T. Trinh. 1989. *Woman, Native, Other*. Indianapolis: Indiana University Press.

———. 1990. "Not You/Like You: Post-Colonial Women and the Interlocking Questions of Identity and Difference." In *Making Face, Making Soul/Haciendo Caras: Creative and Critical Perspectives by Women of Color*, edited by Gloria Anzaldua, 371–75. San Francisco: Aunt Lute Books.

———. 1991. *When the Moon Waxes Red*. New York: Routledge.

Mir-Hosseini, Ziba. 1999. *Islam and Gender: The Religious Debate in Contemporary Iran*. Princeton, N.J.: Princeton University Press.

Moallem, Ali, and Omid Rowhani. 1997 (1375). "Film va majmouch-hay-e mazhabi: Moshkelat, rahe-hal ha va massiri doshvar [Film and Religious Series: Problems, Solutions and a Difficult Path]." *Donyay-e Tassvir*, no. 40: 47–58.

Moallem, Minoo. 2000. "Iranian Immigrants, Exiles and Refugees: From National to Transnational Contexts." *Comparative Studies of South Asia, Africa, and the Middle East* 20, nos. 1–2: 161–64.

———. 2001. "Middle Eastern Studies, Feminism and Globalization." *Signs* 26, no. 4: 1265–68.

———. 2002. "Women of Color in the U.S.: Pedagogical Reflections on the Politics of 'the Name.' " In *Women's Studies on Its Own*, edited by Robyn Wiegman, 368–82. Durham, N.C.: Duke University Press.

Moallem, Minoo, and Iain Boal. 1999. "Multicultural Nationalism and the Poetics of Inauguration." In *Between Women and Nation: Nationalisms, Transnational Feminisms, and the State*, edited by Caren Kaplan, Norma Alarcón, and Minoo Moallem, 243–63. Durham, N.C.: Duke University Press.

Moddaressi Chardehi, Morteza. 1955 (1334). *Zendegi va Falsafe-he Ijtemai va Siamsi Sayyed Jamal-el din Afghani* (The Life and the Social and Political Philosophy of Sayyed Jamal-el din Afghani). Tehran: Iqbal Publishing.

Moghadam, Valentine M., ed. 1994. *Identity Politics and Women: Cultural Reassertions and Feminisms in International Perspective*. Boulder, Colo.: Westview Press.

Moghissi, Haideh. 1999. *Feminism and Islamic Fundamentalism: The Limits of Postmodern Analysis*. London: Zed Books.

Mohanty, Talpade Chandra. 1991a. "Cartographies of Struggle: Third World Women and the Politics of Feminism." In *Third World Women and the Politics of Feminism*, edited by Talpade Chandra Mohanty, Ann Russo, and Lourdes Torres, 1–47. Indianapolis: Indiana University Press.

———. 1991b. "Under Western Eyes." In *Third World Women and the Politics of Feminism*, edited by Talpade Chandra Mohanty, Ann Russo, and Lourdes Torres, 51–80. Indianapolis: Indiana University Press.

Murray, Stephen O., and Will Roscoe. 1997. *Islamic Homosexualities: Culture, History, and Literature*. New York: New York University Press.

Mustaz'afin. 1979. Vol.1. Gorgan: Kanun Farhangi-e Islami-e Gurgan va Dasht (Islamic Culture Unit of Gurgan and Dasht).

Naderi, Nader. 1990. "Max Weber and the Study of the Middle East: A Critical

Analysis." *Berkeley Journal of Sociology* 35: 71–87.

Naficy, Hamid. 1987. "Cinema as a Political Instrument." In *Continuity and Change in Modern Iran,* edited by Michael E. Bonine and Nikki Keddie, 265–83. Albany: New York University Press.

———. 1993. *The Making of Exile Cultures: Iranian Television in Los Angeles.* Minneapolis: University of Minnesota Press.

———. 2001. *An Accented Cinema: Exilic and Diasporic Filmmaking.* Princeton, N.J.: Princeton University Press.

Najmabadi, Afsaneh, ed. 1990. *Women's Autobiographies in Contemporary Iran.* Cambridge, Mass.: Harvard University Press.

———. 1991. "Hazards of Modernity and Morality: Women, State and Ideology in Contemporary Iran." In *Women, Islam and the State,* edited by Deniz Kandiyoti, 48–76. Philadelphia: Temple University Press.

———. 1995. *Hikayat-i dukhtaran-i Quchan* [The Story of the Daughters of Quchan]. Tehran: Entesharat e Rawshangaran.

———. 1997. "Teaching and Research in Unavailable Intersections." *Differences* 9, no. 3 (Fall): 65–78.

———. 1998a. "Feminisms in an Islamic Republic: 'Years of Hardship, Years of Growth.'" In *Islam, Gender, and Social Change,* edited by Yvonne Yazbeck Haddad and John L. Esposito, 59–84. Oxford: Oxford University Press.

———. 1998b. "Crafting an Educated Housewife in Iran." In *Remaking Women: Feminism and Modernity in the Middle East,* edited by Lila Abu-Lughod, 91–125. Princeton, N.J.: Princeton University Press.

———. 2000. "(Un)Veiling Feminism." *Social Text* 18, no. 3 (Fall): 28–45.

Nandy, Ashis. 1983. *The Intimate Enemy: Loss and Recovery of Self under Colonialism.* Delhi: Oxford University Press.

———. 1998a. "The Politics of Secularism and the Recovery of Religious Tolerance." In *Secularism and Its Critics,* edited by Rajeev Bhargava, 321–44. Delhi: Oxford University Press.

———. ed. 1998b. *The Secret Politics of Our Desires.* London: Zed Books.

Navaro-Yashin, Yael. 2002. "The Market for Identities: Secularism, Islamism, Commodities." In *Fragments of Culture: The Everyday of Modern Turkey,* edited by Denize Kandioty and Aysa Saktanber, 221–53. New Brunswick, N.J.: Rutgers University Press.

Nietzsche, Friedrich. 2000. *The Birth of Tragedy.* Translated by Douglas Smith. Oxford: Oxford University Press.

Nillipour, Mehdi. 1998 (1377). *Farhang-e Fatima.* Esfahan: Razmandegan-e Islam Cultural Institute.

Ong, Aihwa. 1995. "State versus Islam: Malay Families, Women's Bodies, and the Body Politic in Malaysia." In *Bewitching Women, Pious Men: Gender and Body Politics in Southeast Asia,* edited by Aihwa Ong and Michael G. Peletz, 159–94. Berkeley: University of California Press.

———. 1999. *Flexible Citizenship: The Cultural Logics of Transnationality.* Durham, N.C.: Duke University Press.

Pahlavi, Reza Shah. 1968 (1346). *Yadgar-e Guzashteh: Majmuah-e Sukhan-raniha-ye Ala-hazrat Faqid Reza Shah Kabir.* Tehran: Sazman-e chap va Intisharat-e Javidan.

Paidar, Parvin. 1995. *Women and the Political Process in Twentieth-Century Iran.* Cambridge: Cambridge University Press.

Pathak, Zakia, and Rajeswari Sunder Rajan. 1989. "Shahbano." *Signs* 14, no. 3 (Spring): 558–82.

Perez, Emma. 1999. *Decolonial Imaginary: Writing Chicanas into History.* Bloomington: Indiana University Press.

Pettman, Jindy Jan. 1996. "Border Crossings/Shifting Identities: Minorities, Gender and the State in International Perspective." *Challenging Boundaries,* edited by Michael J. Shapiro and Hayward R. Alker, 261–83. Minneapolis: University of Minnesota Press.

Pieterse Nederveen, Jan. 1994. "Fundamentalism Discourses: Enemy Images." *Women Against Fundamentalism Journal* 1, no. 5: 2–6.

Probyn, Elspeth. 1993. *Sexing the Self: Gendered Positions in Cultural Studies.* London: Routledge.

———. 1996. *Outside Belonging.* New York: Routledge.

———. 1999. "Bloody Metaphors and Other Allegories of the Ordinary." In *Between Women and Nation: Nationalisms, Transnational Feminisms, and the State,* edited by Norma Alarcón, Caren Kaplan, and Minoo Moallem. Durham, N.C.: Duke University Press.

Pyenson, Lewis. 1993. *Civilizing Mission: Exact Sciences and French Overseas Expansion, 1830–1940.* Baltimore, Md.: Johns Hopkins University Press.

Qavanin va Moqararat-e vizheh dar Jomhouri-e Eslami [Special Law and Regulation on Women in the Islamic Republic of Iran]. 1999. Tehran: Office of the President, Center for Women's Partnership Issues.

Radhakrishnan, R. 1996. *Diasporic Mediations: Between Home and Location.* Minneapolis: University of Minnesota Press.

Rafsanjani, Hashimi, and Ali Akbar. 1981. *Payam-i Shahidan.* Mashhad: Jahad-i Danishgahi-e Khurasan.

Rahnavard, Zahra. 1978. *Piyam-e Zan-e Musluman.* Tehran: Efaf.

———. 1980. *Toloueh Zaneh Mosalman.* Tehran: Mahboubeh Publication.

———. 1990. *The Message of Hijab.* London: Al Hoda Publishers.

Ranger, Terence, and E. J. Hobsbawm. 1983. *The Invention of Tradition.* Cambridge: Cambridge University Press.

Renan, Ernest. 1883. "Islam and Science." *Journal des Débats,* May 18.

———. 1989. *Légendes patriarchales des Juifs et des Arabes.* Paris: Hermann.

Riffat, Hassan. 1990. "The Burgeoning of Islamic Fundamentalism: Toward an Understanding of the Phenomenon." In *The Fundamentalist Phenomenon: A View from Within, a Response from Without,* edited by Norman J. Cohen, 151–71. Grand Rapids, Mich.: W. B. Eerdmans Publishing Co.

Robertson, Roland, and JoAnn Chirico. 1985. "Humanity, Globalization, and Worldwide Religious Resurgence: A Theoretical Exploration." *Sociological Analysis* 46, no. 3: 219–42.

Rodinson, Maxime. 1980. *Europe and the Mystique of Islam*. Translated by Roger Veinus. Seattle: University of Washington.

Rofel, Lisa. 1999. *Other Modernities: Gendered Yearnings in China after Socialism*. Berkeley: University of California Press.

Rouz Shoumar-e Enggelab-e Eslami. 1997 (1376). Vol. 1. Tehran: Sureh Publishers.

Roy, Olivier. 1999. "Le Post Islamisme." *Revue des Mondes Mussulmans et de la Méditerranée*: 85–86.

Roy, Parama. 1998. *Indian Traffic: Identities in Question in Colonial and Postcolonial India*. Berkeley: University of California Press.

Rushdie, Salman. 1990. *In Good Faith*. London: Granta Books.

———. 1991. *Imaginary Homelands*. London: Granta Books.

Sadigi-pur, Abdul Riza, ed. 1967. *Safarnamah-i Mazandaran: Majmu'ah-i Sukhanraniha-yi A'lahazrrat-e Faghid Riza Shah Pahlavi, 1878–1944*. Tehran: Javidan Publishing.

Sahgal, Gita, and Nira Yuval-Davis. 1994. "The Uses of Fundamentalism." *Women Against Fundamentalism Journal* 1, no. 5: 7–9.

Said, Edward. 1979. *Orientalism*. New York: Vintage Books.

———. 1981. *Covering Islam: How the Media and the Experts Determine How We See the Rest of the World*. New York: Pantheon Books.

———. 1983. *The World, The Text, and the Critic*. Cambridge, Mass.: Harvard University Press.

———. 1993. *Culture and Imperialism*. New York: Knopf.

Salecl, Renate. 1992. "Nationalism, Anti-Semitism, and Anti-Feminism in Eastern Europe." *New German Critique* 57 (Fall): 51–65.

Salehi Rad, Hassan, ed. 2001. *Majalis Ta'zieh* [Ta'zieh Assemblies]. 2 vols. Tehran: Soroush Press.

Sanasarian, Eliz. 1982. *The Women's Rights Movement in Iran: Mutiny, Appeasement, and Repression from 1900 to Khomeini*. New York: Praeger.

San'ati, Mahdokht. 1993. "Sadigeh Dawlatabadi: An Intimate Portrayal." *Nimeye Digar: Persian Language Feminist Journal*, no.17 (Winter): 64–76.

Sandoval, Chela. 1990. "Feminism and Racism: A Report on the 1981 National Women's Studies Association Conference." In *Making Face, Making Soul/Haciendo Caras: Creative and Critical Perspectives by Women of Color*, edited by Gloria Anzaldua, 55–71. San Francisco: Aunt Lute Books.

Sarkar, Tanika, and Urvashi Buttalia, eds. 1995. *Women and Right-Wing Movements: Indian Experiences*. London: Zed Press.

Sayyid, Bobby S. 1997. *A Fundamental Fear: Eurocentrism and the Emergence of Islamism*. London: Zed Books.

Schivelbusch, Wolfgang. 1986. *Railway Journey: The Industrialization of Time and Space in the Nineteenth Century*. Berkeley and Los Angeles: University of California Press.

Scott, James C. 1985. *Weapons of the Weak: Everyday Forms of Peasant Resistance*. New Haven, Conn.: Yale University Press.

Shahri, Jafar. 1978. *Tehran-e Khadim*. Tehran: Amir Kabir Publications.

Shari'ati, Ali. 1971. *Fatimah Fatimah Ast*. Tehran: Houssienieh Ershad Publication.

————. 1973 (1352). "Tamadun va Tajaddod (Civilization and Modernity)." Paper read Dec. 13, distributed by the Islamic Association of Students in Europe, Canada and the United States.

————. 1979. *On the Sociology of Islam*. Translated by H. Algar. Berkeley: Mizan Press.

————. 1980. *Ummat va Imamat*. Tehran: Ghalam Publications.

Shayegan, Daryush. 1989. *Le regard motile, schizophrénie culturelle: Pays traditionnels face à la modernité: Sciences et symboles*. Paris: Albin Michel.

Sherkat, Shahla. 1991 (1370). "Cheshmeh-e agahi agar bejoushad [If the Fountain of Consciousness Burst Out]." *Zanan*, no. 1 (Bahman).

————. 2000 (1379). "Shahla Sherkat's Speech at the Berlin Conference." In *Zanan Berlin*, edited by Leili Fahadpour, 120–29. Tehran: Jame'eh-e Iranian.

Shohat, Ella. 1991. "Gender and the Culture of Empire: Towards a Feminist Ethnography of the Cinema." *Quarterly Review of Film and Video* 13, nos.1–3: 45–84.

————. 1992. "Rethinking Jews and Muslims: Quincentennial Reflections." *Middle East Report* 178 (Sept.–Oct.): 25–29.

————. 2002. "Area Studies, Gender Studies, and the Cartographies of Knowledge." *Social Text* 72 (Fall): 67–78.

————. ed. 1998. *Talking Visions: Multicultural Feminism in a Transnational Age*. New York: New Museum of Contemporary Art.

Shohat, Ella, and Robert Stam. 1994. *Unthinking Eurocentrism: Multiculturalism and the Media*. London: Routledge.

Simmel, George. 1904./1971. *On Individuality and Social Forms*. Chicago: University of Chicago Press.

Simons, Jon. 1995. *Foucault and the Political*. London: Routledge.

Skocpol, Theda. 1982. "Rentier State and Shi'a Islam in the Iranian Revolution." *Theory and Society* 11: 266–283.

Slater, Don. 1997. *Consumer Culture and Modernity*. Cambridge: Polity Press.

Slatman, Jenny. 2001. "Tele-vision: Between Blind Trust and Perceptual Faith." In *Religion and Media*, edited by Hent De Vries and Samuel Weber, 216–26. Stanford, Calif.: Stanford University Press.

Smith, H. John. 2000. *Dialectics of the Will: Freedom, Power, and Understanding in Modern French and German Thought*. Detroit, Mich.: Wayne State University Press.

Smith, Pam. 1992. *The Emotional Labour of Nursing*. London: Macmillan.

Sokoloff, J. Natalie. 1980. *Between Money and Love: The Dialectics of Women's Home and Market Work*. New York: Praeger Publishers.

Sommer, Doris. 1991. *Foundational Fictions: The National Romances of Latin America*. Berkeley: University of California Press.

Souroush, Abdlkarim. 1992. *Razdani, Roushanfikri va Dindari*. Tehran: Sarat Publications.

Spivak, Gayatri Chakravorty. 1979–80. "Revolutions That as Yet Have No Model: Derrida's 'Limited Inc.'" *Diacritics* 10, no. 4 (Winter): 758–60.

———. 1988a. *In Other Worlds: Essays in Cultural Politics.* New York: Routledge.

———. 1988b. "Can Subalterns Speak." In *Marxism and the Interpretation of Culture,* edited by Cary Nelson and Lawrence Grossberg, 271–97. Urbana: University of Illinois Press.

———. 1990. *The Post-colonial Critic: Interviews, Strategies, Dialogues,* edited by Sarah Harasym. New York: Routledge.

———. 1993. *Outside in the Teaching Machine.* New York: Routledge.

———. 1999. *A Critique of Postcolonial Reason: Toward a History of the Vanishing Present.* Cambridge, Mass.: Harvard University Press.

Stanley, Mrs. H. M. (Dorothy Tennant). 1890. *London Street Arabs.* London: Cassell.

Starhawk. 1979. "Witchcraft and Woman's Culture." In *Womanspirit Rising: A Feminist Reader in Spirituality,* edited by Carol Christ and Judith Plaskow, 259–68. New York: Harper and Row.

———. 1989. *The Spiral Dance: A Rebirth of the Ancient Religion of the Great Goddess.* San Francisco: Harper.

Stoler, Laura Ann. 1995. *Race and the Education of Desire.* Durham, N.C.: Duke University Press.

Sumic-Riha, Jelica. 1996. "Post-modern Democracy, Politics, and Collective Identities." Paper presented at the conference "State, Nation, Multiculturalism and Citizenship," Centre des Etudes Ethniques à l'Université de Montréal, Montreal, May 30–June 2.

Tabari, Azar, and Nahid Yeganeh, eds. 1982. *In the Shadow of Islam: The Women's Movement in Iran.* London: Zed Press.

Taha, Mahmoud Mohammed. 1987. *The Second Message of Islam.* Translated by Amed an-Na'im Abdullahi. Syracuse, N.Y.: Syracuse University Press.

Talashi dar tassvir-e jebheh [Iran-Iraq War: An Effort to Portray the Battlefield]. 1983 (1362). Tehran: Setade Tablighate Jang.

Taleghani, Alayi Azam, ed. 1991 (1370). *Datftar-e dovom (Zanan).* Tehran: Vajeh.

Tavakoli-Taraghi, Mohamad. 1998. "Modernity, Heterotopia, and Homeless Texts." *Comparative Studies of South Asia, Africa and the Middle East* 18, no. 2: 2–14.

———. 2001. *Refashioning Iran: Orientalism, Occidentalism and Historiography.* New York: Palgrave.

Taylor, Mark C., ed. 1998. *Critical Terms for Religious Studies.* Chicago: University of Chicago Press.

Thomas, Laurie. 1863. *Morning in the Mountains: Woman and Her Savior in Persia.* London: James Nisbet.

Tohidi, Nayereh. 1991. "Gender and Islamic Fundamentalism. Feminist Politics in Iran." In *Third World Women and the Politics of Feminism,* edited by Talpade Chandra Mohanty, Ann Russo, and Lourdes Torres, 251–65. Bloomington: Indiana University Press.

Turani, Behrooz. 1999. "Sahl sazi dar sakht, vaghi'yat Gorizi dar mazmoon/ Carelessness in Structure, Escaping Reality in Content." In *Film-e Farsi Chist?/What is Film-e Farsi?* edited by Hussein Moazzezi Nia, 89–96. Tehran: Saghi Publication.

Turner, Bryan S. 1994. *Orientalism, Postmodernism and Globalism.* London: Routledge.

Vakili, Elaheh. 1991 (1370). *Negaresh-e Tatbighi: Zan dar Ayineh-e Ghoran, Zartusht, Yahoud va Massihiyat* [A Comparative Perspective on Women as Reflected in the Koran, and Zoroastrian, Jewish and Christian Traditions]. Tehran: Sepehr.

Vattimo, Gianni. 1998. "The Trace of the Trace." In *Religion,* edited by Jacques Derrida and Gianni Vattimo, 79–94. Stanford, Calif.: Stanford University Press.

———. 1999. *Belief.* Translated by Luca D'Isanto and David Webb. Stanford, Calif.: Stanford University Press.

Vaziri, Mostafa. 1993. *Iran as an Imagined Nation: The Construction of National Identity.* New York: Paragon House.

Veblen, Thorstein. 1979 [1899]. *The Theory of the Leisure Class.* New York: Penguin Books.

Walby, Sylvia. 1986. *Patriarchy at Work: Patriarchal and Capitalist Relations in Employment.* Minneapolis: University of Minnesota Press.

Walker, Alice. 1990. "Definition of Womanist." In *Making Face, Making Soul/Haciendo Caras: Creative and Critical Perspectives by Women of Color,* edited by Gloria Anzaldua, 370. San Francisco: Aunt Lute Books.

Wallerstein, Immanuel. 1979. "Rise and Future Demise of the World Capitalist System." In *The Capitalist World-Economy,* edited by Immanuel Wallerstein, 1–36. London: Cambridge University Press.

———. 1990. "Culture as the Ideological Battleground of the Modern World-System." In *Global Culture,* edited by Mike Featherstone, 31–56. London: Sage.

———. 1997. "The Unintended Consequences of Cold War Area Studies." In *The Cold War and the University: Toward an Intellectual History of the Postwar Years,* edited by Noam Chomsky, 195–231. New York: New Press.

Wessels, Antonie. 1984. "The So-called Renaissance of Islam." *Journal of Asian and African Studies* 19, nos. 3–4: 190–201.

Whigham, H. J. 1903. *The Persian Problem.* New York: Charles Scribner's Sons.

Williams, Raymond. 1979. *Modern Tragedy.* London: Verso.

———. 1981. *Marxism and Literature.* Oxford: Oxford University Press.

———. 1983. *Keywords: A Vocabulary of Culture and Society.* London: Fontana.

Wilson, Elizabeth. 1992. "Feminist Fundamentalism: The Shifting Politics of Sex and Censorship." In *Sex Exposed: Sexuality and the Pornography Debate,* edited by Lynne Segal and Mary McIntosh, 15–28. New Brunswick, N.J.: Rutgers University Press.

Wolf, Eric R. 1982. *Europe and the People Without History.* Berkeley: University of California Press.

Wuthnow, Robert. 1978. "Religious Movements and the Transition in World Order." In *Understanding the New Religions*, edited by J. Needleman and G. Baker, 63–79. New York: Seabury Press.

———. 1987. *Meaning and Moral Order: Explorations in Cultural Analysis.* Berkeley: University of California Press.

Yaghmaian, Behzad. 2002. *Social Change in Iran: An Eyewitness Account of Dissent, Defiance, and New Movements for Rights.* Albany: State University of New York Press.

Young, Marion Iris. 1987. "Impartiality and the Civic Public: Some Implications of Feminist Critiques of Moral and Political Theory." In *Feminism as Critique,* edited by Seyla Benhabib and Drucilla Cornell, 57–76. Minneapolis: University of Minnesota Press.

Yuval-Davis, Nira. 1992. "Jewish Fundamentalism and Women's Empowerment." In *Refusing Holy Orders: Women and Fundamentalism in Britain,* edited by Nira Yuval-Davis and Gita Sahgal, 198–235. London: Virago Press.

Yuval-Davis, Nira, and Gita Sahgal. 1992. *Refusing Holy Orders: Women and Fundamentalism in Britain.* London: Virago Press.

Zamani niya, Mustafa. 1984. *Farhang-i Sinema-yi Iran: 1308–1362* [The Culture of Iranian Cinema]. Tehran: Kitab-e Adineh.

Zan, Elm, San'at va Tawsi'ah (Woman, Science, Technology and Development). 1995–96 (1374). Tehran: Daftar-I Umur-I Zanan dar Nahad-I Riyasat-I Jumhuri (Presidential Office of Women's Affairs).

Zan dar Ayeneh defa'e Moggadas [Women in the Mirror of the Sacred Defense]. 1990 (1369). Tehran: Sepaheh Passdaran.

Zerinski, P. Michael. 1993. "American Presbyterian Missionary Women in Late Nineteenth and Early Twentieth Century Iran." *Nimeye Digar: Persian Language Feminist Journal,* no.17 (Winter): 38–63.

Index

Abbas, 209–10n10
Abbasid dynasty, 128
Abedi, Mehdi, 24, 199n18
abjectification, 117, 126, 217n15
abjection of urban space, 73–76, 133–35
abortion, 214n9, 220n34
absence, 126, 140, 184; of home, 49–51
absolutism, 39, 136, 151, 164, 171, 173
abstraction: of bodies, 72, 80, 148, 169, 207n31; of women, 167
Abu-Lughod, Lila, 21–22
acid, 138, 214n10
Adam Barfi (film), 142–45, 148–49, 214n12
Adorno, Theodor W., 10, 41, 60
adventure books, 37
advertising, 183, 220n40
affective bonds, 81, 92, 117, 128, 144, 209n8
Al-Afghani, 45–46, 202–3nn16–18
Afghani refugees, 200n27
Afghani women, 161, 164, 186, 217n15, 223n2
Afghan war, 164, 216nn8,10, 217n16
Afrasyab of Turan, 209n4
African women, 168
Afshar, 22, 213n2
agency, 55–56, 185; civic body and, 64, 70, 74, 76, 80–82; feminism and fundamentalism and, 171, 173, 177, 179; politics and religion and, 123, 143, 150; revolution and, 107, 112–14, 211n20
Agnes, Flavia, 205–6n22

Aït Sabbah, Fatna, 219n30
Ajams, 128
akhound, 132
Akrami, Jamshid, 205n18
Alarcón, Norma, 6, 33
Alavi, Ali Reza, 123–24
Alavi Shiism, 107
Alavi Tabar, Ali Reza, 182
Ali, Imam, 86–87, 91–93, 123, 128
Alice, 37–38
alienation, 112, 146, 171, 220nn34,37
Allah, 99–100, 108, 120
Allah-o Akbar, 85, 90, 189
allegory, 84, 116, 213n36
Alloula, Malek, 36
alterity, 126, 170, 176
ambiguities: civic body and, 62, 67, 71, 206–7n30; feminism and fundamentalism and, 166, 171; politics and religion and, 126, 131, 143–44, 146, 148–49; revolution and, 85, 90, 105, 116
ambivalence, 33, 49, 117, 133, 144, 149, 205n19
Amta'eh vatan exhibition, 66
anarchism, 6, 84
ancien régime, 105–7
andarouni, 49, 189, 203n23
Anderson, Benedict, 15, 55, 204n10
andisheh, 92
anti-Arab ideology, 53, 87
anticolonialism, 21, 78, 84, 201n9
antifeminist fundamentalism, 30, 164, 180
anti-imperialism, 174

Text:	10/13 Galliard
Display:	Galliard
Indexer:	Sharon Sweeney
Compositor, printer, and binder:	IBT Global